RENEWALS 458-4574
DATE DUE

**WITHDRAWN
UTSA LIBRARIES**

SOUTH AFRICA'S RACIAL PAST

DAMES
Dansk Center for Migration
og Etniske Studier

**EUROPEAN RESEARCH CENTRE
ON MIGRATION & ETHNIC RELATIONS**

South Africa's Racial Past
The history and historiography of racism, segregation, and apartheid

PAUL MAYLAM
Rhodes University, South Africa

Ashgate
Aldershot • Burlington USA • Singapore • Sydney

© Paul Maylam 2001

All rights reserved. No part of this publication may be reproduced, stored in a retrieval system or transmitted in any form or by any means, electronic, mechanical, photocopying, recording or otherwise without the prior permission of the publisher.

Published by
Ashgate Publishing Limited
Gower House
Croft Road
Aldershot
Hampshire GU11 3HR
England

Ashgate Publishing Company
131 Main Street
Burlington, VT 05401-5600 USA

Ashgate website: http://www.ashgate.com

British Library Cataloguing in Publication Data
Maylam, Paul
   South Africa's racial past : the history and historiography of racism, segregation, and apartheid. - (Research in migration and ethnic relations series)
   1.Apartheid - South Africa - Historiography 2.Apartheid - South Africa - History 3.South Africa - Race relations 4.South Africa - Race relations - Historiography
   I.Title
   323.1'68

Library of Congress Control Number: 2001088770

ISBN 0 7546 1788 2

Printed and bound by Athenaeum Press, Ltd., Gateshead, Tyne & Wear.

Contents

Acknowledgements vi

Introduction 1

PART I: THE EMERGING RACIAL ORDER: PRE-INDUSTRIAL TIMES

1	Before Van Riebeeck: The Early European Legacy	13
2	Differentiation and Discrimination in Cape Dutch Society	29
3	Colonial Expansion and Racial Oppression	67

PART II: THE RACIAL ORDER HARDENS: THE INDUSTRIAL ERA

4	Diamonds, Gold and the Colour Bar	115
5	The Segregation Era	143
6	Apartheid	179

PART III: CONCLUSION

7	South Africa's Racial Order: Historiographical and Historical Reflections	207

Bibliography 245
Index 258

Acknowledgements

Thanks go to Helen Dampier and Carla Tsampiras who acted most ably as research assistants. And to Sandy Rowoldt and the staff of the Cory Library at Rhodes University for their considerable support. Financial assistance from Rhodes University, in the form of research grants, is gratefully acknowledged. Thanks also go to Cherry Charteris and Chris Walwyn for typesetting and page preparation.

Introduction

In 1998 the report of South Africa's Truth and Reconciliation Commission (TRC) declared apartheid to have been a crime against humanity. Few have been moved to dispute that judgement. Even the former practitioners of apartheid have been more or less mildly apologetic – albeit not nearly remorseful enough in the eyes of most, offering little more than the lame concession that apartheid was flawed and unworkable. Indeed, these days one comes across few white people who admit to having supported apartheid. People either deny such support, or hide behind the claim that the horrors of the system were hidden from them by state propaganda and by the largely uncritical media.

So the question arises, how should apartheid – indeed, the whole history of the South African racial order – be remembered? Is there a danger that it might be forgotten? The state of denial among many whites could bring historical amnesia. And does not the cosy 'rainbowism' of the new South Africa require that the horrors of the past be buried, suppressed, in the service of nation-building? The TRC, claim some, has served only to reopen old wounds, and then to leave them to fester. There has been no retribution, no proper reparation, and little reconciliation, it is argued.

These questions are essentially rhetorical. In reality there is little danger of historical amnesia obliterating South Africa's racial past. The horrors of racial oppression – the dehumanisation, death and destruction – will never be forgotten. But how will the historiography of South Africa's racial order evolve in the years ahead? One possibility is that there will be an overriding focus on the plight and misery of the victims of racial oppression. There will be many tragic stories to be told – and they will most certainly need to be told. But where does this leave the endeavour to explain and interpret the racial order? In the academic realm – the stuff of historiography, the terrain of professional historians?

This study is situated, unashamedly, on that terrain. The book has two main concerns: first, to explore the growth of the South African racial order, attempting to periodise it and to examine its various dynamics. Second, to consider the historiography of that racial order, seeing how different writers in particular contexts have analysed and interpreted racial discrimination and oppression in South African history. The book therefore stands at that awkward interface between history and historiography. Interface? Today many would argue that there is no interface, that any distinction between the two is false – that all history is essentially historiography. I go some way with this view. The actual past is just that – past – and cannot be recreated as it actually was. What goes under the name of history amounts only to more or less imperfect, imprecise reconstructions and explanations of the past. However, for the purpose of this work I do retain the distinction, not out of any pretension to gain access to a real past, but in the belief that history cannot simply be collapsed into historiography. One dimension of the book is decidedly historiographical, as I try to capture something of the contestation and debate between different writers on questions pertaining to South Africa's racial past. At the same time I am concerned to highlight the historical evidence that provides clues to the questions under discussion, that enables me to put forward my own explanations.

The book strives to provide an historical overview of South Africa's racial order – an endeavour not unproblematic, a walk across an epistemological minefield. There are pitfalls and hazards. Totalisation, essentialism and reductionism, for instance – trying to explain South Africa's racial order in terms of an overriding grand theory. Or, at another extreme, slipping into a comfortable multicausal approach, throwing a variety of explanations into the melting-pot, arriving at the 'combination of factors' conclusion so favoured by undergraduate students – the approach that fails to weight or prioritise. Then there is the danger of teleology, a kind of inverted whig approach. The whig metanarrative describes the gradual unfolding of British history towards an ultimate goal – the achievement of liberal, parliamentary democracy. So might such a South African metanarrative recount the steady evolution of the South African racial order to its awful summation, the apartheid system. Such a narrative imposes on the past a false sense of continuity, coherence and order.

If, though, one is to compare, analyse, and evaluate the historiography of South Africa's racial order, what is to be the basis of the analysis and evaluation? Might one not end up being 'hoisted with one's own petard'? The writer engaged in historiographical work can present the false appearance of being an aloof, independent surveyor of others' writings, when in reality such a writer, in the process of creating the historiographical survey, is at once becoming part of that very historiography. This is the danger in an historiographical project such as this – that the author, from a seemingly panoramic vantage point, pontificates on the work of others, while at the same time trying to render himself/herself invisible.

Historiographical writing about the work of others can no more be handled from a neutral stance than can more orthodox historical work that tries to record and explain the past. The claims of historians to be objective are always a mere pretence. Indeed the profession at large has long since distanced itself from the tradition of Von Ranke, who claimed some 160 years ago that it was the task of the historian to describe the past 'as it really happened'. However, while most historians have largely abandoned Rankean aspirations, there is still a widespread tendency for historical work to be written in a style that appears to remove the author's voice from the text, creating a false impression of a seemingly neutral observer presenting authoritative accounts and explanations.

So, at the outset, a disclaimer. I do not write from the throne. This is not an authoritative overview produced after life-long research into South Africa's racial order. Rather it is a book born of a deep interest in the history of racism, segregation and apartheid in South Africa – and of a sense that the different strands of this history need to be brought together in a single book. Much of the ground covered in the book will be familiar to those who are well versed in South African history. However, the overall conception of the project is original – nobody has as yet attempted to survey and synthesise the history and historiography of white racism in South Africa throughout its long history. Some might say that this is an over-ambitious project. Certainly my coverage of the literature is not fully comprehensive – there will inevitably be historiographical gaps, texts not brought into the survey.

While there will be gaps I still hope to capture something of this historical contestation – to explore how various writers, from different disciplines and perspectives, have addressed the major theme of white racism in South African history. It is a truism to say that all historical analysis proceeds from basic premises and assumptions – about human behaviour, the historical process, for instance – assumptions that may be implicit or explicit, depending on the style of the individual scholar. So part of the task in this work is to draw out those presuppositions and theories that have guided previous work on these themes.

Nearly all the writing considered in this book was produced before 1994, that is, when the South African racial order was in existence, either emerging, at its peak, or in decline. The writers themselves have been either 'insiders' resident in South Africa, or 'outsiders' observing and analysing the country and its history from afar. The 'insiders' have been either beneficiaries or victims, supporters or opponents of the racial order. Most of the 'insider' writers have been beneficiaries, by virtue of their whiteness (assuming that all whites were advantaged by the system, to a greater or lesser extent), but also opponents of the discriminatory system. Not surprisingly there is also a body of 'insider' work by white beneficiaries who have supported and defended the racial order. However, the work of black victims has concentrated more on the impact of racial oppression, and resistance to it, than on the dynamics of the racial order. The stance of the 'outsiders', neither beneficiaries nor victims in any direct sense, has generally been oppositional.

It would be simplistic to suggest that the particular locations of different writers have determined their mode of explanation and analysis. But clearly the approach of each has been shaped by their own underlying aims and agendas, explicit or implicit. Four such agendas can be identified. First, to represent and explain the South African racial order in such a way as to justify, rationalise and defend it. Second, to examine the racial order critically with a view to its reform or peaceful elimination. Third, to analyse it critically with a view to its wholesale eradication. And fourth, to examine and explain it historically so as to better understand it – the *verstehen* approach often denounced for its lack of commitment to wider, pressing causes.

Such contestations are a standard feature of modern historiography. So too are paradigm conflicts – which have also been most evident in the historiography of the South African racial order. The idealist/materialist divide, with variations on either side, has pervaded the debate. Idealists have tended either towards the conservative position – that races are real entities and that the racial order was therefore natural, simply an expression of the fundamental differences between South Africa's various racial groups. Or towards the liberal position – that racial differences and divisions were at the root of conflict in South African history, but were aggravated by an illiberal racial order that paid scant respect to the worth and rights of individuals. Orthodox materialists on the other hand have dismissed racial categories as artificial constructs, racism as false consciousness, and the racial order as superstructural. Racism, in the materialist view, is essentially an expression of class interests; and in the South African case the racial order was designed largely to further the growth of capitalism. Finally there has been the more eclectic approach which views the racial order as multi-faceted, not reducible to an essential underlying dynamic, not explicable in a single overarching framework – what looks to be a thoroughly sensible position, but also smacks of a rather too comfortable compromise between the idealist and materialist views.

Has the historiography of South African racism been shackled by these positions and paradigms? At times the contestation has been vigorous and lively, especially during the 1970s, at the height of the idealist/materialist debate. But in the last twenty years or so there has been little innovative theorising, few breakthroughs in the historical analysis of the South African racial order. The most significant new dimension has been the greater attention and weight afforded to racial thought and racial theory. This has been partly a reaction against the reductionist, economistic Marxist scholarship of the 1970s, and partly an offshoot of postmodernist thought.

The ideas, language and imagery of racism have come to be stressed at the expense of underlying material interests. This book does not pretend to provide that breakthrough. It is not a paradigm-buster, but rather a stock-taking exercise. The aim is to explore a set of historical questions about the South African racial order, and to examine how those questions have been addressed by others over time. How, for instance is the history of racial discrimination in South Africa best explained: in material terms, as a form of class exploitation? In political terms, as an instrument of domination? In social terms, to maintain separation in the social sphere? In psychological/cultural terms, as fear of racial 'others'?

These questions in turn require a close examination of those South African regions and settings in which racial consciousness and racist practice seemed to be most conspicuous. Some, for instance, have associated white racism more closely with the 'northern tradition' of the nineteenth century boer republics, the Orange Free State and the South African Republic – in contrast to the less racist Cape 'liberal tradition'. Linked to this is the further assumption that white Afrikaners have been more racist than the British settlers and their descendants – an assumption reinforced by the commonly held view that apartheid was essentially the product of the post-1948 Afrikaner-dominated National Party government. These assumptions have to be questioned. Did racism vary in intensity from region to region? And did it flourish in some settings rather than others – on the frontier, for instance? Has it been more of a rural phenomenon, or has racism been embedded in city life? Such questions, though, cannot be properly addressed without considering closely the conditions and contexts that appeared to give rise to racism. Are the most fertile conditions those where there is competition for scarce resources? Or where a dominant group seeks to exploit and control labour for its own advantage and profit? Or where social problems arise – such as crime and disease – and take on racial overtones?

Then there are questions of periodisation. To what point in South African history can one trace the source of racial discrimination and separation? To the beginning of white settlement at the Cape – where there seemed to be early signs of racial stratification and segregation, whether it be Van Riebeeck's hedge, slavery, or the treatment of the indigenous Khoi? Or to the frontier era of the eighteenth and nineteenth centuries, when the expansion of white settlement brought contact and conflict between communities – and perhaps too a growing sense of racial identification along with the practice of discrimination? Or to the mineral revolution, when the demand for cheap labour necessitated the implementation of policies based on racial differentiation?

These questions of periodisation have wider implications. There is more to the issue than the age-old exercise of weighing up the historical discontinuities against the continuities. Any stress on discontinuity in the history of the South African racial order might lead to the conclusion that apartheid, post-1948, was an aberration, a monstrous departure from what had gone before, rather than a culmination of a long history of racial oppression. Such a view tends naturally towards a demonisation of the National Party, particularly Verwoerd and his henchmen, and a softer stance on pre-1948 patterns of discrimination and oppression. However, it can also be argued that an emphasis on the continuities, on the steady growth of the racial order over time, serves to mitigate the evils of apartheid. Does it not make those who laid the building-blocks of the racial order no less guilty than those who strove to bring that order to its hideous completion? These are large, complex questions. In this book the continuities are highlighted – not in any way to absolve successive apartheid regimes of their crimes, but to draw proper attention to the roles of earlier colonial structures and white overlords in the making of the racial order. At the same time, though, the breaks, the disjunctures, and the watersheds are brought out. This is not a teleological study.

All these issues raise further questions of a conceptual nature. The very use of terms like 'race' and 'racism' has become increasingly problematic. Some would say that the mere mention of the word 'race' is itself racist, seemingly implying that different races do actually exist as distinct categories within humankind. I hold to the view that racial categories are social constructs, and that use of the term 'race' or 'race group' can reify those categories in a dangerous way. At the same time, though, it is impossible to write a text such as this without using the concept. Hereafter I shall be using words like 'race', 'racial', 'racism', without inverted commas. I do this to avoid excessive use of punctuation. I do not wish to imply that the concept of race is anything other than a social construct.

But if the term is to be used, it is still necessary to clarify its meaning. After all, the word 'race' has had over the years a number of different meanings – indeed, so many different meanings that David Goldberg has been 'tempted to say that race is whatever anyone in using that term or its cognates conceives of collective social relations'.[1] Or, as Kenan Malik has observed, 'everyone "knows" what a "race" is, but no one can quite define it'.[2] Michael Banton has traced the first English usage of the term to the early

---

1 David Theo Goldberg, *Racist Culture* (Oxford, 1993), p.81.
2 Kenan Malik, *The Meaning of Race* (New York, 1996), p.2.

sixteenth century.³ Over the next three centuries 'race' was generally used to denote a group – of animals or plants, perhaps, as well as persons – sharing a common descent. But in the past two hundred years or so the concept of race has come to rest on a variety of defining characteristics, including physical type, skin colour, genes, historical origin, language and culture.⁴ Variations in meaning have occurred according to broader ideological contexts or prevailing states of knowledge at particular times. The conceptualisation of race was, for instance, greatly influenced by Darwinian theory for some decades from the later nineteenth century. It will be one of the concerns of this book to keep constantly in view the way in which writing about race in South African history has, over the years, fallen into certain paradigms that had leverage, or followed patterns of thought that were hegemonic at the time.

Just as the term 'race' has had different meanings, so has the notion of racism. According to Banton, the term 'racism' was first used in the 1930s, 'to identify the doctrine that race determines culture'. In recent times the word has come to be used in a more generalised sense, 'to refer to almost anything connected with racial discrimination, prejudice, inequality, or with apartheid'.⁵ For Fredrickson, 'racism' is an 'ambiguous and loaded' word: 'Narrowly defined, racism is a mode of thought that offers a particular explanation for the fact that population groups that can be distinguished by ancestry are likely to differ in culture, status and power'.⁶ Goldberg offers a general definition of racism as 'the irrational (or prejudicial) belief in or practice of differentiating population groups on the basis of their typical phenomenal characteristics, and the hierarchical ordering of the racial groups so distinguished as superior or inferior'.⁷

It is one of the central contentions of this book that racism cannot be understood properly if treated as a monolithic phenomenon. Racial orders take on different forms at different times. There are various dimensions to the phenomenon of racism. In this book I take racism to comprise four main elements, not all of which may be present in a racial order at any one time. Two of the elements lie in the realm of belief, attitude and thought; the other two relate to social, legal, and institutional practice.

The first element can be termed racial consciousness. This refers to a set of beliefs about perceived differences between human groupings based on

---

3   Michael Banton, *Racial Theories* (Cambridge, 1987), p.1.
4   *Ibid.*, pp.xi-xii, Goldberg, *Racist Culture*, pp.81-2.
5   Michael Banton, *Racial Consciousness* (London, 1988), p.26.
6   George M. Fredrickson, *White Supremacy* (Oxford, 1981), p.xii.
7   Goldberg, *Racist Culture*, p.93.

colour, physical type and culture. Such beliefs may be widely held, but they tend to be loosely articulated, expressed in popular attitudes and behaviour patterns, but not systematised in a body of theory or scientific discourse. In other words these beliefs stop short of the second element – racial theory or scientific racism. This refers to a body of ideas expounded by intellectuals, politicians or publicists. These ideas would assume, at the very least, the existence of different race groups, and might proceed to stress the correlation between racial and cultural differences, or go further and postulate a hierarchical ordering of race groups. Such ideas often carry weight, authenticated by experts, scientists or authority figures.

Fredrickson has also drawn this distinction between these first two elements – between 'the explicit and rationalized racism that can be discerned in nineteenth and early twentieth century thought and ideology and the implicit or societal racism that can be *inferred* from actual social relationships'.[8] It is an important distinction that is well illustrated in the history of modern South Africa. Until a few years ago racial doctrine was widely propagated in South Africa, and deeply embedded in the official discourse of apartheid. Now, in the post-apartheid era, racial ideology is rarely articulated explicitly or formally. Even the far right seems to have abandoned it, preferring the discourse of nationalism and ethnicity. However, assumptions about racial difference and racial superiority still remain inscribed in white popular consciousness. Even though it has become common for whites to distance themselves from the apartheid past, these racist assumptions remain very much alive in the private discourse of family and friends. And they remain implicit in such terms as 'incompetence', 'corruption', 'violence', all of which have significant racial connotations.

This distinction between racial consciousness and racial theory is paralleled in the distinction between the third and fourth components of racism – informal racial practice and formalised racial policy. Racial practice, like racial consciousness, is not prescribed or formally laid down. It is rather implicit in the way that people interact, or limit their interaction, with those who are presumed to be racial others. It may be expressed through avoidance or maintaining social distance from those perceived to be physically different or culturally alien. Racial policy, the fourth element, refers to the formalisation and institutionalisation of racial differentiation and

---

8 George M. Fredrickson, *The Arrogance of Race* (Middletown, 1988), p.189; also quoted in Saul Dubow, "Afrikaner Nationalism, Apartheid and the Conceptualization of 'Race'", *Journal of African History*, 33, 1992, p.210.

discrimination. It is more rigid, state-driven, enforced by law – epitomised most obviously in the post-1950 apartheid system.

This four-dimensional conceptualisation of racism is crucial to this book. One of my key arguments is that in much of the new historiography South African racism has been represented as too monolithic. Or else historians and others have generally failed to draw out the interconnections between the different components of South African racism. There is a sizeable body of writing on South African racial policy, particularly the legislation and institutionalisation of racial discrimination in the twentieth century. In recent years there has been a growing interest in the development of racial theory in South Africa. But very few historians have considered the linkages between the different elements of the racial order.

So one of my concerns is to explore these linkages. How, for instance, did informal racial practice come to be solidified into racial policy? Has racial theory shaped racial policy, consciousness and practice? Or has such theory served merely to legitimate and systematise pre-existing policy, consciousness and practice? These will be central questions. Idealists have stressed the importance of attitudes and beliefs in the construction of South Africa's racial order. Others have emphasised the legitimating function of racial ideology, making segregation and apartheid appear as something other than a crude system of labour exploitation. Both views are oversimplified. It will be necessary to emphasise the complexity of the history of South Africa's racial order, and to show that each of the different elements of racism have tended to come to the fore at different times, in particular contexts.

In this preliminary exploration a number of questions have been raised. It could be argued that the questions themselves are inherently essentialist, inviting answers that amount to no more than loose generalisation or broad totalisation. Some would argue that it is a futile quest to seek out the point of origin of South Africa's racial order. To do so would be to assume a process of sequential development from a single source – creating an artificial metanarrative that blurs the discontinuities and complexities. However, many of these questions have been at the forefront, explicitly or implicitly, in numerous works of South African history. This is not surprising. At one level writers of history may strive to satisfy a common curiosity as to when racism began in South Africa and why it persisted. Then there is the more academic interest in making sense of South Africa's past by giving it some shape and coherence. At another level there has been a political, ideological concern – to identify the sources and causes of South Africa's diseased racial order so as to be better able to prescribe the appropriate remedy.

This is a study only of white racism. It does not explore forms of black racial consciousness. Such an undertaking would have made the project too large. Nor do I examine the horrendous impact of racial oppression on the black victims of that oppression. This is a study of the nature and dynamics of a racial order constructed by whites. Although the white colonisers and power-holders have at various points in South African history made use of black collaborators it would be utterly invidious to suggest that people of colour bear some responsibility for the making of South Africa's racial order.

I adhere to the view that racial, national, and ethnic identities are constructed, made and manipulated in particular historical contexts for various social, political, and economic reasons. The politicisation of such identities in this country, and elsewhere, has wrought extraordinary destruction in the fabric of South African society. At the same time I see cultural variety – which may to a greater or lesser extent correspond to presumed racial or ethnic differences – as a positive, enriching characteristic. Implicit in this second assumption is my firm belief in the important role of historical analysis in trying to make sense of racism in South Africa. Certainly one can draw insights from anthropology, sociology, psychology, politics, philosophy, and other disciplines, but ultimately, I would argue, the process of identity formation cannot be properly understood unless it is contextualised historically.

These are all assumptions – 'correct' ones, I believe – but assumptions all the same. They are the major assumptions that inform my approach to the writing of this book. There will, too, be other underlying premises upon which this book is built. A 'soft materialism', for instance – not a crude economic determinism, but a belief that one cannot properly understand history if one ignores material forces. The influence of paradigmatic shifts in South African history since the 1970s will be evident, but I remain committed to the critical tradition – so materialist analyses do not escape critical review.

The book makes no search for essential truths. These are unattainable. Our understanding of racism in South Africa will surely remain approximate, clouded, uncertain. The book is rather an attempt to capture something of states of knowledge, analytical approaches, and discursive practice, both in the more distant and recent past. The product may bring more confusion than clarity, as I shall resist the temptation to draw firm conclusions that might elucidate the essential character of racism. I must also beware of an indulgent self-deprecation that might seem to undermine the project from the outset. I have seen the need for a synthesising work such as this. It ought to contribute to our understanding of crucial themes in the South African past and present – until its flaws come to be exposed more fully in the context of new paradigmatic or discursive shifts.

PART I:

THE EMERGING RACIAL ORDER: PRE-INDUSTRIAL TIMES

PART I

1 Before Van Riebeeck: The Early European Legacy

There is a long tradition of historical writing that handles the past within a grand narrative framework. To reconstruct the past is to tell a story. And all stories have a beginning. So in this tradition there has been a constant concern to identify points of origin, to dig down to the roots of the issue or phenomenon under investigation. This concern has been very apparent among scholars striving to explain the history of racism in the European and colonial world. When and where did race prejudice and racist practice begin? Can its origin be traced back to the time of the earliest contacts between black and white? Did racism become evident only in the context of European colonial expansion and exploitation? Were pre-existing racist attitudes transported to the colonies by the colonisers? Or did racism first evolve in colonies among white settlers who came to believe in their own natural superiority following contact with indigenous communities? Should racism be viewed as a premodern phenomenon with deep roots in European culture? Or, in the way that many scholars now interpret nationalism and ethnicity, should it be explained as a product of modernity, as embedded in the history of scientific and economic 'progress' during the last two centuries?

These questions cannot be addressed in isolation from other related issues. Any attempt to periodise the history of racism inevitably implies, too, some kind of causative analysis – the context in which racism is presumed to have developed will suggest reasons why it developed. If, for instance, one is to stress a sixteenth century origin, then it is likely that racism is being explained as a product of imperial expansion. Emphasis on the seventeenth century would probably be implying a link between slavery and racism. In both cases a further connection is suggested – between racism and the colonial exploitation of indigenous people. But the nature of that connection has been a matter of contestation between scholars, giving rise to a variety of interpretations that range along a continuum between the poles of idealism and materialism. Idealists tend to stress the psychological and cultural dimension of racism, claiming that the economic exploitation of people of colour tends to arise from and follow upon the development of racist attitudes and racial ideology. For the materialist, racism tends to be no more than a form of ideology trying to justify material interests. This area of contestation goes to the heart of the issues that are central to this study. Here the idealist-materialist divide is presented as a rather simple polarisation. The real complexity of this debate should become apparent in the remainder of this book.

A colonial aberration? Or deeply rooted in European history and culture? Ancient, medieval, early modern, or modern? How far back have scholars traced the origins of European racism? Can one perhaps look to the classical era as a possible source?

The weight of scholarly opinion exonerates the ancient Greeks and Romans. In classical society discrimination and exclusion were practised, but not along racial lines. Indeed, race seems to have been a category that had little significance or meaning. The Greeks looked down upon 'barbarians' – outsiders whose culture and language were alien. Similarly, among the Romans social hierarchies were not at all based on divisions of colour. 'Barbarians' were those who did not belong to the Roman Empire. The written evidence suggests that skin colour was not an issue in Roman society.[1]

So colour does not seem to have been a factor in classical society. There was no theory of black racial inferiority. This is not to say that colour differences were not observed and commented upon. It was the Greeks who first labelled blacks from Africa as 'Ethiopians'.[2] But the overall image of 'Ethiopians' in Greek and Roman literature is generally favourable. As Snowden has observed, 'There was clear-cut respect among Mediterranean peoples for Ethiopians and their way of life. And, above all, the ancients did not stereotype all blacks as primitives defective in religion and culture'.[3] There seems to be little dispute on this point among scholars who have investigated the history of racism.[4]

Why this absence of colour prejudice in the classical world? A brief exploration of this question may offer some clues as to the conditions and contexts in which racism does emerge. It is often argued that racism develops when the 'racial other' is perceived as a threat or as a competitor. This is an argument that tends to rest on numbers – the larger the 'alien' population, the

---

1 Frank M. Snowden, *Before Color Prejudice* (Cambridge, Massachusetts, 1983), p.63; Goldberg, *Racist Culture*, p.21; Lloyd A. Thompson, *Romans and Blacks* (London and Oklahoma, 1989), pp.6, 157-60.
2 Snowden, *Before Color Prejudice*, p.26.
3 *Ibid.*, p.108.
4 In addition to the work of Snowden and Goldberg, see also A.N. Sherwin-White, *Racial Prejudice in Imperial Rome* (Cambridge, 1967), p.1; Oliver C. Cox, *Caste, Class and Race* (New York, 1970), pp.323-25.

greater the supposed threat. Snowden rejects this argument. In classical Greece and Rome the size of the black population was almost certainly larger than is usually thought. Other considerations better explain the non-racialism of the time. Blacks were not naturally associated with abject servility, as the vast majority of slaves were white. Nor were they associated with material poverty or cultural backwardness. Indeed, Snowden suggests that white-black relations in the classical world were based on a long and easy familiarity, and on mutual respect.[5]

Did this tradition of non-racialism continue into the medieval era? Snowden believes it did, at least into the early Christian period. During the first few centuries of Christianity people of colour were welcomed as converts into the Christian family, and treated as equals.[6] Pieterse, on the other hand, stresses how the Christian symbolism of light and darkness came to take on racial connotations: 'Black became the colour of the devil and demons'.[7] But there is no firm evidence for this connection between Christian symbolism and discrimination against people of colour. Rather does it seem that in the medieval era discrimination came to be based far more on religious differentiation than on colour. Antipathy was directed against non-Christians, or infidels, with Muslims being the main target. From the twelfth century anti-Jewish prejudice became more evident in western Christendom. As Gossett has observed, 'From then on, the Jews became the most frequent scapegoat of Christian societies'. And this prejudice was not dissimilar to modern racism: 'Jews were frequently regarded by Christians as loathsome creatures who had bad physical, mental, and moral characteristics which they apparently inherited and passed on to their descendents'.[8] Or else cultural and social differences lay at the base of prejudice towards 'others'. From the twelfth century the English, for instance, commonly expressed their contempt for the 'wilde Irish'.[9] Generally, though, before the sixteenth century in western Europe there was little attempt to categorise groups, or differentiate between them, on the grounds of race or colour.[10] 'In the Middle Ages ...' asserts Oliver Cox, 'we find no racial antagonism in Europe'.[11]

---

5 Snowden, *Before Color Prejudice*, pp.65-73.
6 *Ibid.*, pp.106-8.
7 Jan Nederveen Pieterse, *White on Black* (New Haven, 1992), p.24.
8 Thomas F. Gossett, *Race: The History of an Idea in America* (Dallas, 1963), pp.10-11.
9 Pieterse, *White on Black*, p.31.
10 Goldberg, *Racist Culture*, pp.21-24.
11 Cox, *Caste, Class and Race*, p.326.

If white racism cannot be traced back to the classical or medieval eras, surely the age of European maritime exploration and imperial expansion, from the late fifteenth century, would be a more likely source. A number of writers have thought so. Cox, writing in the late 1940s, is quite precise on this point: 'If we had to put our finger upon the year which marked the beginning of modern race relations we should select 1493-94. This is the time when total disregard for the human rights and physical power of the non-Christian peoples of the world, the colored peoples, was officially assumed by the first two great colonizing European nations'[12] – Spain and Portugal. Ruth Benedict makes a similar claim, just a few years before Cox: 'European expansion overseas, therefore, set the stage for racist dogmas and gave violent early expression to racial antipathies without propounding racism as a philosophy'.[13] For Benedict, though, these antipathies were more of a carryover of medieval discrimination against non-Christians – it was not as yet discrimination based on skin colour.[14] David Goldberg goes further, pinpointing the emergence of the concept of race, a concept which 'seeped into European consciousness more or less coterminous with the exploratory voyages of discovery, expansion, and domination in the latter part of the fifteenth century'. The first English usage of the term 'race' was in a poem of 1508. Through the sixteenth century the word 'race' came to be used increasingly to denote different human groups who could be distinguished according to physical and cultural characteristics, lines of descent, geographical locations.[15] The 'other' was gradually being constituted.

The search for the origins of white racism has not surprisingly brought a sharp focus on the Americas in the early colonial era. The connection between racism and slavery – a 'chicken-or-egg' question – has been extensively debated. One seminal text has been Winthrop Jordan's *White Over Black*, published in 1968. Working within a broadly idealist paradigm, Jordan traces the history of white American race attitudes from the sixteenth century. He argues that prejudice towards people of colour was deep-seated in the culture of Elizabethan England and imported into North America by English colonisers: 'From the first, Englishmen tended to set Negroes over against themselves, to stress what they conceived to be radically contrasting qualities of colour, religion, and style of life, as well as animality and a

---

12   *Ibid.*, pp.331-32.
13   Ruth Benedict, *Race: Science and Politics* (New York, 1945), p.111.
14   *Ibid.*, p.108.
15   Goldberg, *Racist Culture*, pp.62-63.

peculiarly potent sexuality'.[16] For Jordan this racism grew out of symbols, associations and images that came to be ingrained in an English mind-set. Blackness was at the heart of this symbolism: 'Long before they found that some men were black, Englishmen found in the idea of blackness a way of expressing some of their most ingrained values'.[17] These were negative values: 'Black was an emotionally partisan color, the handmaid and symbol of baseness and evil, a sign of danger and repulsion'.[18] Blackness symbolised the devil, heathenism, cultural depravity, unrestrained animality.[19]

According to this view the roots of race prejudice and race discrimination are to be found in differences of skin colour and culture – what Allen calls 'the psycho-cultural argument'.[20] Attitudes of white superiority and distaste towards 'others' grew, in part at least, out of this dark symbolism and the negative connotations of blackness. The attitudes became more ingrained as white colonisers and traders sought the land, labour and commodities of indigenous peoples. But the racism predated the exploitation. This is a position argued quite vigorously by Carl Degler in an article exploring the connection between racism and slavery in British North America. Writing a few years before Jordan, Degler asserts that race prejudice came before slavery: '... long before slavery or black labor became an important part of the Southern economy, a special and inferior status had been worked out for the Negroes who came to the English colonies'.[21]

Degler and Jordan had their followers. Writing soon after Jordan, Gary Nash and Richard Weiss were others to ascribe a distant origin to American racism: 'Racial attitudes have shaped the American experience since Europeans first set foot in the New World', they assert.[22] Nash himself, like Jordan, looks back to the culture of Elizabethan England as a major source of these attitudes.[23] The emergence of this Elizabethan culture of racism has been explored and unpacked by James Walvin. He notes an outpouring of

---

16 Winthrop D. Jordan, *White Over Black: American Attitudes Towards the Negro, 1550-1812* (Baltimore, 1968), p.43.
17 *Ibid.*, p.7.
18 *Ibid.*
19 *Ibid.*, pp.27-35.
20 Theodore W. Allen, *The Invention of the White Race* (New York, 1994), vol.1, p.4.
21 Carl N. Degler, "Slavery and the genesis of American race prejudice", *Comparative Studies in Society and History*, 2, 1959-60, pp.61-62.
22 Gary B. Nash & Richard Weiss (eds), *The Great Fear: Race in the Mind of America* (New York, 1970), p.iii.
23 Gary B. Nash, "Red, White and Black: The Origins of Racism in Colonial America", in Nash and Weiss (eds), *The Great Fear*, p.1.

foreign travel literature from the 1570s, including accounts of Africa. This writing revealed the existence of peoples whose culture and values appeared to contrast strikingly with the dominant moral ethos of the English. No matter that the literature was full of errors, fantasies and myths – these lived on, coming to be 'absorbed and embellished by later generations of Englishmen'.[24]

The psycho-cultural argument came under serious questioning during the 1970s and 1980s. The idea that English settlers transplanted their deeply ingrained racist attitudes on North American soil did not hold in the eyes of many critics. One should not, it is argued, generalise too readily about a racist culture in Elizabethan England, where one could identify a range of attitudes towards people of colour. For instance, the English explorers, Drake and Raleigh, sometimes portrayed native Americans as noble, godlike creatures.[25] What was evident at the time, say Jordan's critics, was not so much a virulent racism based on colour difference, but rather a strong ethnocentrism directed against 'others' whose culture and religion were considered strange and alien. As Fredrickson has put it, 'In the absence of sustained contact, the negative attitude towards Africans that Elizabethan Englishmen sometimes manifested was, in all likelihood, the casually held and somewhat fluid impression of a remote and exotic form of humanity rather than an expression of a fixed and deeply rooted colorphobia'.[26]

The contours of the debate are taking shape. The origins and dynamics of white racism is a matter of historical contestation in which the analytical, conceptual and methodological pitfalls are many. The Degler/Jordan psycho-cultural approach at once highlights a fundamental problem – has white racism been the expression of deep-seated attitudes, or has it been the product of circumstances? The Degler/Jordan thesis suffers from a rather static idealism. In viewing white racism as ingrained, fixed, and enduring the thesis loses the opportunity to differentiate between various forms of racism and to show how the phenomenon changes over time. If applied to the South African case the Degler/Jordan approach would imply that the Dutch and British colonisers simply imported their ingrained racism and planted it on Cape soil. As we shall see, this view does have its adherents, but falls far short

---

24 James Walvin, *Black and White: The Negro and English Society 1555-1945* (London, 1973), pp.22-28.
25 Allen, *Invention of the White Race*, pp.6-7; Gossett, *Race*, pp.24-25.
26 Fredrickson, *White Supremacy*, p.74; see also Oscar and Mary Handlin's letter to the editor, in *Comparative Studies in Society and History*, 2, 1959-60, pp.488-90.

of an adequate explanation. Any attempt to historicise racism requires careful attention to specificity and context. Racial attitudes have varied according to circumstances. Some suggest that racism arises from ignorance, and ignorance from insularity and isolation. Others stress that racism develops in situations of contact – especially, perhaps, where the nature of the contact is threatening, giving rise to fear and hostility. One must, too, assess carefully the significance of skin colour in the shaping of racism. Which has been the more crucial – difference of colour, or difference of culture? Furthermore, has racism been more pronounced in some colonial countries than others?

Spanish and Portuguese colonialism, argue some, was not marked by virulent racial prejudice. Certainly this is a claim firmly maintained by the Portuguese. As Boxer has put it, '... it is an article of faith with many Portuguese that their country has never tolerated a colour-bar in its overseas possessions and that their compatriots have always had a natural affinity for contacts with coloured peoples'.[27] It is a claim that has been supported by scholars across an ideological spectrum. Oliver Cox, for instance, stresses that the Portuguese did not indulge in racial hatred, did not develop racial theories.[28] Moreover, there was seemingly no Portuguese antipathy towards intermarriage or interracial sexual liaisons. Indeed, there is much evidence of Portuguese colonists assimilating indigenous cultures. In Africa many Portuguese traders and adventurers became Africanised. Spanish colonialism has similarly been credited with a certain racial tolerance. Some argue that both Spain and Portugal had experienced a long history of contact with peoples of diverse cultures – with Muslims, Jews, Berbers, among others, since the eighth century. Intermarriage and social interaction had thus given rise to a widespread attitude that differences of colour did not matter.[29]

Such a view is almost certainly too lenient. Notwithstanding a seemingly 'soft' stance on racial 'mixing' there is evidence that racism was a characteristic of Portuguese and Spanish culture. Russell-Wood has pointed to the racist discourse of much fifteenth and sixteenth century Portuguese writing – a discourse which represented blacks as savage, degenerate and libidinous.[30] Spanish writers were particularly contemptuous of indigenous Amerindians, who were often likened to beasts. They were sometimes

---

27 C.R. Boxer, *Race Relations in the Portuguese Colonial Empire 1415-1825* (Oxford, 1963), p.1.
28 Cox, *Caste, Class and Race*, pp.327-28.
29 Nash, "Red, White, and Black", p.13; Degler, "American race prejudice", p.50.
30 A.J.R. Russell-Wood, "Iberian expansion and the issue of black slavery: changing Portuguese attitudes, 1440-1770", *American Historical Review*, 83, 1, 1978, pp.38-39.

portrayed as savage cannibals – a representation that seemed to justify Spanish conquest.[31] Boxer notes that among the Portuguese, in the colonial era, '... the prevailing social pattern was ... one of conscious white superiority'.[32] He also stresses what he sees as an 'obvious fact' – namely, 'that one race cannot systematically enslave members of another on a large scale for over three centuries without acquiring a conscious or unconscious feeling of racial superiority'.[33] This can hardly be called a 'fact'. Boxer is making a speculative point – and touching upon an issue that was to become an important area of debate: the connection between slavery and racism. Which came first? The implication of Boxer's assertion is that racism grew out of slavery. This issue has been extensively debated in American historiography. And, as we shall see, it has a bearing on the historiography of South African racism.

The main focus of this study is on South Africa. So if we are searching for a pre-existing European racism as a source of segregation and apartheid in South Africa, our attention should be directed first and foremost to the Netherlands, whence came South Africa's first white settlers. Did these Dutch settlers bring with them ingrained prejudices which they simply transplanted on Cape soil? Can a Degler/Jordan type of analysis also be applied to the Dutch? In emphasising the metropolitan sources of colonial racism is one thereby placing insufficient stress on the particular colonial conditions in which racist consciousness and practice emerged?

Leonard Guelke is one proponent of the view that the Dutch brought their prejudices with them to the Cape. He argues that 'white supremacy is not an essentially South African product, but rather has its origin in a pre-existing Dutch colonial vision, which was premised on European dominance and a sense of racial superiority. This vision was the basis of the first European settlement at the Cape, and predated its founding by many decades'.[34] This Dutch sense of superiority, continues Guelke, 'was made manifest in colonial settings in institutional racism and slavery'.[35] Guelke builds his argument around the idea that Dutch East India Company officials saw the colonial world as distinct from that of their metropolitan base in the Netherlands. The Company, for instance, tolerated interracial marriages between its European

---

31 Goldberg, *Racist Culture*, pp.25; Gossett, *Race*, p.12.
32 Boxer, *Race Relations*, p.40.
33 *Ibid.*, p.56.
34 Leonard Guelke, "The Origin of White Supremacy in South Africa: An Interpretation", *Social Dynamics*, 15, 2, 1989, p.40.
35 *Ibid.*, p.41.

employees and women converts of Asian origin. However, such couples were not permitted to return to the Netherlands – an indication of racial attitudes in the home country. This attitude of European superiority was apparently so deep-seated that the Dutch came to South Africa with the expectation to be served rather than to serve. This was why Van Riebeeck was so quick to ask for slaves.[36] Thus, concludes Guelke, 'the original impulse to maintain racial exclusivity was not a colonial-born settler impulse but rather a home impulse transferred to an overseas setting'.[37]

Guelke's position is strikingly original, even unique in South African historiography. It has few other adherents. Some historians accept that racism existed in the Netherlands before the era of Dutch colonial expansion, but also stress that racism was fuelled by particular colonial conditions. Elphick and Giliomee, for instance, recognise that 'even before 1652 the Dutch had developed a strong aversion to Africans, attributing to them sexual licence, savagery and a diabolical religion'.[38] But the overall concern of Elphick and Giliomee's analysis is to show how racial consciousness and discrimination developed in the Cape from the mid-seventeenth century. They move some way beyond Guelke's rather rigid interpretation, recognising the colonial, rather than metropolitan, origins of racism.[39]

Van den Boogart, like Elphick and Giliomee, differs from Guelke, questioning the Jordan/Degler approach. He sees the attitudes of the Dutch as being shaped by their own cultural norms and by their perceptions of black communities. But these attitudes were also strongly influenced by 'forms of contact'.[40] In their first contact with Africa, from the late sixteenth century, the Dutch seem to have developed ambivalent attitudes. Dutch interests were primarily commercial. So, argues Van den Boogart, 'there was much in the ways of Africans that was bound to remain strange and threatening. On the other hand, the dependencies and reciprocity of the trading contact allowed Dutchmen to develop some sympathetic interest and a feeling that Africans

---

36 *Ibid.*, pp.41-42.
37 *Ibid.*, pp.43-44.
38 Richard Elphick & Hermann Giliomee, "The origins and entrenchment of European dominance at the Cape, 1652-c.1840", in Richard Elphick & Hermann Giliomee (eds), *The Shaping of South African Society, 1652-1840* (Cape Town, 1989), p.525.
39 See below for a further discussion of this issue.
40 Ernst van den Boogart, "Colour prejudice and the yardstick of civility: The initial Dutch confrontation with black Africans, 1590-1635", in R. Ross (ed.), *Racism and Colonialism* (The Hague, 1982), p.40.

could not be totally different from themselves'.[41] Van den Boogart accepts Jordan's view that blackness had negative connotations for the Dutch at the time, as it did for other Europeans, but these dark images and connotations tended to gain expression only when the Dutch felt threatened by black Africans. Moreover, Van den Boogart sees cultural difference rather than skin colour as the basis of an emergent Dutch racism. Africans were generally perceived by the Dutch to be living in a state of savagery. But Van den Boogart concedes that the Dutch 'also discovered that Africans were not entirely savage' – they were considered to be superior to Amerindians in political organisation, agriculture and craftsmanship.[42] He advances beyond the straightforward idealist position that presents racism as the expression of ingrained attitudes derived from differences of skin colour. For him culture was more significant than colour in shaping Dutch attitudes. And to understand Dutch racism one had to look closely at the context in which those attitudes were formed.

Fredrickson takes a similar position in his brief analysis of pre-1652 Dutch racial attitudes. For him, the Dutch colonial project of the seventeenth century was not imbued with a deep-seated racism. The Dutch did not set out with ingrained racial attitudes. Rather was Dutch colonialism shaped by hard-nosed commercial concerns. The Dutch East India Company was not set on conquest and colonisation.[43] So, in the East the Dutch 'showed little racial prejudice'. They tolerated intermarriage between colonists and indigenous women who had been converted. Some children of mixed marriages rose to high positions in the Company.[44] But the Company dealt ruthlessly with indigenous communities that resisted or undermined its commercial interests.[45] In Fredrickson's account of early Dutch colonialism one sees little of the ingrained Dutch prejudice towards people of colour so stressed by Guelke.

Guelke's thesis has hardly provoked a major debate. Indeed the issue at hand has been somewhat removed from the mainstream of South African historiography. Few historians have even explored the possibility that the roots of South African racism might be found in the early seventeenth century Netherlands. Authors of South African historical surveys, from De Kiewiet

---

41 *Ibid.*, p.43.
42 *Ibid.*, p.54.
43 Fredrickson, *White Supremacy*, p.19.
44 *Ibid.*, pp.108-10.
45 *Ibid.*, p.19.

through to Davenport and Thompson, have generally avoided the question. There are some exceptions. Sparks, for instance, seems to follow the Guelke line, claiming that the Dutch showed contempt 'toward the indigenous inhabitants of Africa from the day they landed'.[46] One recent survey-writer who has paid greater attention to the early metropolitan European dimension is Moleah. He begins his text by arguing that 'To understand the colonizing European, one has to look at his conditioning experiences'.[47] He proceeds to outline those experiences, in a somewhat generalised way. He points to the negative, destructive forces that shaped seventeenth century western Europe – violence, warfare, brutality, inequality. Warfare was endemic: 'This ubiquity of war engendered a culture of war, cruelty and violence which presages European behaviour in the colonies'.[48] More specifically, 'The Netherlands emerged out of the cauldron of European violence to be the most energetic colonizer of non-European lands'.[49] Moreover, advances in the technical field had led Europeans to develop a strong belief in their own innate superiority. And 'This sense of superiority transmitted into a sense of entitlement, a sense of priority which in the colonial world translated into racism, pillage and murder'.[50] Moleah asserts his position vigorously and unequivocally. The position is a variant of the Jordan thesis, stressing the continuity of European attitudes and practices before and through the era of colonial expansion.

The conclusions to be drawn from this brief historiographical survey are somewhat ambivalent. On the one hand it is erroneous to suggest that a ready-made racism, or an embryonic racial order, was brought to the Cape by the Dutch in the seventeenth century. There was no systematic body of racial thought. Notions of racial difference and racial superiority were as yet undeveloped and would only evolve more fully in specific colonial contexts, as we shall see. On the other hand, it would be equally misleading to separate the history of South Africa's racial order from the rise of capitalism, Protestantism and imperialism in early modern Europe. The colonisers were bearers of values and interests that would become significant ingredients in the making of that racial order.

---

46   Allister Sparks, *The Mind of South Africa* (London, 1991), p.29.
47   Alfred Tokollo Moleah, *South Africa: Colonialism, Apartheid and African Dispossession* (Delaware, 1993), p.2.
48   Ibid., p.6.
49   Ibid., p.22.
50   Ibid., p.26.

This brief historiographical exploration has so far centred on one main question: can one detect a long continuity in the history of white racism, stretching back perhaps 500 years? The counter-arguments, resting on the view that racism is best understood as a modern phenomenon or as a product of specific colonial conditions, still have to be considered. But this continuity/discontinuity question is only one of the issues that make up the larger debate surrounding the history of racism. Many would say that at the heart of this debate is the more fundamental division between idealist and materialist interpretations: in other words, is racism best explained as a product of attitudes and ideas, or in terms of material interests?

This division will be constantly in view as we traverse the historiography of South African racism. But it is too simplistic to reduce the debate to a straightforward polarised contestation between idealist and materialist approaches. Some writers sit easily in one camp or the other, but some do not. Moreover, each position has its own internal complexities. There are, for instance, idealists who see racist attitudes as arising mainly from colour differences. Others stress the prime importance of cultural division. Among the former one can count Winthrop Jordan, with his stress on the symbolic associations attached to whiteness and blackness in western culture over many centuries. For writers like Van den Boogart, on the other hand, racism rather grew out of a general European contempt for 'other' cultures that were deemed to be inferior, primitive, uncivilised. Because cultural differences often coincided with colour differences this contempt came to be expressed more and more in a racist discourse.

It is not helpful to proffer easy generalisations about the complex phenomenon of European racism in the early modern era. The very notion of 'European' racism is itself misleading as it obscures national and regional differences. Some have argued, for instance, that the English and Dutch exhibited more intense forms of racism than did the Spanish and Portuguese. As we have seen, it is often claimed that race relations in Spanish and Portuguese colonies were more relaxed than in their English and Dutch counterparts. This seemed to be exemplified by widespread intermarriage and easier interracial sexual relations between Spanish and Portuguese colonists and indigenous inhabitants. Various reasons are put forward to explain this supposed difference. There was the religious factor. It is suggested that the Roman Catholic Church, dominant in Spain and Portugal, espoused the spiritual unity and equality of all Christians, regardless of race.[51] By contrast

---

51 Degler, "American race prejudice", p.50.

Protestantism had gained a hold in England and the Netherlands during the sixteenth century. The Calvinism of the Dutch in particular gave rise, supposedly, to strong beliefs in divine election. These beliefs translated easily into the racist presumption that the enterprising white colonisers were 'chosen people' and that the members of 'backward' indigenous communities were not.[52] It has also been pointed out by Gossett that Protestant conversion standards were more rigorous than those required by Catholic missionaries. While the latter would often accept conversions which were merely nominal, Protestant missionaries generally insisted on a more wholehearted, genuine adherence to their faith on the part of converts.[53] The Catholic approach was thus more easily assimilationist, allowing for the relaxation of racial barriers in the religious sphere.

However, a straightforward differentiation such as this, along national and denominational lines, is also too much of a simplification. One cannot ascribe particular race attitudes to specific nationalities. To do this is to stereotype. There was not a racial attitude that can be described as characteristically English. Some scholars have, for instance, highlighted the different attitudes towards miscegenation adopted by English colonists in the West Indies from those in North America. In the British West Indies interracial sex was widely practised and tolerated, whereas in the North American colonies it was largely condemned.[54] Similarly one should not make easy generalisations about the supposedly more relaxed racial attitudes of the Portuguese. Bender calls this the myth of lusotropicalism: 'The proponents of lusotropicalism maintained that because of the [asserted] historically unique absence of racism among the Portuguese people, their colonization of tropical, non-European territories was characterized by racially egalitarian legislation and human interaction'.[55] This claim had flimsy foundations. It rested largely on the high level of miscegenation between Portuguese colonists and Amerindians and Africans in Brazil. But Bender argues that the Brazilian experience was somewhat exceptional in the Portuguese colonial world. Apart from the small islands of Cape Verde, Sao Tomé and Principe, there were low levels of miscegenation in Portugal's other colonies: '... the percentage of mestiços in Portugal's African colonies

---

52 Elphick & Giliomee, "European dominance", p.525.
53 Gossett, *Race*, p.24.
54 Nash, "Red, White, and Black", pp.18-19; Gerald J. Bender, *Angola under the Portuguese: The Myth and the Reality* (London, 1978), pp.35-38.
55 Bender, *Angola under the Portuguese*, p.3.

was relatively insignificant, while in the Portuguese Indian and Asian colonies the percentage of mestiços was barely negligible'.[56]

The myth of lusotropicalism also seems to rest on the false assumption that the easy practice of interracial sex is an accurate gauge of relaxed racial attitudes. The connection between racism and sexuality is a complex one – and one that will require further exploration in this study of South African racism. It does appear to be a connection marked by ambivalence. Ideas, myths and perceptions of black sexuality could induce both aversion and desire among those who held such ideas. As Noyes has observed, colonial discourse could produce 'elaborate fantasies of naked brown women free for the taking, or syphilitic black women waiting enticingly in the shadows, or potent black men stalking white virgins'.[57] Walvin notes how centuries ago the belief emerged in Europe that African men had unusually large penises – a myth that 'came to form the basis for much sexual excitement, resentment and, ultimately, racial antagonism between black and white'.[58] Bender detects a similar ambivalence among the Portuguese who 'openly fornicated with Indians', but also despised them 'as savages, barbarians and animals'.[59] Moleah explains this ambivalence in terms of the repressed European personality. European colonisers projected their own repressed desires on to indigenous people, so that the supposed sexual potency of the latter became a source of both fear and envy for the former.[60] When we come to examine the specificities of South African racism we can expect to find a similar ambivalence.

Any one explaining the connection between sexuality and racism would most likely be working within the idealist tradition – the tradition that emphasises the power of beliefs, ideas, attitudes in shaping the course of history. It is an approach that gives explanatory primacy to ideological, psychological and cultural factors. As we have seen in this brief preliminary survey, attempts to find the roots of western racism have produced a variety of idealist interpretations. And when we come to explore the historiography of South African racism we will encounter many such interpretations. We will also find that materialist approaches have had a prominent place in this historiography.

---

56   *Ibid.*, p.32.
57   John K. Noyes, "Rainbow Nation", *South African Review of Books*, 41, 1996, p.15.
58   Walvin, *Black and White*, p.22.
59   Bender, *Angola under the Portuguese*, p.40.
60   Moleah, *South Africa*, p.30.

Before Van Riebeeck: The Early European Legacy

An early, and unequivocal, exponent of the materialist position was Oliver Cox. His classic text, *Caste, Class and Race*, was first published in 1948. For Cox racism 'was not an abstract, natural, immemorial feeling of mutual antipathy between groups, but rather a practical exploitative relationship'.[61] Racism is viewed as an instrument used by the dominant class to facilitate labour exploitation. So the 'capitalist exploiter ...' continues Cox, 'will devise and employ race prejudice when that becomes convenient'.[62] Racism thus becomes a justification, a legitimating ideology, for exploitation:

> The capitalist exploitation of colored workers ... consigns them to employments and treatment that is humanly degrading. In order to justify this treatment the exploiters must argue that the workers are innately degraded and degenerate, consequently they naturally merit their condition.[63]

Cox goes even further, offering a bold counterfactual: namely, the probability 'that without capitalism, a cultural chance occurrence among whites, the world might never have experienced race prejudice'.[64]

The notion that there has been a close connection between capitalism and racism came, especially in the 1970s, to gain significant support from radical South Africanist social scientists, as we shall see. More recently, though, the materialist analysis of racism has been criticised as too mechanical, too reductionist. Postmodernists go further, largely dismissing the materialist approach for its essentialism and its tendency to totalise. A complex phenomenon like racism, it is argued, cannot be explained in terms of a single overarching theoretical model.

Postmodernists would also rail against any account that surveyed the history of racism in a teleological vein. The search for a single point of origin, an evolutionary model implying a gradual unfolding towards an ultimate destiny – such are the teleological assumptions challenged by postmodernists who might place greater emphasis on the discontinuities and disjunctures in the history of racism, than on the continuities.

There is, too, another postmodernist theme that has a bearing on our subject. Up till now we have considered, albeit sketchily, the history of racism in classical, medieval and early modern times. And we have seen that there is

---

61   Cox, *Caste, Class and Race*, p.332.
62   *Ibid.*, p.333.
63   *Ibid.*, p.334.
64   *Ibid.*, p.345.

a body of literature that stresses a connection between the emergence of racist thought and European colonial expansion in early modern times. Postmodernists, on the other hand, would tend to view racism as more a product of modernity. The eighteenth century Enlightenment, with its assumption that reason and science would triumph and bring future progress to humankind, failed in its grand objectives. So, as we shall see, some historical analyses now claim that the development of racial theory went hand-in-hand with scientific thought, especially from the nineteenth century.

This idea, in turn, raises further questions. What is the connection, for instance, between racial theory and racial consciousness? And how has racial theory influenced the practice of racial discrimination, legislated and institutionalised? These questions compel us to investigate more closely our South African case-study. After all it is in twentieth century South Africa that one finds what has been perhaps the most rigid, systematised and abhorrent practice of anti-black racial discrimination that has ever been known in history. It is to this case-study that we must now turn.

2 Differentiation and Discrimination in Cape Dutch Society

Blame it on Van Riebeeck – the title of a satirical book by Leo Marquard and Joel Mervis – goes to the heart of our problem. If the Dutch did not bring with them an embryonic racial order to the Cape in the seventeenth century, how soon after their arrival did such an order begin to take shape? Or did it evolve gradually over several decades? Did there emerge a formal, institutionalised racial order, or was racial discrimination more informal, *de facto* rather than *de jure*? To what extent did perceived racial differences give rise before 1800, to race consciousness, racial ideology, racial categorisation, even racial theory? Assuming that some kind of racial order did emerge in the early Cape, why did it emerge? Did it grow out of cultural differences, or out of white attitudes of superiority and repugnance towards others? Or should one look to a materialist explanation, stressing the connection between labour exploitation, especially slavery, and racism? Is it possible to detect a continuity between an evolving racial order in the pre-1800 Cape and the segregation and apartheid policies of the twentieth century? Or does such a whiggish, teleological approach conceal discontinuity and disjuncture?

These are the central questions for consideration in this chapter. What is particularly striking is that for decades these questions were not addressed in any thorough or substantial way by historians. It was not until the publication in 1979 of the first edition of a book edited by Richard Elphick and Hermann Giliomee, *The Shaping of South African Society, 1652-1820*, that these questions were brought to the fore. This collective work brought the issue of apartheid's distant origins firmly into the arena of South African historical debate. Up till that time no historian had attempted an in-depth exploration of the emerging racial order at the Cape in the seventeenth and eighteenth centuries. Earlier writing on the subject had tended to make large assumptions and generalisations with little analytical or empirical substantiation. For all his prolific historical output, G.M. Theal, for instance, merely assumed that the racial order was a natural, normal state of affairs that had long existed and did not require investigation.[1] This

---

1 Christopher Saunders, *The Making of the South African Past* (Cape Town, 1988), p.70.

assumption particularly suited Afrikaner nationalists – historians, social scientists and politicians alike – as it seemed to confirm that apartheid was more a product of historical reality, with deep roots in the past, rather than the appalling contrivance of post-1948 National Party governments. Thus two apartheid apologists, N.J. Rhoodie and H.J. Venter, writing in the late 1950s, could claim that racial separation in South Africa was 'a process which began three centuries ago with "natural apartheid" between White and Black ... . During the earliest years of settlement in South Africa, White and Black existed as two autonomous, free-flowing units living side by side, each in its own territory'.[2]

Before 1970 most writers, across the ideological spectrum, had assumed that the South African racial order was taking shape by the late eighteenth century. The pioneering liberal historian, W.M. Macmillan, put forward the view that white racism developed in the eighteenth century, but without really substantiating his position.[3] Similarly, De Kiewiet asserted in his general history that 'South Africa took the policy of racial segregation seriously from the very start'.[4] One finds a similar assertion, made at about the same time, the late 1940s, in *Time Longer Than Rope*, the famous work of Edward Roux, the former Communist Party activist. For him, too, white racist attitudes originated in the eighteenth century. Among earlier writers I.D. MacCrone was exceptional in paying close attention to the origins of racism in South Africa.[5]

The emergence of a new generation of radical South Africanist scholars in the 1970s prompted a deeper intellectual engagement with historical questions relating to the country's racial order. These writers challenged long-held assumptions and previous approaches to these questions. Legassick's pioneering article on the frontier tradition did much to stir debate and open up avenues of inquiry.[6] As is well known, in the 1970s many radical writers stressed the connection between mining capitalism and the development of race discrimination in South Africa. The necessary corollary of this view was to play down the extent of race consciousness and racial

---

2   N.J. Rhoodie and H.J. Venter, *Apartheid: A Socio-historical Exposition of the Origin and Development of the Apartheid Idea* (Cape Town, 1960), p.vii.
3   Saunders, *South African Past*, p.70.
4   C.W. de Kiewiet, *A History of South Africa* (London, 1957), p.20.
5   Edward Roux, *Time Longer Than Rope* (London, 1964), p.24. See below for an examination of MacCrone's analysis.
6   Martin Legassick, "The frontier tradition in South African historiography", in *Societies of Southern Africa*, vol.2 (Institute of Commonwealth Studies, London, 1971), later published in Shula Marks and Anthony Atmore (eds), *Economy and Society in Pre-industrial South Africa* (London, 1980).

practice in the pre-industrial era. However, like much earlier writing, this corollary also came to rest largely on premise and assumption rather than on substantial research. Radical historians generally steered clear of the early Cape. One exception was Bill Freund, the only historian to offer a clear-cut exposition of the radical view on race in the early Cape.[7]

The challenge to explore in greater depth the history of race in the early Cape was taken up by scholars who did not fall squarely in the radical tradition. Elphick and Giliomee's collective project was conceived in 1973, two years after the appearance of Legassick's frontier paper, which must surely have been a major stimulus for their project. Two chapters in the first edition of the book explicitly examined race relations and racial policy in the early Cape.[8] Two years later there appeared George Fredrickson's comparative study of racial segregation in American and South African history. In this there is a close examination of the early Cape.[9] Robert Ross was another historian to look at the early Cape, with similar questions in mind, soon after Fredrickson.[10] The authors of these seminal works – Elphick, Giliomee, Fredrickson and Ross – adopted similar approaches and reached similar conclusions. Although the works show an openness to radical perspectives, none accept the radical position that played down the white segregationist impulse in the pre-industrial era. For all of them there were clear signs of an emerging racial order in the Cape long before the industrial era. And in all their works there is a refusal to subordinate the race factor to an overriding class analysis.

The first question: to what extent was early Cape society, during the era of the Dutch East India Company, marked by racial ideology and consciousness, and by the practice of racial discrimination? And if a racial order emerged at this time how can it be periodised? We have already seen that a small group of scholars argue that the first white colonists brought with

---

7   W.M. Freund, "Race in the social structure of South Africa, 1652-1836", *Race and Class*, 18, 1, 1976.
8   Richard Elphick and Robert Shell, "Intergroup relations: Khoikhoi, settlers, slaves and free blacks, 1652-1795", and Hermann Giliomee and Richard Elphick, "The structure of European domination at the Cape, 1652-1820", in Richard Elphick and Hermann Giliomee (eds), *The Shaping of South African Society 1652-1820* (London, 1979).
9   Fredrickson, *White Supremacy*.
10 Robert Ross, "Pre-industrial and industrial racial stratification in South Africa", in Ross (ed.), *Racism and Colonialism*; Robert Ross *Beyond the Pale* (Hanover, 1993) - first published (in Dutch) in 1983. See also Hermann Giliomee, "Eighteenth century Cape society and its historiography: culture, race and class", *Social Dynamics*, 9, 1, 1983.

them to the Cape from Europe racial preconceptions and attitudes of superiority towards racial 'others'. The obvious corollary of such a view is that this imported racism would have immediately given rise to discriminatory practice in the colonial situation.

Is there evidence to support this corollary? Some of the writings of Van Riebeeck, in the months after his arrival at the Cape in 1652, suggest a fairly virulent racist outlook on his part. Within a few days of his arrival he issued a proclamation to regulate interaction between Dutch East India Company employees and the indigenous Khoikhoi. The language of the proclamation reveals something of Van Riebeeck's attitude towards the latter. The Khoikhoi are described as 'very brutal', and as a '... wild nation ... very bold, thievish, and not at all too be trusted ...'.[11] A year later his impressions were largely unchanged, when he wrote of '... these dull, stupid, lazy, stinking people ...'.[12] Great significance has been attached to these writings by some. Rhoodie and Venter, for instance, describe this initial Dutch attitude, exemplified by Van Riebeeck, as one of 'noticeable aloofness' and see it as 'one of the earliest origins of apartheid'.[13] Other historians have made much of the early attitudes and policies of Van Riebeeck and the Dutch East India Company administration. Early attempts to impose territorial segregation have been highlighted. In 1659, for instance, the Company administration tried to create a border from the Salt River mouth to the mountain – a fence and an almond hedge, to separate the white inhabitants of the Cape peninsula from the Khoikhoi. Eric Walker, a prominent South Africanist historian from the 1920s to the 1960s, saw this as 'the first attempt at apartheid', as did Rhoodie and Venter.[14]

The almond hedge as an embryonic group areas measure? This idea had an obvious appeal to Afrikaner nationalists from the 1950s, concerned as they were to legitimate apartheid by stressing its deep historical roots. But most writers have played down any seventeenth century origin for South African racism. In 1937 there appeared I.D. MacCrone's important study, part historical and part psychological analysis, *Race Attitudes in South Africa* – a text often referred to in the South African race debate. MacCrone argued that the identity of the early Dutch colonists at the Cape was shaped much more by religion than by race: 'Throughout these early, as well as subsequent, race

---

11 Quoted in I.D. MacCrone, *Race Attitudes in South Africa* (London, 1937), p.19.
12 *Ibid.*, p.22.
13 Rhoodie and Venter, *Apartheid*, p.43.
14 Eric A. Walker, *A History of Southern Africa* (London, 1965), p.41 n.3; Rhoodie and Venter, *Apartheid*, p.46.

contacts, the great dividing line which ran between European and non-European was that of religion'.[15] There was no notion of superior and inferior races. MacCrone believed that there was 'ample evidence' to show that race and skin-colour 'played little or no part' in determining white attitudes towards people of colour.[16] For about three decades MacCrone's book was viewed as an authoritative text on the subject of South African race relations. Other writers came to adopt his claim that religion rather than race was the key differentiating factor in the early colonial era at the Cape.[17]

Although MacCrone played down the early significance of race, his stress on religion still placed him firmly in the idealist tradition: identity was shaped more by beliefs and attitudes than anything else. This idealist premise was vigorously confronted by a new generation of materialist scholars in the 1970s. Materialist analysis had come very much to the fore when research and writing on race in the early Cape gained momentum in the late 1970s and early 1980s. However, most of the writers engaged in this flurry of research did not operate in the materialist paradigm. Nor, though, did they write material considerations out of their analyses. We also see these writers supporting MacCrone's contention that race was not a crucial factor in the seventeenth century Cape – but on different grounds from MacCrone.

Fredrickson, for instance, stressed the commercial considerations that shaped early Dutch attitudes at the Cape. The Dutch East India Company was first and foremost a trading operation, not an agent of conquest and colonisation. The Company's treatment of indigenous communities was therefore dictated largely by commercial interests: the Company's aim 'was control of what these societies produced rather than direct domination of their territories and population'.[18] Trade did not require conquest or control of the Khoikhoi, and allowed for a permissive rather than discriminatory policy in the matter of racial interaction. Initial attempts to regulate this interaction were designed more to protect trade with the Khoikhoi than to institute white domination. This, though, would change later, when the Cape became an expanding colony of settlement – a development that would impact on race attitudes and policy.

---

15 MacCrone, *Race Attitudes*, p.6.
16 *Ibid.*, pp.8-9, 40-41.
17 See, for instance, "Mnguni" (Hosea Jaffe), *Three Hundred Years* (Cape Town, 1952), p.37; Sheila Patterson, *The Last Trek* (London, 1957), p.9; Pierre L. van den Berghe, *South Africa: A Study in Conflict* (Middletown, 1965), p.14.
18 Fredrickson, *White Supremacy*, p.19.

Ross, Elphick and Giliomee also rejected the claim that apartheid existed in embryonic form from the 1650s. Ross stated emphatically that 'the racial order of modern South Africa was in no way inherent in colonial society from its foundation'.[19] Elphick and Giliomee reached a similar conclusion: 'Notwithstanding the racial assumptions embedded in the legal status system – such as the assumption that Asians and Africans, but never Europeans could be enslaved – the VOC had no intention of establishing a rigid European – dominated society at the Cape'.[20] They accepted that whites were dominant in the seventeenth century Cape, but also stressed that by the early eighteenth century it was not clear how or whether that domination would be sustained.[21] The future racial order was, by that time, in no way prefigured or preordained.

Only some Afrikaner nationalist writers, and a few others, chose to stress the early beginnings of racial segregation in the seventeenth century Cape. A much greater body of writing has played down the significance of this period in the long-term evolution of South African racism. Considerable emphasis has, though, been placed on the eighteenth century. MacCrone was among the first to stress the significance of the eighteenth century, which he saw as 'the formative period' in the shaping of white race attitudes.[22] MacCrone was to have his followers. For the next thirty to forty years after the publication of his book in 1937, MacCrone's position became standard fare. Patterson, for instance, stated that by the end of the eighteenth century the earlier Christian-heathen dichotomy had given way to a racial divide.[23] Others, like Keppel-Jones and Roux, also followed MacCrone on this issue.[24]

When the new wave of research into early Cape history was initiated in the mid-1970s the question of periodising the development of South African racism was explored more closely. The question was firmly addressed by Elphick and Giliomee. Like MacCrone, they also stressed the importance of the eighteenth century. They saw 'the racial order as largely in place by the

---

19 Ross, *Beyond the Pale*, p.90.
20 Richard Elphick and Hermann Giliomee, "The origins and entrenchment of European dominance at the Cape, 1652-c.1840", in Richard Elphick and Hermann Giliomee (eds), *The Shaping of South African Society, 1652-1840* (Cape Town, 1989). It should be noted that a second, revised and extended, edition of this book appeared ten years after the first edition. Hereafter all references are to the second edition, unless otherwise indicated.
21 *Ibid.*, p.532.
22 MacCrone, *Race Attitudes*, p.136. See below for a discussion of MacCrone's reasons for stressing the importance of the eighteenth century.
23 Patterson, *Last Trek*, p.9.
24 A. Keppel-Jones, *South Africa* (London, 1963), p.41; Roux, *Time Longer Than Rope*, p.24.

end of the eighteenth century'.²⁵ But they reached their conclusion by a route different from that taken by MacCrone. MacCrone argued that racist attitudes were shaped on the frontier (see below). Elphick and Giliomee saw the racial order taking shape across the Cape. And it seemed to be a clear-cut process of racial stratification: 'Throughout the eighteenth century Europeans held almost all the land and exercised all the power in the vast agricultural regions of the colony, Khoisan and slaves laboured in the service of others'.²⁶ Just as MacCrone's ideas and conclusions were adopted by subsequent writers, so has the Elphick and Giliomee position found its way into survey texts on South African history.²⁷

This stress on the eighteenth century origins of South African racism has come to be associated with what is loosely labelled the 'liberal' school of South African historiography – although we have also seen that Afrikaner nationalist historians favoured the idea that the origins of apartheid could be traced back to the beginning of white settlement. The opposing view – emphasising the more recent late nineteenth century origins of the racial order – is generally associated with the 'radical' school. The concomitant of this latter position was to play down the extent of racism in the pre-industrial era. Freund offered a forceful exposition of this view in an article that appeared three years before the first edition of Elphick and Giliomee's book. He stated the position unequivocally:

> Race became in the twentieth century the obsessive theme of South African politics. Until well into the nineteenth, it was not. Only an extremely thorough investigation informed by hindsight can ferret out the colour line at the Cape, as late as the 1820s. In part, this is because the determination of strict racial categories is entirely a modern preoccupation in South Africa.²⁸

Freund's article represents an interesting historiographical moment. The piece followed upon and reinforced Legassick's pioneering article on the 'frontier tradition'; it provided an uncompromising assertion of the 'radical' view, a few years before 'radicals' began to rethink and refine their position in the 1980s; and it remains one of very few pieces of writing on the early Cape to reflect that fairly stark 1970s position.

---

25 Elphick and Giliomee, "Origins and entrenchment", p.522.
26 *Ibid.*, p.560.
27 See, for instance, T.R.H. Davenport, *South Africa: A Modern History* (London, 1991), p.30; H.J. van Aswegen, *History of South Africa to 1854* (Pretoria, 1990), pp.153-54.
28 Freund, "Race in the social structure of South Africa", p.56.

Attempts to periodise the history of South Africa's racial order have been beset by shortcomings. Political and ideological agendas have clouded the issue. Afrikaner nationalists have used history in an effort to legitimate apartheid. By arguing that the racial order had deep roots in the past they hoped to show that apartheid was the logical culmination of a lengthy process of historical evolution. Some Marxist analysts, on the other hand, have been determined to establish that racism was essentially the product of capitalism. This required them to deny the existence of a racial order in the precapitalist era. Other historians less driven by such agendas have also handled the periodisation inadequately. This is because they have generally failed to provide a sufficiently complex conceptualisation of racism. Only when the racial order is broken down into its component elements – four of which I am emphasising in this study – can one offer a more nuanced periodisation. As one surveys the history of South African racism once can see some of these elements coming to the fore, while others remain underdeveloped. So the question of periodising the development of the South African racial order cannot really be explored in isolation. There is little point in arguing for an eighteenth or nineteenth century origin, unless one considers carefully the much larger question – what is the evidence for racist thinking and practice in the Cape before 1800? This is a difficult question. Racism is not easily measured. Race discrimination may be *de jure* – institutionalised and legalised – or it may be *de facto* – practised informally. Similarly racist thought may be explicitly articulated, even theorised, or it may be more hidden, embedded in people's consciousness and implicit in their behaviour. So we must explore the Company era of Cape history in the light of these different dimensions.

First, to what extent was racial discrimination formalised, legalised, institutionalised at the Cape in the seventeenth and eighteenth centuries? The evidence suggests that such *de jure* discrimination was very limited. One can find few laws that explicitly discriminated against people on racial lines at that time. Some writers have drawn attention to anti-miscegenation regulations introduced at the Cape in 1685. These were designed to prohibit Dutch men from marrying freed slaves of colour, and to prevent 'illicit intercourse between European males and female slaves or natives'. Two historians in particular, Hosea Jaffe and W.P. van Schoor, have claimed that these regulations marked the beginning of formalised colour discrimination.[29]

---

29 Mnguni (Hosea Jaffe), *Three Hundred Years*, p.40; W.P. van Schoor, "The origin and development of segregation in South Africa", in Maurice Hommel (ed.), *Contributions of Non-European Peoples to World Civilization* (Johannesburg, 1989), p.105.

Both were members of the Unity Movement, writing in the early 1950s. And they wrote explicitly from a Marxist perspective – something of a paradox, given that later Marxist historians were to play down the significance of race discrimination in the Cape before 1800. The emphasis that Jaffe and Van Schoor placed on these 1685 regulations seems to have been somewhat misplaced, as the regulations were never implemented in a serious way.[30]

Jaffe highlighted the institutionalisation of discrimination during the Company period. He pointed to the decision of Governor Tulbagh in 1755 to open segregated hospitals after a scarlet fever and smallpox epidemic, reversing the earlier practice of blacks and whites sharing the same ward. From 1780 policemen of colour were generally not permitted to arrest whites. This apparent trend prompted Jaffe to conclude that 'Under the period of slavery the policy of segregation became the official State policy'.[31] Subsequent research has shown Jaffe's conclusion to be too stark, too far-reaching. Elphick and Giliomee, for instance, arrived at more nuanced conclusions. For them the Company era was not characterised by the development of a clear-cut, legalised system of racial discrimination. But they did see at that time the emergence of a racial order, which was not defined explicitly in racial terms but rather rested on differences between 'legal status groups'. The Company created four main status groups: Company servants (employees), freeburghers, slaves and 'Hottentots' (Khoisan). In this legal status system there was a close, but not complete, correlation of race and class. The first two groups were almost entirely white; and no whites belonged to the other two groups. Members of the various groups received differential treatment from colonial officials and courts 'in many areas of daily life, such as domicile, right of marriage, right of movement, taxation, militia service, land ownership, and so on'.[32] Moreover,

> In the official view one's legal status – more than one's race, religion, origin, culture or colour – determined one's opportunities for advancement: most important, before 1795 only Company servants, freeburghers and free blacks could hold land on secure tenure or gain political power in the official hierarchy of the colony.[33]

---

30 Elphick and Shell, "Intergroup Relations", p.195.
31 Mnguni, *Three Hundred Years*, pp.41-42.
32 Elphick and Giliomee, "Origins and entrenchment", pp.522-23, 528-30.
33 *Ibid.*, p.529.

From this analysis it is apparent that the system of differentiation was not explicitly race-based, nor was it clear-cut. But there was an emergent racial order that had some basis in the legal system, albeit limited.

Racial differentiation and discrimination were not readily discernible in the legal, institutional structures of the Cape in the seventeenth and eighteenth centuries. The emergent racial order rested much more on informal practice, evident in everyday thought, behaviour and patterns of interaction. But the historian who moves into this realm faces difficulties. It is hard enough to capture popular consciousness in the modern era, so much more daunting a project when going back more than 200 years into the past. How can the historian reconstruct behaviour and thought patterns from the past with any kind of precision? Will there not be a tendency to draw general conclusions from fragments of evidence, conclusions that are way out of proportion to that evidence? Moreover, how can one make generalisations about such a vast region as the Cape? Would there not have been regional differences? Indeed, many scholars have drawn a distinction between racial attitudes and practices in the western Cape and those manifested on the frontier. Then, too, there is the problem of determining to what extent attitudes and behaviour have been a response to perceived physical, racial or cultural differences? Such considerations will have to be kept in mind in our historical exploration of racism during the Company era at the Cape.

There is evidence – and agreement among a number of writers – that the Dutch, from the 1650s, held attitudes of contempt and repugnance towards the indigenous Khoisan. Fredrickson noted that 'the Dutch regarded the Khoikhoi as abject savages'; indeed, early reports from the Cape 'gave the "Hottentots" the general reputation of being the most bestial people yet encountered by Europeans in the course of discovering and conquering new lands'.[34] Travellers who visited the Cape and recorded their impressions generally wrote about the Khoisan in denigrating terms. Negative stereotypes came to abound; particular attributes came to be associated with the indigenous inhabitants – drunkenness, dirtiness, barbarism. This stereotyping spread far beyond the borders of the Cape, into Europe and elsewhere, and survived well into the twentieth century.[35]

One should not read too much into this negative stereotyping of the Khoisan. As Ross has argued, this was not racial ideology. Attitudes of contempt and repugnance were not transferred wholesale to other persons of

---

34 Fredrickson, *White Supremacy*, p.34.
35 Ross, *Beyond the Pale*, pp.81-82.

colour. Early white accounts of the Xhosa and Tswana were 'far from derogatory'.[36] Although whites were dominant, they did not develop at this time a racial ideology to justify their domination. There was no rigid system of racial classification, no clear-cut dichotomisation between whites and 'others'.[37] Elphick and Giliomee were in some agreement with Ross. It is true that Elphick and Giliomee saw a strong correlation between race and status groups, and perceived that whites developed a strong collective identity during the seventeenth and eighteenth centuries.[38] But they also conceded that 'Racial attitudes were not systematically expressed. Although Europeans frequently expressed disgust at the appearance of Khoisan and (less frequently) of slaves, these groups were not lumped together and castigated as different and inferior'.[39]

So far this exploration has revealed little evidence of a clear-cut racial order at the Cape during the Company era. An explicit racism is not to be found in the legal system of the time; nor can one detect racial ideology or a body of racial theory. But the exploration must proceed beyond these realms, into the domestic sphere and the work-place, as we focus our attention on two fundamental human activities – sex and work. Both themes lie at the core of the debate about racism at the Cape. Writers engaged in this debate have had much to say about the two issues of miscegenation and slavery. Both can be viewed as test cases. The widespread practice of miscegenation, if proven by the evidence, would seem to undermine the idea that racism was rife before 1800. And was slavery an instrument of class exploitation or a form of racial domination?

In the twentieth century the majority of white South Africans have deemed interracial sex to be repugnant and repulsive. Indeed, these attitudes, together with laws prohibiting such sexual relations, have been viewed as a key indicator of racism in South Africa. Not surprisingly therefore, when researchers seek out the origins of the South African racial order they look carefully at the evidence for miscegenation at the Cape before 1800. If sex across colour lines can be shown to have been widespread at that time, then the case for an early beginning to apartheid would seem to be weaker. If the practice can be shown to have been uncommon the argument that apartheid simply grew out of longstanding attitudes and behaviour patterns appears stronger.

---

36   *Ibid.*, p.85.
37   *Ibid.*, pp.85-86.
38   Elphick and Giliomee, "Origins and entrenchment", pp.523-24.
39   *Ibid.*, p.532.

However, the issue is not as straightforward as this. How far can the incidence of miscegenation be used as a measure to gauge the degree to which a society is racist or not? The low incidence of miscegenation may not be an indicator of racism. Because people choose sexual partners of the same colour as themselves does not necessarily make them racist. Conversely a greater incidence of miscegenation may not necessarily suggest a high level of racial tolerance. White men may sexually exploit black female bodies while at the same time holding deeply racist attitudes. The correlation between miscegenation and non-racism, or between anti-miscegenation attitudes and racism, is not so clear-cut. With this qualification in mind, a study of interracial sexual relations ought to provide some clues into racial thinking and practice at the Cape before 1800.

That miscegenation occurred from the early years of white settlement at the Cape is confirmed by an overwhelming body of evidence. Sexual relations were particularly common between white men and slave women. By 1672 75% of children born to Company slaves had white fathers.[40] The Company's slave lodge served as a brothel – indeed, as the main brothel in Cape Town in the seventeenth and eighteenth centuries, frequented by soldiers, sailors, Company employees, and freeburghers alike. And slave women were there to be abused. As Shell has put it,

> ... local officials turned the Lodge into a brothel for an hour every night, with female slaves compelled to act as prostitutes, at the very time that the male slaves (among whom were the spouses of these women) were set to the demeaning and melancholy chore of carrying the town's slurry to the beaches and hence were not around to object.[41]

Slave women may have actively sought white male partners as a possible route to freedom. But such relations were more likely characterised by high levels of coercion. The Cape authorities did not question the right of single slave-owners to exploit the bodies of their female slaves. Indeed, throughout the 180-year history of Cape slavery no slave-owner was ever convicted of raping a slave.[42] Teenage sons from respectable Cape families would sometimes become involved with slave women.[43] Masters frequently entered

---

40   Fredrickson, *White Supremacy*, p.112; MacCrone, *Race Attitudes*, p.68.
41   Robert C.-H. Shell, *Children of Bondage* (Hanover, NH, 1994), pp.71-72. See also Fredrickson, *White Supremacy*, p.112; Elphick and Shell, "Intergroup Relations", p.195.
42   Ross, *Beyond the Pale*, p.114.
43   Elphick and Shell, "Intergroup Relations", p.197.

into relationships – some stable, some casual – with slave women.[44] There were cases of a married slave-owner living with his wife and a slave concubine.[45] Even Van Riebeeck, so contemptuous in his attitude towards the Khoikhoi, may have had an intimate relationship with his Khoikhoi maid, Eva.[46] Interracial marriage, between white men and women of colour, was common at the Cape before 1800. Among such women were former slaves. It is reckoned that between 1652 and 1795 over 1000 ex-slave and 'native' women married white free burghers.[47] Fredrickson claims that between 1652 and 1806 one-fifth of male German immigrants to the Cape married women who had been born slaves, and he notes the 'surprising frequency and social acceptability of legal intermarriage'.[48]

What can be made of this kind of evidence? And what has been made of it? In the apartheid era, for obvious reasons, the revelation that miscegenation was widespread in the early Cape was politically explosive. Some writers made every effort to embarrass the NP government and its supporters, for whom white racial purity was such a cherished ideal.[49] The 1950 Population Registration Act demanded that racial categories be distinct and clear-cut. Historical research revealing past miscegenation and mixed ancestry clearly indicated otherwise. Heese, for instance, reckoned that in 1984 there were over 1000 white Afrikaner families who were descended from slave women.[50]

When historians like Elphick, Giliomee, Shell, Fredrickson and Ross came, from the late 1970s, to explore the issue of miscegenation at the early Cape they were guided more by academic historical concerns. By that time, too, the issue was taking on less political importance. The NP government was striving to preserve its power by building multi-racial alliances to counter the rise of internal and external opposition. White racial purity was not an important component of the government's 'total strategy' and its survivalist ideology. The police were less obsessive than they had been in the 1960s and early 1970s in hunting down mixed couples. In 1986 the government felt able

---

44 Fredrickson, *White Supremacy*, p.114.
45 Shell, *Children of Bondage*, p.316.
46 Julia C. Wells, "Eva's Men: Gender and Power in the Establishment of the Cape of Good Hope, 1652-74", *Journal of African History*, 39, 1998, p.422.
47 Shell, *Children of Bondage*, p.324.
48 Fredrickson, *White Supremacy*, pp.114-15.
49 See, for instance, Anon, "The origin and incidence of miscegenation at the Cape during the Dutch East India Company's regime, 1652-1795", *Race Relations Journal*, 20, 1953; and H.F. Heese, *Groep Sonder Grense* (Bellville, 1984).
50 Shell, *Children of Bondage*, p.321.

to abolish the legal prohibition on mixed marriages and interracial sexual relationships.

Elphick and Shell, in particular, were able to produce a much more dispassionate, nuanced analysis of the issue. Given the evidence, it was now easy to dismiss out of hand the hoary Afrikaner nationalist myth that it was not the early white settlers but passing sailors and soldiers who were responsible for miscegenation at the early Cape. Clearly, too, the position at the other extreme does not hold: that race and colour were not factors in the choice of sexual partners. While miscegenation was widespread at the early Cape, the picture does need to be qualified in a number of ways. First, there seem to have been few sexual relationships between black men and white women. This was not just a product of demography – the low proportion of white women among the population. Such relationships appear to have been distasteful to whites. Black men found guilty of raping white women were subjected to the most brutal forms of execution, while white men who raped black women were given light, rarely enforced, sentences.[51]

Second, in their choice of sexual partners white men seem to have had a preference for certain racial and physical types. Women of mixed ancestry or Asian women were preferred. Bengali women, for instance, were favoured partners in the seventeenth century.[52] According to Elphick and Shell liaisons between white men and Khoi women were rare; but Fredrickson claims that by the late eighteenth century in more remote rural areas it was common for white farmers and trekkers to take Khoi concubines.[53] Third, most liaisons occurred in Cape Town, and involved lower paid company servants, soldiers and sailors (but not exclusively, as some would like to have it). Intermarriage seems to have been rare in the rural hinterland of the western Cape where white sex ratios were more equal. In the more remote pastoral regions, where white sex ratios were less equal, miscegenation occurred on some scale, but not intermarriage.[54]

To say that interracial relationships were initiated largely by deviant white males in transit rather than by permanent settlers is just as much an oversimplification as to claim that white men were colour-blind in choosing sexual partners. Miscegenation and intermarriage clearly did occur, even if more so in some areas than others. But how much can be read into this? Writers like Elphick, Shell and Giliomee have tended to play down the

---

51 Elphick and Shell, "Intergroup Relations", pp.199-200.
52 *Ibid.*, p.197.
53 *Ibid.*, pp.194, 201; Fredrickson, *White Supremacy*, p.123.
54 Elphick and Shell, "Intergroup Relations", p.204.

significance of miscegenation in the larger scheme of things. Elphick and Shell state emphatically that 'Miscegenation and intermarriage scarcely ever threatened European dominance at the Cape'.[55] By marrying white men or bearing their children women of colour did not necessarily obtain enhanced status or privileges. Few slave women, for instance, gained their freedom as a result of extramarital relationships with white men.[56] And the offspring of such unions were usually treated as members of the slave class, like their mothers.[57] An extramarital liaison or intermarriage does not therefore seem to have been a means of upward mobility for women of colour. In other words, the social structure of early Cape society was not significantly affected in this way.

But what does miscegenation tell us about white racial attitudes at the Cape before 1800? It has commonly been argued that miscegenation was largely the product of demography – that it was more widespread in those areas where there was a low ratio of white women to white men. This is emphasised by Fredrickson who states that 'many European men would not have found mates at all had they not been willing to establish liaisons with nonwhite women'.[58] This is a seemingly obvious point. Less obvious is the implicit assumption which it carries – that had the white sex ratio been equal there would have been less miscegenation, if any. In other words, the assumption is that white men had a natural preference for white women as partners, and that demographic reality denied them the chance to realise that preference. This assumption does not necessarily hold. There is some evidence, for instance, that British men in the West Indies, where there was not a shortage of white women, found black women particularly attractive.[59] Moreover, relationships with slave women or other subordinated women of colour may have been especially appealing to white men because of the power, domination and control that such relationships would normally have afforded them. One cannot therefore assume that for white men miscegenation was the product of necessity – of white sex ratios – rather than a matter of preference.

---

55   *Ibid.*, p.203.
56   *Ibid.*
57   Giliomee, "Eighteenth century Cape society", p.24.
58   Fredrickson, *White Supremacy*, pp.126-27; see also, Freund, "Race in the social structure of South Africa", p.58.
59   Robert J.C. Young, *Colonial desire: Hybridity in Theory, Culture and Race* (London, 1995), pp.151-52.

What about the attitudes of whites in general to interracial sexual relationships? Could such attitudes provide evidence of a more pervasive racism at the early Cape? Again, the picture is not all that clear. Guelke suggests that in frontier districts white men who cohabited with Khoi women were ostracised by the white community.[60] But the literature suggests rather that white attitudes ranged between tolerance and mild disapproval. The Dutch authorities generally tolerated miscegenation. In 1685 there was an attempt to prohibit marriage between white men and slave women. But the prohibition was not enforced, and it did not apply to non-slave women of colour.[61] What does seem apparent is that at the Cape before 1800 there was no coherent racist ideology, such as emerged in the nineteenth century. Notions of racial purity were not explicitly articulated. There is little evidence of fears being expressed about racial contamination – that interracial unions would inevitably lead to racial degeneration. This line of thinking was to be much more a feature of the nineteenth century. Indeed, as Ross has noted, the very word miscegenation was not even coined until the mid-nineteenth century.[62]

In the nineteenth and twentieth century the interracial sex taboo was to become an obsessive concern of racial ideologists. It seems that before 1800 at the Cape the picture was rather different. There were no strict taboos, no legal prohibitions on interracial partnerships. A white male's choice of female partner may have been guided by physical attributes, including colour, but ultimately the choice was made in a demographic context. It was not racial consciousness, but rather the demographic reality of male:female ratios, together with assumptions about gender roles and relations, that determined marital and extramarital relationship patterns.

So far it has not been possible to produce a precise delineation of the racial order at the Cape before 1800. The picture is ambivalent. Two of our four main elements of racism were not present. There was no coherent body of racial theory, no clearly articulated racial ideology. Moreover, legalised, institutionalised racial discrimination and segregation – the fourth element – was minimal. What about the other two? While whites did not express their sense of difference from 'others' in explicitly racial terms, they did believe themselves to be superior to those 'others'. Such attitudes were particularly pronounced among the white elite, but less easily measurable among

---

60 Leonard Guelke, "Freehold farmers and frontier settlers, 1657-1780", in Elphick and Giliomee (eds), *Shaping*, p.99.
61 Fredrickson, *White Supremacy*, pp.112-13, 128-29.
62 Ross, *Beyond the Pale*, p.74.

lower-class whites. At the same time the lack of formalised discrimination must not be allowed to hide the fact that the social, political and economic structure of early Cape society was dominated and controlled by white men. There was an emergent *de facto*, if not *de jure*, racial order.

Was, though, this white dominance and sense of superiority necessarily born of racial difference? Was it perhaps an outcome of economic relationships, a product of class exploitation? This is a fundamental question which will remain at the forefront throughout this book. At this juncture the question requires a careful look at the significance of slavery at the early Cape.

There is a vast international literature on the history of slavery. The connection between slavery and racism is one of the many themes that permeate this literature. It is a problematic connection – a 'chicken-or-egg' type of question. Did the enslavement of millions of people of colour grow out of a deep-seated, pre-existing racism that enabled that enslavement? Or did slavery come first, racial thought being developed later as a means to justify the institution? As we have seen, this has been an ongoing debate in US historiography. Degler and Jordan have been two prominent exponents of the former position, the psycho-cultural approach. Degler argued unequivocally that blacks were treated as inferior from the outset of white colonisation; so slavery was simply the institutionalisation of an already existing race prejudice.[63] Degler's critics retorted that there was little evidence to support his claim that racism was endemic before slavery. Moreover, he failed to explain why it was that free blacks in the British West Indies were treated better than their counterparts in North America – which should not have been the case if racism was embedded in the British colonial psyche. It is worth noting that Degler was writing in the late 1950s at a time when racial segregation was still deeply entrenched in the USA. His historical interpretation of racism was thus pessimistic, informed by the firm belief that white racism was deep-rooted, endemic, immutable, and ineradicable.[64]

This rather steadfast idealist view has never gained significant support. The opposing position, more materialist-inclined, putting slavery first, has come to carry greater weight. For the latter school a key historiographical moment was the publication of Eric Williams' classic text, *Capitalism and Slavery*, in 1944. In this book Williams put forward the challenging claim that

---

63 Degler, "Slavery and the genesis of American race prejudice", pp.52-66; Allen, *Invention of the White Race*, pp.4-9. See also Alden T. Vaughan, *Roots of American Racism* (New York, 1995), pp.136-76.
64 Allen, *Invention of the White Race*, pp.4, 63.

'slavery was not born of racism; rather racism was the consequence of slavery'.[65] A similar position was adopted by Oscar and Mary Handlin in a seminal article published in 1950. They argued that in early colonial Virginia not all blacks were servile, and not all servile people were black – there was no clear correlation between colour and discrimination. But the situation changed in the second half of the seventeenth century. The large-scale importation of black slaves aroused a sense of social insecurity among the colonists. In this situation a white group identity came to be consolidated, and so too did there develop an increasing correspondence of race and status: 'Color then emerged as the token of the slave status; the trace of color became the trace of slavery'.[66] The socio-economic approach gained strength from the 1970s, at a time when materialist, political-economy analysis was becoming more fashionable in western historiography.[67] Emphasis was placed on the control and exploitation of slave labour – and on race discrimination as a means to secure that objective. More recently Walvin has argued along these lines. For him racism largely grew out of slavery, especially in the Americas: 'Slavery became a defining institution, creating the image that to be black was to be a slave'.[68] It was slavery that changed whites' image of black Africans – from objects of cultural curiosity into non-persons, chattels to be possessed and utilised. In British colonial discourse the negative stereotyping of black slaves was developed to justify the continuation of slavery which was so crucial to British economic prosperity. When the abolition of slavery became a major issue in the eighteenth century ideas about race permeated the debate, as anti-abolitionists drew upon notions of black inferiority to defend slavery.[69]

The racism/slavery debate in South African historiography does not parallel exactly that carried on elsewhere. One does not, for instance, come across an obvious South African equivalent of Degler's psycho-cultural approach. It is not argued by anybody that Cape slavery was a natural consequence of a pre-existing racism – that dark-skinned people were enslaved because of their colour. Moreover there were significant differences between slavery in the Americas and Cape slavery. Most Cape slaves were

---

65 Eric Williams, *Capitalism and Slavery* (Chapel Hill, 1944), p.7.
66 Oscar and Mary F. Handlin, "The Origins of Negro Slavery", in Noel (ed.), *American Slavery and Racism*, p.33. This article was originally published in *William and Mary Quarterly*, 7, 1950.
67 See Allen, *Invention of the White Race*, pp.15-21.
68 James Walvin, *Questioning Slavery* (London, 1996), p.73.
69 *Ibid.*, pp.72-92.

not black Africans, whereas nearly all slaves in the Americas were black Africans or their descendants. In the Americas slavery was crucial to the prosperity of the plantation economy; in the Cape slavery was not of such vital economic importance. However, the possible connection between Cape slavery and the growth of the South African racial order still requires consideration. After all, it has been widely held that Cape slavery gave rise to racism – not the sole cause maybe, but certainly a significant factor. The general argument runs like this: only people of colour came to be enslaved; and so whites came to assume that servitude was a natural, normal state for such people, and that whites (one may say 'white men') were naturally masters; and there is a further corollary – that white men as a consequence of slavery, developed the attitude that menial, servile types of work were beneath their dignity.

This argument pervades South African historiography. It can be found in numerous texts, across the historiographical spectrum. How have the various components of this argument been substantiated by historians and other scholars? Again, one can discern a certain drift. There seems, for instance, to be a fair degree of agreement that although slaves were first introduced into the Cape in the 1650s there was no firm commitment at that time, on the part of the Company authorities, to a labour system based on racial slavery. That commitment only came later, in the early eighteenth century.

There was a significant moment, duly stressed by historians – a debate conducted within the upper echelons of the Dutch East India Company during 1716 and 1717. In 1716 the directors of the Company in Amsterdam asked the governor and Council of Policy at the Cape to consider whether white immigration to the Cape should be encouraged, with a view to establishing a white labour policy. All except one member of the Council opposed the suggestion. The overwhelming weight of opinion was that the use of slave labour should be maintained. This was the decision, taken largely on the basis of economic considerations. It was argued that slaves were more easily controlled, while lower-class white immigrants tended to become lazy and dissipated.[70] In this debate there was another contention: that whites had developed an antipathy for manual work, believing it to be beneath them. This antipathy further underlined the impracticality of a white labour policy. It is interesting that the Council members did not argue that such a policy was

---

70   Fredrickson, *White Supremacy*, pp.66-67; Nigel Worden, *Slavery in Dutch South Africa* (Cambridge, 1985), pp.16-17.

inappropriate because they themselves believed that menial work was demeaning to whites. Their arguments were based not on considerations of colour or race, but rather on economic and social grounds. Slaves would be cheaper than white labour. And a large class of exploited, discontented whites could be potentially dangerous.[71]

As directors of a large enterprise the members of the Company's Council of Policy were more concerned about profitability than about any incipient colour bar. In opting for the continuation of slave labour they were not trying to protect whites or preserve whites' sense of dignity. However, this decision taken in 1717 did have important consequences – and has, hence, often been regarded as a major turning-point in South African history. The decision amounted to confirmation that the colonial economy would be slave-based, and to the continuation of racial slavery. Through the remainder of the eighteenth century there was to be a growing correspondence between race and class – sufficient to suggest that a kind of racial order was taking clearer shape. Many historians, across the ideological spectrum, have attested to this. The view was stated in the starkest possible terms by the Marxist writer, Hosea Jaffe, in the early 1950s. Writing about the Cape in the early eighteenth century, he contended that 'There were in actual fact not only two colours, but also two classes: the slave-owning Whites and the enslaved Blacks'.[72] This is too bald an assertion, as clearly not all whites were masters, and not all people of colour were enslaved. But many later historians have concurred with the broad idea – that there was a strong connection between slavery and racism. Fredrickson argues that 'More than any other single factor, it [Cape slavery] established a presumption that whites were naturally masters and members of a privileged group while nonwhites were meant to be their servants and social inferiors'.[73] Worden is also in no doubt about the impact of slavery: 'The most significant feature of Cape slavery was that it shaped much of the society of early colonial South Africa'.[74] In the shorter term, he argues, a sense of group consciousness and racial solidarity developed, particularly among slave-owning farmers in the western Cape.[75] In the longer term there grew more entrenched racial divisions which

---

71 Fredrickson, *White Supremacy*, pp.68-69; Worden, *Slavery in Dutch South Africa*, pp.16-17.
72 "Mnguni", *Three Hundred Years*, p.38.
73 Fredrickson, *White Supremacy*, p.93.
74 Worden, *Slavery in Dutch South Africa*, p.4.
75 *Ibid.*, p.138.

'coincided with the distinctions that had emerged within the slave society of the Dutch Cape'.[76] A pattern had been set.

This has become a fairly standard position in South African historiography – that racial slavery at the Cape gave rise to a more far-reaching racist outlook and discriminatory practice on the part of white settlers during the eighteenth century and beyond. This racism, so the argument goes, was marked not only by certain attitudes towards people of colour, but also by a refusal to perform menial tasks that were considered to be beneath the dignity of whites. Generations of historians have readily assumed this white contempt for manual labour and brought it into their writing. Indeed, it was an assumption that goes back way beyond the earliest historical writing about South Africa. It was voiced, for instance, in the Council of Policy debate of 1716: one of the reasons given for continuing to use slave labour was that whites refused to perform certain types of manual work because it was beneath their dignity.[77] Then there is the oft-quoted comment of Baron van Imhoff, a governor-general of the East Indies who inspected the Cape settlement in 1743 and found that 'having imported slaves every common or ordinary European becomes a gentleman and prefers to be served rather than serve'.[78] This perception of white work-place snobbery was shared by later travellers, such as Barrow who visited the Cape in 1797.[79] And the perception seemed to be confirmed by the changing role of white *knechts* in the farming districts of the south-western Cape. Once employed as manual labourers these *knechts* increasingly, during the eighteenth century, took on the function of overseers or farm managers.[80]

This assumption is to be found in numerous twentieth century historical texts on South Africa. MacCrone in the 1930s, and De Kiewiet in the 1940s both asserted that in white eyes manual labour was the function of servile dark-skinned people.[81] The assumption lived on, and can still be found in recent writings.[82] It even survived the radical historiographical challenge in the 1970s. Only Davies, writing on white labour in the gold-mining industry,

---

76 *Ibid.*, pp.4-5.
77 Fredrickson, *White Supremacy*, p.67.
78 *Ibid*; Worden, *Slavery in Dutch South Africa*, p.139; van Schoor, "Origin and Development of Segregation", p.104; A. du Toit and H. Giliomee, *Afrikaner Political Thought* (Cape Town, 1983), i, p.7.
79 Worden, *Slavery in Dutch South Africa*, p.139.
80 *Ibid.*, pp.139-40.
81 MacCrone, *Race Attitudes*, p.86; De Kiewiet, *History of South Africa*, p.21.
82 See, for instance, van Aswegen, *History of South Africa to 1854*, p.131; Sparks, *Mind of South Africa*, pp.43-44.

was prepared to dismiss this supposed white aversion to manual labour as 'a myth of bourgeois ideology'.[83] But Davies was not writing about the Cape in the eighteenth century – indeed, radical writers generally had little to say about white attitudes towards labour at that time.

What is to be made of this assumption? Even if there really was this strong white aversion to manual labour, as claimed by generations of historians, is that evidence of white *racism*? It depends on how one views the connection between these two attitudes – the prejudice towards people of colour, and the aversion to manual labour. Was it a case of the latter being a natural consequence of the former – a contempt for dark-skinned people giving rise to a corresponding aversion to the work performed by such people? If so, one is viewing the antipathy to manual work as being part-and-parcel of a broader racist attitude. On the other hand one could argue that this antipathy was more a manifestation of a class attitude – that a relatively privileged position in the socio-economic order could be gained and preserved for whites through voicing ideological objections to performing 'kaffir work'. This is a complex question that is not easily answered. How can the historian enter the consciousness and capture the attitudes of people who lived two to three hundred years ago? There is a very limited body of source material offering clues to the attitudes of lower-status whites in the Cape at that time.

Even those historians who have explored these questions more closely have not been able to come up with firm conclusions. However, a survey of the historical literature does reveal one interesting paradox. Most of the historians who have examined the connection between slavery and racism at the Cape would not generally be considered to fall in the materialist tradition of South African historiography. Yet their approach to this connection appears to be more materialist than idealist. I have not come across any historian who has argued that racism preceded Cape slavery – that people were enslaved because of prejudiced white attitudes towards people of colour. On the contrary, the most widely held view is that racist attitudes grew out of slavery – that certain patterns of labour exploitation gave rise to white prejudice and antipathy towards dark-skinned people. Moreover, strongly implicit in this interpretation is the idea that these racist attitudes did not develop to preserve white racial purity or identity, but rather to protect a privileged class position.

---

83 Robert H. Davies, *Capital, State and White Labour in South Africa 1900-1960* (Brighton, 1979), p.54.

A rich body of historical writing on Cape slavery has been produced in the past fifteen years or so. However, in this writing surprisingly little attention has been paid to the relationship between slavery and racism. There is no equivalent of the American debate in South African historiography. Strong assertions have been made. Shell, for instance, states that 'Slavery, not the frontier and certainly not the process of industrialization, shaped South Africa'. He is struck by the 'compelling legal and demographic similarities' between Cape slavery and apartheid: both were violent, coercive systems that denied basic human rights and tried to eliminate the political identities of those who had been subjugated.[84] Similarly Fredrickson has argued that 'a slaveholding mentality remained the wellspring of white supremacist thought and action long after the institution that originally sustained it had been relegated to the dustbin of history'.[85]

These are bold claims. It is noticeable, though, that hardly any historians have attempted to analyse closely the connection between slavery and racism. To what extent, it should be asked, did contempt for slaves come to be expressed in racial terms? This is a question that has barely been addressed. Why this omission? Might this neglect be explained perhaps by an apparent paradox – that the heartland of slavery, the western Cape, has also been the supposed heartland of South African liberalism? If Cape slavery is deemed to be a key foundation-stone of the South African racial order, then the liberal pretensions of the western Cape might be dented. There is, though, another more likely reason for the omission. In South Africa the prime target of white racism came to be black Africans. But in the Cape the majority of slaves were not black Africans. Indeed, the Cape slave population was ethnically diverse. It was therefore difficult to denigrate in racial terms those condemned to abject servility. The kind of racial ideology that grew out of slavery in the Americas would therefore be less evident at the Cape. Cape slavery was an obvious form of class exploitation, but its role in the making of the South African racial order remains open to question and further research.

Until now our discussion has focused largely on the early development of a racial order at the Cape. But one must be wary about talking of 'the Cape' in a single breath. As is well known, white settlement expanded outwards from the western Cape during the seventeenth and eighteenth centuries. White settler land occupation extended further and further towards the east

---

84 Shell, *Children of Bondage*, pp.xix-xx, 395.
85 Fredrickson, *White Supremacy*, p.93.

and the north. Some scholars have argued that distance from the western Cape metropole gave rise to different, harsher attitudes and social relations among these remote communities of colonists. This is the so-called 'frontier thesis' – a thesis which has for over sixty years been central to the whole debate around the making of South Africa's racial order.

The original 'frontier thesis' is generally ascribed to the American, Frederick Jackson Turner, who in the 1890s argued that the North American frontier experience did much to shape American society, giving rise to a democratic, egalitarian culture. When applied to South African history the 'frontier thesis' took on far more negative connotations. From the 1920s a succession of historians, who in time came to be classified as 'liberal', adapted the Turner thesis, arguing that the frontier represented a crucial point of origin in the making of South Africa's racial order.

One of the first historians to suggest this connection between the frontier experience and racism was W.M. Macmillan. In his book, *The Cape Colour Question* (1927), he painted a picture, somewhat stereotyped, of the character of the eighteenth century boer frontiersmen: 'Hardy and venturesome', and fiercely independent in spirit, they deeply resented government control over their activities, particularly in their dealings with indigenous people. 'Liberal views', stated Macmillan, 'were hardly to be looked for, least of all in their attitude towards the Native races'.[86] A more forthright statement of the South African frontier thesis was presented by Eric Walker in a lecture at Oxford University in 1930. He argued that the Cape trekboers left civilisation behind them as they ventured further and further away from the western Cape metropole. The isolation of the frontier bred in the trekboers a deeply racist outlook – 'a denial in the sight of God and man of all equality between white and non-white'.[87]

A few years later I.D. MacCrone developed the thesis more fully in a book which was part history, part psychology – *Race Attitudes in South Africa* (1937). He further emphasised the isolation of frontierspeople from western civilisation. The frontier environment was isolated, rough and crude. Such conditions gave rise to a certain lifestyle, attitudes and ways of thinking among the trekboers. A fierce individualism and a tendency to take the law into their own hands were just two characteristics. Together with these came 'narrow, hard, and intolerant' attitudes, especially towards people of colour.[88]

---

86 W.M. Macmillan, *The Cape Colour Question* (London, 1927), pp.20-21. See also, Saunders, *South African Past*, p.114.
87 Eric A. Walker, *The Frontier Tradition in South Africa* (London, 1930), pp.12-13.
88 MacCrone, *Race Attitudes*, pp.98-101, 108-9, 114, 117.

The Walker/MacCrone thesis gained a strong following among other writers in South Africa through the 1940s, 1950s, and 1960s. Although few of these writers devoted any special attention to the frontier and its impact, the basic assumption of the Walker/MacCrone thesis found its way into their work. There is, for instance, a much-quoted sentence in De Kiewiet's classic survey, *A History of South Africa*, first published in 1941. In this De Kiewiet stretched the impact of the frontier era into the early twentieth century, arguing that '... the Union Constitution, in native policy at all events, represented the triumph of the frontier, and into the hands of the frontier was delivered the future of the native peoples. It was the conviction of the frontier that the foundations of society were race and the privileges of race'.[93] De Kiewiet also believed that the migration of the trekboers into the Cape interior left them in severe isolation, removed from the progressive influence of the eighteenth century European Enlightenment.[94] A similar assumption was shared by Sheila Patterson (1957) who described the frontier boers as 'untouched by a century of European thought'. She also attributed to them the characteristic stereotypes: 'In general then, the frontier Boers were independent, self-reliant, unimaginative, tenacious, enduring, roughly courteous, hospitable, devout, restless in their movements, but narrowly conservative in their thinking'.[95] Moreover, South Africa's future racial order was shaped in large part by the frontier experience: 'Slavery initiated the basic socio-economic division in South African society, but it was the frontier that made it sharp and irrevocable'.[96] Pierre van den Berghe, in his socio-political study of South Africa (1965), carried this thinking into the 1960s. He was unequivocal about boer race attitudes on the Cape frontier: 'Africans or Hottentots who were not reduced to the status of slaves or serfs, the only status for a Black person which was acceptable to the Boers, were automatically treated as enemies. We shall later see how this outlook has been carried into the present'.[97] Again we see here the 'carry-over' argument – the assumption of an evolving pattern of race attitudes from the frontier through to apartheid.

---

93   De Kiewiet, *History of South Africa*, pp.150-51; see also Saunders, *South African Past*, p.92; and Legassick, "Frontier tradition" in Marks and Atmore (eds), *Economy and Society*, p.45.
94   De Kiewiet, *History of South Africa*, pp.17-81.
95   Patterson, *The Last Trek*, p.19.
96   *Ibid.*, pp.9-10.
97   Van den Berghe, *South Africa*, p.25.

The Walker/MacCrone thesis gained a strong following among other writers in South Africa through the 1940s, 1950s, and 1960s. Although few of these writers devoted any special attention to the frontier and its impact, the basic assumption of the Walker/MacCrone thesis found its way into their work. There is, for instance, a much-quoted sentence in De Kiewiet's classic survey, *A History of South Africa*, first published in 1941. In this De Kiewiet stretched the impact of the frontier era into the early twentieth century, arguing that '... the Union Constitution, in native policy at all events, represented the triumph of the frontier, and into the hands of the frontier was delivered the future of the native peoples. It was the conviction of the frontier that the foundations of society were race and the privileges of race'.[93] De Kiewiet also believed that the migration of the trekboers into the Cape interior left them in severe isolation, removed from the progressive influence of the eighteenth century European Enlightenment.[94] A similar assumption was shared by Sheila Patterson (1957) who described the frontier boers as 'untouched by a century of European thought'. She also attributed to them the characteristic stereotypes: 'In general then, the frontier Boers were independent, self-reliant, unimaginative, tenacious, enduring, roughly courteous, hospitable, devout, restless in their movements, but narrowly conservative in their thinking'.[95] Moreover, South Africa's future racial order was shaped in large part by the frontier experience: 'Slavery initiated the basic socio-economic division in South African society, but it was the frontier that made it sharp and irrevocable'.[96] Pierre van den Berghe, in his socio-political study of South Africa (1965), carried this thinking into the 1960s. He was unequivocal about boer race attitudes on the Cape frontier: 'Africans or Hottentots who were not reduced to the status of slaves or serfs, the only status for a Black person which was acceptable to the Boers, were automatically treated as enemies. We shall later see how this outlook has been carried into the present'.[97] Again we see here the 'carry-over' argument – the assumption of an evolving pattern of race attitudes from the frontier through to apartheid.

---

93 De Kiewiet, *History of South Africa*, pp.150-51; see also Saunders, *South African Past*, p.92; and Legassick, "Frontier tradition" in Marks and Atmore (eds), *Economy and Society*, p.45.
94 De Kiewiet, *History of South Africa*, pp.17-81.
95 Patterson, *The Last Trek*, p.19.
96 *Ibid.*, pp.9-10.
97 Van den Berghe, *South Africa*, p.25.

At the same time there developed among these isolated communities of boer colonists a strong group consciousness: '... the intense and exclusive group consciousness of the frontier found expression in a consciousness of race and social supremacy which coincided almost uniformly with the distinctions based upon creed and colour'.[89] MacCrone was not alone in stressing the importance of religion – more specifically Calvinism – in the worldview of the Cape frontierspeople. Walker had already made the point: 'The Cape colonists, seventeenth-century Calvinists, with something of the self-confidence bred of the still vigorous doctrines of election and predestination, were confirmed in their consciousness of superiority by daily contact with beings obviously less fortunate than themselves'.[90]

Coming out of this work of the 1920s and 1930s was a picture, even a stereotype, of the boer frontier character: rugged, individualist, independent, outside the law, Calvinist – and racist. At the same time a contrast was drawn between frontierspeople and western Cape colonists. While the former lacked the attributes of civilisation, the latter were altogether more enlightened and refined, and less racist.

The South African version of the frontier thesis carried another far-reaching assumption that was to have significance in the wider historiography of racism, segregation and apartheid – the assumption that the frontier era represented a key formative phase in the evolution of South Africa's racial order. The racist attitudes that became so evident in the frontier environment were apparently carried over into the nineteenth and twentieth centuries, eventually becoming entrenched and institutionalised in the apartheid system. This boer frontier tradition, with its accompanying racism, was transported by the voortrekkers into the interior where the boer republics would strive to maintain a strict racial divide. As MacCrone put it, '... those same attitudes, more particularly in the form in which they were developed on the frontier, were to be one of the main factors in shaping nineteenth-century history in South Africa'.[91] The continuity of the frontier tradition extended into the twentieth century. Walker even saw the 1922 Rand Revolt by white mineworkers as 'an attempt by Labour, in very great measure Afrikander Labour fresh from the soil and with the frontier tradition hot within it, to save the colour bar which kept down the rising tide of colour'.[92]

---

89   *Ibid.*, p.130.
90   Walker, *Frontier Tradition*, p.7. See also, Macmillan, *Cape Colour Question*, pp.23-24; S.F.N. Gie, "The Cape Colony under Company Rule, 1708-1795", in *The Cambridge History of the British Empire*, vol.viii (Cambridge, 1936), p.165.
91   MacCrone, *Race Attitudes*, p.135.
92   Walker, *Frontier Tradition*, p.23.

In the 1970s the South African 'frontier thesis' came to be heavily criticised, as we shall soon see. Even so, the thesis has lived on. It could still be found in work being written in the 1980s and 1990s. Although Leonard Guelke refined the thesis in a subtle way, his 1985 article still contained some of its basic assumptions: 'Frontier attitudes', he wrote, 'encapsulating many early eighteenth century notions of government and justice, had hardened into a rigid ideology of white supremacy. That ideology became the foundation of the boer republics, founded by the descendants of the early Cape frontiersmen'.[98] Here can be seen the idea of continuity, and the teleology – the view that South Africa's racial order evolved gradually over a long period of time, and that the frontier was one of its most crucial sources. The accompanying view – that, in part at least, the isolation of the frontier accounts for the growth of race attitudes – appears even more recently in Allister Sparks' *The Mind of South Africa* (1991). Sparks perpetuates the long-held claim that the Cape boers 'missed the momentous developments of eighteenth century Europe, the age of reason in which liberalism and democracy were born ...'. Indeed Sparks goes further, stereotyping the boers as 'a people who became, surely, the simplest and most backward fragment of Western civilization in modern times'.[99] The implication of this is very evident – that had the boers fallen under the rational, civilising influence of the eighteenth century Enlightenment, South African history might have taken a very different course, one that was altogether more benign and less racist. As we shall see in due course such assumptions have come to be seriously questioned, but they must still be viewed as integral components of an historiographical lineage that ran from the 1920s through to the 1990s.

Historiographical discourse can require the convenience of easy categorisation – placing historians in schools or camps. This has been true of South African historiography, especially in the last thirty years. The Walker/MacCrone lineage has, for instance, come to be labelled as 'liberal' – a term that often carries more polemical purchase than conceptual weight. Not all 'liberal' scholars have adhered rigidly to the South African 'frontier thesis' with its emphasis on racial polarisation and conflict. Some writers, generally recognised as belonging to the liberal tradition, have drawn attention to forms of peaceful, cooperative interaction between black and white in frontier zones. As early as 1934-35, for instance, H.M. Robertson published a

---

98 Leonard Guelke, "The Making of Two Frontier Communities: Cape Colony in the Eighteenth Century", *Historical Reflections*, 12, 3, 1985, p.442. See below for a further discussion of Guelke's article.
99 Sparks, *Mind of South Africa*, p.42.

two-part article entitled '150 years of economic contact between black and white'. He argued that the attempts of the Dutch East India Company to restrict contact between white colonists and the indigenous inhabitants generally failed.[100] The latter could supply commodities and services – cattle, trade goods, land and labour – that the colonists sought to acquire. This inevitably gave rise to interaction, peaceful and violent. A much later version of this view is to be found in Monica Wilson's chapter on the eastern Cape frontier in the *Oxford History of South Africa*. While recognising that the 'basic fact of frontier history' was black-white conflict over land, Wilson also emphasised areas of peaceful black-white interaction. She identified four kinds of interaction: 'economic, religious, aesthetic and political'. More particularly she highlighted trade, missionary endeavour, and social intercourse as the most likely points or contexts of such interaction.[101]

The Walker-MacCrone frontier thesis remained largely unchallenged until the early 1970s when Martin Legassick produced a pioneering essay in which he developed a vigorous critique of the thesis.[102] This was a seminal piece, not only heralding a new wave of radical South African historiography, but also arousing a new interest in the origin and dynamic of South Africa's racial order. Legassick rejected the idea that in the unfriendly environment of the eighteenth century Cape frontier white colonists developed both a strong group consciousness and, accordingly, hostile attitudes towards the out-group – people of colour. There was, argued Legassick, little cohesion among the white colonist population at the time. The patriarchal family was the basic social unit; and this would tend to pursue its own individual interests rather than those of some ephemeral colonial community.[103]

Given this evident lack of group consciousness and out-group hostility among the colonists Legassick went on to paint a different picture of black-white relations on the frontier. Like Robertson and Wilson he saw evidence of interracial cooperation which belied the idea of the frontier as the breeding-ground for a virulent racism. Legassick pointed to trading relations across the frontier. Moreover, white frontiersmen – or transfrontiersmen as they have become called – sometimes moved away from their fellow

---

100   H.M. Robertson, "150 years of economic contact between black and white", part one, *South African Journal of Economics*, 2, 4, 1934; part two, *ibid.*, 3, 1, 1935.
101   Monica Wilson, "Co-operation and conflict: the eastern Cape frontier", in Monica Wilson and Leonard Thompson (eds), *The Oxford History of South Africa* (Oxford, 1969), i, pp.238-40, 268.
102   Legassick, "Frontier tradition".
103   *Ibid.*, pp.60-62.

colonists, exploring opportunities on the other side of the frontier. Some lived in Xhosa territory under the rule of chiefs. Interracial military alliances were formed – frontier struggles were not simply white-against-black conflicts.[104] Indeed, as Legassick put it, 'Enemies and friends were not divided into rigid, static categories; non-whites were not regarded implacably as enemies'.[105] Therefore it followed for Legassick that the frontier era could not be accorded any real long-term significance in the making of South Africa's racial order: 'It was not ... the frontier, seen as a social system distinct and isolated from a parent society, which produced a new, or even intensified an old, pattern of racial relationships'.[106] In attributing so much significance to the frontier legacy liberal explanations of segregation and apartheid in twentieth century South Africa were off the mark.

Legassick's essay on the 'frontier tradition' aroused great interest, and stimulated further research and writing. Much of this subsequent writing more or less accepted the main points of his argument, which has never been subjected to a vigorous, thorough-going critique.[107] Writers who came to be loosely labelled as 'radical' generally supported Legassick. Freund, for instance, argued that one could not better understand modern South African realities by trying 'to mine earlier periods for pristine and disembodied "racial attitudes" on the lines of MacCrone's work ...'.[108] More importantly, historians who were not generally labelled as 'radical' (a rather loose label of convenience) came to support Legassick's rejection of the Walker-MacCrone argument. Giliomee and Elphick, for instance, believed that racial prejudice and discrimination increased at the Cape during the eighteenth century, but could not accept MacCrone's view that the frontier was 'primarily responsible' for this. Prejudice and discrimination were equally evident in the southwestern Cape.[109] The influence of Legassick could also be seen clearly in Saunders' essay on the South African frontier. For Saunders, 'There was no

---

104 *Ibid.*, pp.64-67.
105 *Ibid.*, p.65.
106 *Ibid.*, p.67.
107 Harrison Wright tried to pick holes in the essay, but failed to address the main issues raised by Legassick. See Harrison M. Wright, *The Burden of the Present* (Cape Town, 1977), pp.63-67.
108 Freund, "Race in the social structure of South Africa", p.65.
109 Hermann Giliomee and Richard Elphick, "The structure of European domination at the Cape, 1652-1820", in Richard Elphick and Hermann Giliomee (eds), *The Shaping of South African Society 1652-1820* (London, 1979), first edition, p.383. On this specific point Giliomee and Elphick stuck to their position in the second edition of this book: Elphick and Giliomee, "Origins and entrenchment", pp.551-52.

simple, dichotomized white-black frontier with two monolithic, antagonistic blocs facing each other ...', and, on the frontier 'relationships were naturally fluid and cross-cutting alliances joining white and black factions common'.[110]

By the late 1970s the South African frontier debate had become polarised. The Walker-MacCrone thesis and Legassick's critique seemed to represent two starkly opposing positions. In the past fifteen years or so, some have tried to break free from this polarity. Leonard Guelke, for instance, has adopted a compromise position. As the white frontier population expanded during the eighteenth century, he argues, there emerged 'two distinct frontier communities. The one community, which I will term the "orthodox" settler community, was dedicated to the maintenance of an exclusivist "European" way of life; the other community involved the blending of cultures and peoples within an informal social framework'.[111] Guelke's two communities clearly corresponded to the two polarised representations offered by MacCrone and Legassick. The first, the 'orthodox' frontier community, was essentially middle class in outlook, striving to maintain a 'respectable', 'civilised' way of life, and seeing themselves as separate from and superior to the indigenous Khoisan 'on account of their religion, race and culture'. This community made up what Guelke calls the 'frontier of exclusion'.[112] The other component of the white frontier community formed the 'frontier of inclusion'. These were the people, mainly men, who were prepared to adapt their lifestyle to frontier conditions, who exploited the opportunities offered by the frontier – the chance to forge 'a variety of social-sexual relations'. They were most likely hunters or traders, many of whom would have cohabited with or married Khoi women. They 'created for themselves a new way of life in which the customs of Europe were blended with those of the Khoikhoi among whom many of them lived and found sexual partners'.[113] Implicit in Guelke's dichotomisation of the frontier community is an acknowledgment of Legassick's contribution to our understanding of the South African frontier. However, Guelke also gives the last word to MacCrone. The final sentence of his article seems to endorse the main thrust of MacCrone's thesis: 'The early eighteenth-century autocratic, bourgeois, slave-owning values of the southwestern Cape found a fertile ground on the

---

110 Christopher Saunders, "Political Processes in the Southern African Frontier Zones", in Howard Lamar and Leonard Thompson (eds), *The Frontier in History* (New Haven and London, 1981), pp.150, 156.
111 Guelke, "Two Frontier Communities", p.434.
112 *Ibid.*, pp.434-42.
113 *Ibid.*, pp.443-46.

frontier, and these values shaped the attitudes of generations of white settlers'.[114]

Another kind of distinction has been drawn by Giliomee – between the open frontier and the closing frontier. The former was characterised by fluidity. There was no central authority, colonial or indigenous, that was able to exercise firm control over the frontier zone. There was thus a rough balance of power between the different frontier communities. Interethnic relations were marked by cooperation, as well as by competition and rivalry. There was no set pattern of racial interaction: 'Europeans were not all masters, non-Europeans were not all servants'.[115] Giliomee's open frontier is in many respects Legassick's frontier. The closing frontier, on the other hand, was marked by a decline in the freedom of individuals to pursue their own interests. This was partly because political authority came to be exercised more strongly in the frontier zone. At the same time, control over black labour was being developed in a stricter, more racialised form.[116]

Giliomee applied this open/closing distinction to the eastern Cape frontier, focusing his attention on the extreme easterly end of that zone where colonist and Xhosa came into increasing contact in the last quarter of the eighteenth century. In Giliomee's interpretation the years 1770-93 marked the open phase of this frontier. This was a time when 'interracial' relations across the frontier were fluid, characterised by forms of cooperation as well as conflict. Trade was one form of peaceful interaction to have been highlighted. Giliomee states that 'Barter was the tie which initially brought colonists and Xhosa together'. Xhosa-owned cattle were exchanged for copper, iron and beads.[117] Giliomee also notes that conflict on this eastern frontier was not always a straightforward clash between black and white. There were instances of Xhosa chiefs allying with groups of colonists in conflicts with other Xhosa chiefs.[118] Other scholars have stressed the fact of miscegenation as further evidence that racial consciousness was weakly developed on the

---

114 *Ibid.*, p.448.
115 Hermann Giliomee, "The Eastern Frontier, 1770-1812" in Elphick and Giliomee (eds), *Shaping* (second edition, 1989), pp.426-30; see also Hermann Giliomee, "Processes in Development of the Southern African Frontier", in Lamar and Thompson (eds), *Frontier in History*, pp.77-79.
116 Giliomee, "Eastern Frontier", p.449; Giliomee, "Processes in Development", pp.78-79.
117 Giliomee, "Eastern Frontier", p.432. See also J.B. Peires, *The House of Phalo* (Johannesburg, 1981), pp.98-103, and Clifton C. Crais, *The Making of the Colonial Order* (Johannesburg, 1992), pp.36-38.
118 Giliomee, "Eastern Frontier", p.429. See also, Timothy Keegan, *Colonial South Africa and the Origins of the Racial Order* (Cape Town, 1996), p.34.

eastern frontier in the late eighteenth century. It has been estimated (probably underestimated) that in 1798 in the Graaff-Reinet district 5-6% of married couples were 'mixed' in that one of the partners had a grandparent who was not white.[119] In addition there were the many interracial partnerships outside marriage.

Generally, though, in his study of the eastern frontier Giliomee makes only a few concessions to the Legassick position. Even in its open phase Giliomee's frontier was characterised by interracial conflict over land and cattle, and by mutual suspicion, growing into bitterness and hatred.[120] When the frontier closed – that is, when land became scarcer, greater governmental authority was exercised over the frontier zone, and individual freedom and opportunity was accordingly curtailed – so did these tendencies become more pronounced. For Giliomee the eastern Cape frontier went through its closing phase in the two decades after 1793. This was a time marked by a hardening of racial attitudes:

> ... contemporaries overwhelmingly perceived conflicts in racial terms. The poorer whites vigorously stressed their racial identity, believing that this qualified them for membership in the dominant group. Xhosa and colonists distinguished themselves from others mainly by their perceptions of racial and ethnic differences. They had come to see each other more as racial adversaries as well as economic competitors, and conflict occurred mainly along racial lines.[121]

Giliomee plays down the counter-tendencies emphasised by Legassick. There were interracial military alliances, but they tended to be 'temporary and opportunistic', and short-lived. There was miscegenation and acculturation between colonists and the Khoi, but this 'did not lead to the removal of ethnic distinctions'. Moreover miscegenation and acculturation between colonists and the Xhosa was minimal.[122]

In the end Giliomee's interpretation of the eastern frontier is quite far removed from Legassick's position. However, Giliomee, together with Elphick, also rejects many aspects of the MacCrone thesis. For instance, they do not accept MacCrone's argument that frontier conflict was a source of racial ideology and policy in South Africa – that could be traced just as much

---

119 Keegan, *Colonial South Africa*, p.31.
120 Giliomee, "Eastern Frontier", p.438.
121 *Ibid.*, p.461.
122 *Ibid.*, pp.459-61.

to 'the settled southwestern Cape'.¹²³ Moreover, argues Giliomee, frontier society did not become stratified simply along racial or ethnic lines. There were other criteria determining people's status – baptism, control of land and livestock – even though these criteria often corresponded to racial divisions.¹²⁴

As the interest aroused by Legassick's essay began to fade, so did the frontier debate, after some years, become a less significant issue in South African historiography. Some recent writers have touched upon the theme without delving into it in great depth. These have inclined more towards Giliomee's modified position than to either Legassick or MacCrone. Crais, for instance, suggests that the slave-owning mentality of the western Cape was carried over to the eastern frontier, where 'The relationship between blacks and whites ... became increasingly oppressive during the course of the eighteenth century'.¹²⁵ He also gives greater emphasis to growing black-white conflict over land and cattle in the late eighteenth and early nineteenth centuries than to the more fluid, cooperative dimensions of frontier life emphasised by Legassick.¹²⁶

Keegan, the most recent historian to have commented on the frontier debate, also inclines towards the Giliomee position. Keegan recognises that Legassick had 'effectively challenged' the MacCrone thesis, but proceeds towards conclusions somewhat removed from Legassick's own line of argument. Keegan sees the frontier trekboers essentially as cultural chauvinists. They had a sense of Christian exclusiveness – and for them Christians were generally people of European origin. The trekboers may not have openly proclaimed doctrines of racial superiority, 'but race was implicit in the self-definition of the colonists. In practice, competition over land and the resources of water and grazing reinforced attitudes of inclusiveness and exclusiveness'. Thus, 'There was never any doubt that for most colonists, the Xhosa, like the Khoi, were cultural outsiders, separated from people of European origin by an unbridgeable gulf, of which heathenism was an explicit and physiology an implicit element'.¹²⁷ In both Crais and Keegan little of Legassick's frontier is to be found. The emphasis is more on racial exclusiveness and domination than on the fluid, cooperative forms of racial interaction.

---

123 Elphick and Giliomee, "Origins and entrenchment", p.551.
124 Giliomee, "Eastern Frontier", p.457.
125 Crais, *Colonial Order*, p.44.
126 *Ibid.*, p.48.
127 Keegan, *Colonial South Africa*, pp.26-27, 34.

Legassick's broader critique of the Walker-MacCrone frontier thesis grew out of his more specific, detailed study of the Cape northern frontier. This northern zone was more amenable to Legassick's line of analysis than was the eastern Cape frontier. The work of Legassick and Penn shows that in the eighteenth century race, colour and physical type mattered little in the northern frontier region (located in the area of the present Northern Cape and North-West provinces). Penn notes, for instance, that in this zone miscegenation 'was the rule rather than the exception'.[128] There was 'extensive intermarriage' between white colonists and Khoikhoi, and the resultant growth of a sizeable mixed population. Such people, who came to be called 'Bastaards', would often have Dutch surnames, might have been baptised, and enjoyed the right to acquire farms. But during the course of the eighteenth century their status declined and they became increasingly subject to the exaction of labour and military service.[129]

The northern frontier, beyond the range of any effective colonial or indigenous authority, attracted opportunistic bandit-types and their followers – groups that survived by hunting, robbing and raiding. Some leaders of these bands were white, others were not. One such leader, Jan Bloem, was a German who built up a following among the Kora and used his band to raid other Kora and Sotho-Tswana communities. Another warlord was Klaas Afrikaner, an Oorlam (that is, a Khoi from a more northerly region). He conducted raiding operations in the southern region of modern Namibia.[130] This was a frontier of ruthless opportunism. But it was not only a raiding frontier. Hunting and trading were other activities that brought profit to these acquisitive leaders and their followers. They can be likened to warlords or bandits. And they operated in a zone in which differences of colour counted for little and racial divisions were barely apparent.

It is now a commonplace to say that the past and the present are closely intertwined – that our views of the past are shaped, to a considerable extent, by concerns and ideas about the present. This holds for the South African frontier debate, as it does for the larger debate about the nature and evolution of South African racism. When Walker, Macmillan and MacCrone, from the late 1920s and through the 1930s, began to offer their historical

---

128 Nigel Penn, "The Orange River Frontier Zone, c.1700-1805", in Andrew B. Smith (ed.), *Einiqualand: Studies of the Orange River Frontier* (Cape Town, 1995), p.34.
129 *Ibid.*, pp.34-45.
130 Martin Legassick, "The Northern Frontier to c.1840: The rise and decline of the Griqua people" in Elphick and Gilliomee (eds), *Shaping*, pp.368-69.

interpretations of racial interaction, they were doing so in a particular context which influenced their historical thinking. By the 1930s white South African liberals were becoming increasingly conscious that racial integration, especially in the economic sphere, was an irreversible trend. Industrialisation and urbanisation were bringing black and white together, in the workplace and in the towns and cities. This was a reality that had to be acknowledged. Segregationism, which had shaped the policies of successive South African governments since 1910, flew in the face of this reality. Even leading white English-speaking liberals, like Howard Pim, Charles Loram and Edgar Brookes, had been advocating segregationism during the first three decades of the twentieth century. But by the 1930s such thinking was going out of favour in these circles. Historical writing on the frontier in the 1930s has to be viewed in this context. It has been suggested that Walker's essay on the frontier tradition, originally delivered as a lecture at Oxford in 1930, was largely a reaction to a segregationist speech given by Smuts in Britain the year before.[131]

There were two rather different strands to the liberal frontier thesis, as we have seen. One emphasised interracial cooperation on the frontier; the other stressed conflict and the hardening of white racial attitudes. Both could be harnessed to support liberal opposition to segregationism in the 1930s. H.M. Robertson had emphasised interracial cooperation in South African history in two articles in the mid-1930s.[132] It was a theme later taken up by De Kiewiet. Their intention was to show that such cooperation had occurred in the past, and therefore could be restored in the future.[133] Growing racial integration in the economic sphere could be viewed as the continuation of these earlier forms of cooperation. The contrasting stress on the conflictual, racist character of white frontier life also served the liberal position as it evolved during the 1930s. The concern was to represent the early white frontier communities as removed from civilising agencies and the influence of the eighteenth century Enlightenment. These communities thus slipped into an outlook that was pre-modern, unenlightened, irrational – and hence racist – and an outlook that survived into the twentieth century. Not only was this mindset unenlightened, it was also out of touch with reality – the reality of growing integration. Such an outlook, and the segregationist policies that embodied it, would surely yield to the modernising forces of industrialisation

---

131   Legassick, "Frontier Tradition", p.64; Saunders, *South African Past*, p.114.
132   See above, n.100.
133   Legassick, "Frontier Tradition", p.63.

and urbanisation – in time existing and future realities would finally vanquish the surviving frontier mentality. This in turn implied that that mentality was not so deeply rooted in history, nor so embedded in the white psyche as to be ineradicable. The liberal frontier thesis was in some sense a message of hope. The ugly trajectory of the country's past – the growth of racism – could be stalled and reversed, while the more positive strand – the history of cooperation – could be emulated or sustained as the country modernised.

There was perhaps another agenda underlying the liberal frontier thesis: to pin the blame for racism, segregation (and later, apartheid) on to the boers/Afrikaners. The thesis implied gradual evolution and continuity in the making of South Africa's racial order: the continuity ran from the trekboer frontier mentality, which was carried by the voortrekkers into the interior in the nineteenth century, and culminated in the apartheid system established by the National Party after 1948. Such a view deflected attention away from any racist attitudes or practices that could be associated with the English-speaking colonists and British imperial administrations in the nineteenth century. It is also significant that the liberal frontier thesis was developed in the early 1930s, at a time when some English-speaking liberals, like Edgar Brookes, were dropping their earlier support for segregationism. From the late 1920s there was growing concern in some English-speaking intellectual and political circles that interracial cooperation be fostered. This was the time when the South African Institute of Race Relations was established, when the Joint Councils were striving to promote such cooperation, and when social anthropologists were beginning to focus more attention on culture contact and its implications. In this context the frontier thesis served to reinforce the idea that 'Englishness' epitomised a modern, liberal outlook, in contrast to the unenlightened, irrational, racist worldview of white Afrikaners.

Implicit in the South African frontier thesis is a set of binary opposites. As Legassick put it, '... the "frontier tradition" thesis imposed a dichotomy – sometimes the dichotomy of missionaries and officials versus colonists, sometimes of Afrikaner nationalists against their (largely British) opponents, sometimes of Cape liberalism against Republican frontierism'.[134] It was also a dichotomy between the Enlightenment and irrational forces, between town and country, between industrialisation and pastoralism, between the modern and the pre-modern world.

These dichotomies came to be challenged by a new wave of radical historical writing in the 1970s. No longer could apartheid be blamed simply

---

134   *Ibid.*, p.47.

on the boer frontier outlook, on the voortrekkers, or on the National Party. The particular context of the 1960s, when apartheid reached its zenith, forced a re-think among some scholars and intellectuals. The liberal tradition, usually associated with the western Cape and the more enlightened section of the white English-speaking population, had failed to prevent the racial order becoming entrenched and systematised during the twentieth century. There were even suggestions of liberal complicity in the making of that order. Those modernising forces – industrialisation and urbanisation – had not been the catalysts that would destroy an archaic racism, but had served only to strengthen and reinforce racial discrimination. This line of thinking led Legassick and others to attack the frontier thesis. There was also a sense among some radical scholars in the 1970s that, contrary to the liberal view, the frontier thesis gave rise to fatalist attitudes – that racism was so embedded in South African history and the white consciousness that its elimination was virtually impossible. As Freund wrote in 1976, the MacCrone thesis '... offers little help in comprehending modern realities, and ultimately encourages a passive acceptance of the givens of contemporary South African society'.[135]

The South African frontier has ceased to be a subject of intense, historical enquiry in recent years. In effect the South African 'frontier debate' has died away. But the topic still invites the occasional reflection. Among the more recent reflections those of Keegan are particularly judicious.[136] So what is the current state of play on the issue? MacCrone's arguments continue to be widely rejected. Few would now see the frontier as the wellspring of apartheid. The frontier did not produce a particular set of racist attitudes and practices that came to be carried over into the nineteenth and twentieth centuries, culminating in the post-1948 apartheid order. Nor can one entirely go along with Legassick's alternative characterisation of the frontier. His critique of the Walker-MacCrone view was necessary and highly effective. But like Walker and MacCrone before him, Legassick too was writing in a particular political and ideological context that shaped his thinking. He was rightly concerned to break down the false dichotomy between, on the one hand, racism, segregation and apartheid, and, on the other, British imperialism, liberalism and capitalism. But in doing so he overstated his case. The frontier was not an arena of racial mixing and mutual acculturation to the extent that Legassick suggested. Indeed Legassick himself has recently acknowledged that his early 1970's argument '... in the light of more recent work, was an over-corrective to the idea of the

---

135 Freund, "Race in the social structure of South Africa", p.65.
136 Keegan, *Colonial South Africa*, pp.26-34.

frontier as the crucible of race consciousness'.[137] One would now have to recognise that white frontierspeople did have a sense of their racial identity and did maintain a degree of exclusiveness. Neither trade, nor interracial military alliances, nor even miscegenation, can be taken as evidence of early colonial non-racialism. That people of different colour trade or do business with each does not necessarily indicate an absence of racism. Similarly, interracial military alliances were more likely born of necessity than of non-racial solidarity. After all, in the early 1990s the far right, the embodiment of a virulent racism, did at various times align itself with black bantustan leaders like Buthelezi and Mangope.

The South African frontier debate can be characterised as a kind of historiographical dialectic. There was the original Walker/MacCrone thesis which was challenged by the Legassick antithesis. The more recent synthesis has both abandoned some of the more far-reaching claims of the original protagonists, while restoring some elements of the Walker/MacCrone thesis and incorporating some of Legassick's analysis. Historiography often proceeds in this way.

Neither slavery nor the frontier produced a racial order in South Africa. Neither gave rise to any coherent body of racial ideology or racial theory. The ethnic diversity of slaves militated against the kind of racial ideology that is associated with slavery in the Americas. Frontier colonists were more concerned with daily survival than with theorising. However, it is evident that in the era of slavery and the frontier whites had a sense of their physical and cultural difference from racial 'others'; and difference generally meant superiority. But generalisations such as this cannot be made too readily. Patterns of interaction across racial boundaries varied from region to region, and within regions. There was greater fluidity on the Cape northern frontier than on the eastern frontier. And Guelke's point is well taken – that some white frontierspeople were less inclined than others to adopt racially exclusivist or discriminatory forms of behaviour. But of all the generalisations that have been made, one of the least acceptable is that which represents boers/Afrikaners as the archetypal racists, to be contrasted with the supposedly more urbane, enlightened English-speakers. This is one of the great (and many) myths of South African history. To expose this myth we now have to turn our attention to the nineteenth century and the era of British imperialism and colonisation in South Africa.

---

137 Martin Legassick, "The State, Racism and the Rise of Capitalism in the Nineteenth Century Cape Colony", *South African Historical Journal*, 28, 1993, p.339.

3 Colonial Expansion and Racial Oppression

In this quest to understand better the origin, evolution and dynamic of South Africa's racial order, a study of the nineteenth century ought to provide clues. At the beginning of the century a new force comes into the picture – British imperialism – bringing with it institutional change, further settler colonisation, and territorial expansion. During the middle decades of the century this expansion, together with boer migration, creates a set of new frontier zones across southern Africa. In the last third of the century mineral discoveries set the region on the path to industrial capitalism, which would be connected in significant ways to the twentieth century racial order – as we shall see in the final part of this book.

British imperialism is a theme that has generated a great deal of heat in South African historiography. For much of this century it provided fuel for Afrikaner nationalist historical writing, which viewed British imperial intervention in southern Africa as an evil inflicted upon the boer/Afrikaner people. A more recent generation of radical writers has examined more closely the destructive impact of British imperialism on indigenous African societies in southern Africa. Writers with liberal leanings have varied between either being mildly critical of the British imperial record in southern Africa or defending the positive British impact on the region. It is this latter grouping in particular that has ignored or glossed over the racist character of British imperialism and its part in the evolution of racial domination and segregation.

The historiography of British imperialism in South Africa is both extensive and lacking – extensive in quantity of output, but lacking in any incisive overall assessment of the imperial impact. Historical writing on British imperialism was for a long time clouded by Afrikaner nationalism's own particular anti-imperialist agenda. Later, liberal writers became overly preoccupied with interpreting the motives of British imperialism, à la Robinson and Gallagher. Nobody has attempted to produce a balance-sheet of the British imperial record. There is no single work which examines in a general way the contribution of British imperialism to the making of a racial order. To get the broader picture one has to draw upon the findings of many informative monographs and case-studies. The aim of this chapter is to produce such a synthesising overview.

In exploring the connection between British imperialism and evolving racial policy and practice in nineteenth century South Africa a number of questions will arise. Was British imperialism essentially a benevolent, humanitarian force, protecting indigenous communities against the depredations of white colonists, or did it aid and abet those depredations and promote racial discrimination? Were racist ideas and policies exported from the British metropole to South Africa? Or was it the particular conditions of the colonies – competition for resources, cultural difference, physical insecurity – that produced racist attitudes and discriminatory measures? How significant was the development of racial theory in the nineteenth century? Did it shape the colonial outlook and influence official policy? Why and how have different writers at different times come to view British imperialism more or less favourably or to represent it as a negative, destructive phenomenon?

There has been in South African historiography a widely held view that British imperialism was a liberalising force in nineteenth century South Africa. It is a view that was generally expounded by Afrikaner nationalist historians, for whom liberalism was utterly anathema. They argued that British imperial administrations pursued liberal policies towards indigenous people – policies that were inappropriate for colonial conditions and which alienated the boer population. Generally though, Afrikaner nationalist historians were more concerned about the destructive impact of British imperialism on boer communities through most of the nineteenth century. They focussed their attention on the British acquisition of boer-claimed territory, on the British suppression of boer republican independence. That British imperialism was impacting on indigenous African communities in similar ways mattered not at all to Afrikaner nationalist historians. They were only concerned with the adverse effects of British imperialism on the boers and Dutch – and one of these adverse effects was deemed to be liberal race policies. Implicit in the Afrikaner nationalist view was the idea that British imperial policy ran counter to the principles of untrammelled white supremacy and racial separation.

Scholars and commentators with liberal leanings have reached a similar conclusion to Afrikaner nationalist historians, but for very different reasons. Whereas Afrikaner nationalists viewed the supposedly liberal character of British imperial policy in a negative light, liberal scholars have generally recorded and represented this in a positive way. De Kiewiet, for instance, writing in the late 1930s, argued that the humanitarian character of British imperial policy in South Africa in the nineteenth century had to be recognised: 'Not all the penetration into the shadier and more obscure processes of imperial action can seriously disturb the conviction that there was in England a genuine feeling of concern over the native tribes'.[1] If De Kiewiet was critical of the imperial government it was for its parsimony, its unwillingness to spend more money to establish more securely a British administrative and judicial system in the region.

Through the 1950s and 1960s this view of British imperialism became fairly standard. In the first half of the nineteenth century the British, so the story goes, introduced sound administrative and judicial structures to the Cape, abolished slavery, and passed other measures that gave greater freedom and equality to indigenous people.[2] When Van den Berghe in the 1960s wrote his sociological study of racial conflict in South Africa, these assumptions found their way into his introductory historical survey. The British government at the Cape introduced 'a series of liberalizing measures', culminating in the abolition of slavery in 1834. What is more, in Van den Berghe's view these measures were heavily influenced by missionaries and 'dictated by humanitarian considerations'[3] – another standard assumption held by liberal and Afrikaner nationalist historians alike.

J.S. Galbraith was another to hold that British imperial policy in southern Africa was influenced by 'humanitarian considerations' – had the British not intervened in the region the boers and indigenous Africans would have slugged it out in a merciless confrontation, at the end of which the latter would either have been subjugated or exterminated. Galbraith also took further De Kiewiet's criticism that the British were too parsimonious, arguing that colonial conditions, with their potential for instability and conflict, required stronger British intervention. This the British were unwilling to provide because of the government's concern to keep expenditure to a minimum in southern Africa, which was seen as being of limited economic value to the mother country.[4]

Galbraith's analysis remained within the idealist view of British imperialism – a view that held sway for over 30 years from the 1930s. Although this idealist interpretation came to be questioned and challenged in

---

1   C.W. De Kiewiet, *The Imperial Factor in South Africa* (New York, 1966), p.6.
2   See, for instance, Leo Marquard, *The Peoples and Policies of South Africa* (London, 1962), p.9. See below for further discussion of these measures.
3   Van den Berghe, *South Africa*, pp.26-27.
4   J.S. Galbraith, *Reluctant Empire: British Policy on the South African Frontier 1834-1854* (Los Angeles, 1963), pp.4-9.

the 1970s, it has lived on and its underlying assumptions can still be found in more recent work. Van Aswegen, for instance, has as recently as 1990 upheld the idea that British imperialism was essentially humanitarian and non-racial: 'Influenced by the spirit of enlightenment of the time and under pressure from philanthropic circles, after 1806 the British gradually started to propagate the idea of equal social rights and to apply it in practice'.[5] To support this view Van Aswegen highlights measures, policies and tendencies that underlined the liberalising impact of British imperialism: the abolition of slavery and other measures that ostensibly protected labourers; the introduction of a qualified, non-racial (but still sexist) municipal franchise in Cape Town in 1839; application of the principle of equal, non-racial education in government schools – a principle confirmed in a government memorandum of 1839.[6]

Such views must be put to the test. The record of British imperialism in South Africa has to be critically examined – and the specific measures and policies, as well as the actions and attitudes of Cape governors and other leading imperial administrators, carefully scrutinised. Many of the measures to be considered dealt with labour relations, but also had a wider significance in the evolution of racial domination. Three years after the second British occupation of the Cape in 1806 the first such set of measures was imposed under the authority of the Cape governor, the Earl of Caledon. The so-called Caledon Code of 1809 was designed to regulate relations between white colonial employers, or 'masters', and their Khoisan labourers. The language of the Code gave the appearance that the Khoisan were to be accorded greater freedom, equality and protection. But in practice this was far from the case, as the measure, more than anything, secured a labour supply for the colonists. The Code gave Khoisan a fixed place of residence, which they could leave only with official permission and when carrying a pass. This severely curtailed freedom of movement and effectively tied Khoisan labourers to their colonial masters. The Code was also designed to give labourers some rights and protection: the right to complain against ill-treatment, and a contract stipulating the wages to be paid. In practice such protection was rarely available as labourers lacked easy access to the relevant officials, who would anyway naturally tend to side with the colonists where labour disputes arose. Ultimately, the Code has to be viewed as a discriminatory measure promulgated in a developing racial order. Although it ostensibly subscribed to

---

5 Van Aswegen, *South Africa to 1854*, p.212.
6 *Ibid.*, pp.206-13.

notions of equality before the law, it continued to withhold the right of Khoisan to own land. And the Code clearly accorded differential treatment to groups of people distinguished on putative racial grounds. 'Hottentots' were viewed as a distinct category of people who should be subject to specific regulations and prohibitions.[7]

There are few single measures that have been given more attention in South African historical writing than Ordinance 50 of 1828 (apart, perhaps, from the 1913 Natives' Land Act). Ordinance 50, promulgated by the Lieutenant-Governor of the Cape, General Bourke, overturned the Caledon Code and appeared to herald a new liberal direction in imperial policy. The measure abolished the requirement that Khoisan carry passes, and granted 'Hottentots and other free Persons of colour' the right to purchase and own land. Ordinance 50 has been accorded considerable historical significance, and it has been the subject of debate. According to one view the measure represented a landmark in South African history, indicating a new direction in imperial policy at the Cape – towards a 'colour-blind', egalitarian dispensation. It also appeared to reflect the triumph of the humanitarian, philanthropist lobby, led by missionaries, over the crude exploitative racism of the white colonists. Van Aswegen has provided a clear, recent exposition of this view:

> Ordinance 50 of 1828 was of great importance in the history of intergroup relations in the Cape Colony. It was the first real attempt by an authority to embody in law the principle of equality between white and non-white. The act made no distinction between people on the basis of race, colour or status and gave to the Khoikhoi the status of full and equal colonial subjects.[8]

Implicit in this view is the idea that the measure emanated from an enlightened metropole and was imposed upon recalcitrant, unenlightened white colonists wanting a free hand in managing their labourers and persons of colour.

---

7   Ross, *Beyond the Pale*, p.95; Macmillan, *Cape Colour Question*, pp.156-57, 160-62; Crais, *Making of the Colonial Order*, pp.59-60; Susan Newton-King, "The labour market of the Cape Colony, 1807-28" in Marks and Atmore (eds), *Economy and Society*, pp.176-77.
8   Van Aswegen, *South Africa to 1854*, p.204. See also De Kiewiet, *History of South Africa*, p.46, and J.S. Marais, *The Cape Coloured People 1652-1937* (Johannesburg, 1962), p.157.

An early challenge to this view came from Macmillan who closely examined the origins and impact of Ordinance 50. Macmillan played down the influence of the humanitarian, missionary lobby in the passing of the measure. Nor did the ordinance, in his view, bring complete legal equality to all, as many, before and after him, claimed that it did. Macmillan was also perceptive to observe that 'the very wording of the law gives it special application only to 'Hottentots and other free persons of colour'.[9] Further reinterpretation of Ordinance 50 was to follow some years after Macmillan's writing on the subject. Newton-King examined the measure in the context of the colony's acute labour shortage. By granting Khoisan greater labour mobility and by freeing the labour market it was envisaged that the labour supply could be improved. This was not essentially a measure dictated by humanitarian considerations.[10] And Ross has distinguished between the *de jure* and *de facto* significance of the measure. Implementation was left in the hands of local authorities whose sympathies lay with the white colonists: 'The intentions [behind the ordinance] may have been worthy, but no means were provided to realize them'.[11] In effect, the pattern of labour exploitation in the Cape continued after 1828 much as it had before.

The emancipation of slaves, enacted by the British parliament in 1833 and coming into effect in British colonies in 1834, could be seen as a blow struck not only against the institution of slavery, but also against racism, in that slaves were persons of colour. Recent work, however, suggests that the opposite may have been the case – that the abolition of slavery may well have fuelled racism at the Cape. A slave system enabled the stringent control of slave labour. It did not require racial ideology to reinforce that control. Moreover not all persons of colour were enslaved – so the main distinction would have been between the free and unfree, rather than between black and white. With the abolition of slavery the situation changed. As Ross has put it,

> There was no longer any legal mechanism to maintain the control of the owners of agricultural or other property over their labour force. The measures adopted then were likely to apply to all those who were dark of complexion since this became the main signal for subordination.[12]

---

9 Macmillan, *Cape Colour Question*, pp.211-13.
10 Newton-King, "The labour market of the Cape Colony", pp.197-200.
11 Ross, *Beyond the Pale*, p.102.
12 Ross, "Pre-industrial and industrial racial stratification in South Africa", p.85.

Slave emancipation aroused fear among the master class, almost exclusively white – the fear that freed slaves would become idle, undisciplined, even dangerous. It was in this context that racial ideology became more pronounced. The former legal domination exercised through slavery came to be replaced by ideological and cultural domination that rapidly took on a racist character.[13]

Both Ordinance 50 and the emancipation of slaves appeared to be liberalising measures, bringing greater freedom and equality to people of colour. In a *de jure* sense this was indeed the case – a reading of their terms reveals greater freedom for formerly servile or enslaved persons. However, this liberalisation did not bring deracialisation. Both measures, concludes Ross, 'in no way hindered the development of a society divided racially between a white upper stratum and a coloured lower stratum, composed primarily of unskilled labourers'.[14]

In the years following the emancipation of slaves the British colonial administration at the Cape passed further labour measures that had the effect of sharpening this racial divide – thereby strengthening the view that the abolition of slavery brought in its wake not greater freedom and racial equality, but rather heightened white domination and racial oppression. A key measure was the 1841 Masters and Servants Ordinance. This tightened employers' control over their workers. The contract was to be the instrument of control. Although the contract would lay down the obligations of the employer as well as the labourer, its effect was to tie the latter more tightly to the former, as magistrates invariably sided with employers when disputes arose. Breach of contract became a criminal offence; and desertion would be severely punished. Race was not explicitly mentioned in the ordinance, but the measure was clearly directed at persons of colour who made up the labouring class.[15] The subordination of black labourers, albeit in the guise of a non-racial measure, had been taken a step further.

So far there is little to suggest that during the early decades of British imperialism at the Cape the growth of a racial order was in any way stalled. This can be further confirmed by an examination of the attitudes, policies and

---

13 Pieterse, *White on Black*, p.2. See also Edna Bradlow, "Emancipation and Race Perceptions at the Cape", *South African Historical Journal*, 15, 1983, p.23.

14 Ross, *Beyond the Pale*, p.105.

15 *Ibid.*; Ross, "Pre-industrial and industrial racial stratification in South Africa", pp.85-87; Clifton Crais, "Race, the State, and the Silence of History in the Making of Modern South Africa: Preliminary Departures" (unpublished paper, University of Cape Town, 1992), p.11.

actions of successive Cape governors, the chief agents of imperial authority. These governors were generally military men, autocratic in style and racist in outlook. Such men commonly viewed Xhosa communities beyond the frontier as irredeemable savages who posed a serious threat to the security of the colony. They were especially concerned to demarcate and secure boundaries – lines that would prevent the intrusion of the Xhosa into the colonial world, lines separating civilisation from barbarism.[16] Cradock, who became governor in 1811, five years after the second British occupation of the Cape, epitomised this outlook. The Great Fish River was just such a boundary that had to be secured. He thus instructed Lieutenant-Colonel John Graham to drive out those Xhosa remaining west of this boundary. Graham was happy to oblige, viewing the Xhosa as plundering savages.[17] He led the operation with relish, destroying Xhosa crops, seizing their cattle, 'and shooting every man who can be found'.[18] Cradock expressed his satisfaction with the outcome of the 1811-12 Frontier War: '... had we yielded the ancient boundary of the Great Fish River, the weakness we had evinced would only have added contempt to the operation of their [Xhosa] thirst for plunder and other savage passions'.[19]

Cradock's attitude was typical of most Cape governors in the first half of the nineteenth century. Lord Charles Somerset, governor for most of the period 1814-1826, was another military man fiercely determined to shore up the colonial boundary against alien 'others'. For him, the Xhosa beyond the boundary were savages who required a clear demonstration of colonial superiority and power. This meant a vigorous defence of the border, and the expansion of colonial settlement.[20] Sir Benjamin D'Urban, Cape governor in the mid-1830s, was even more racist in outlook and action than his predecessors. In his view the Xhosa were a 'barbarous' people with an 'inherent propensity ... to rob and pillage'. D'Urban showed his ruthlessness in 1835 when he ordered the colonial forces to drive the Xhosa beyond the Kei. Following this successful military action he at once opened up the

---

16   Alan Lester, "The Margins of Order: Strategies of Segregation on the Eastern Cape Frontier, 1806-c.1850", *Journal of Southern African Studies*, 23, 4, 1997, p.637.
17   Andrew Bank, "Liberals and their Enemies: Racial Ideology at the Cape of Good Hope, 1820 to 1850" (unpublished Ph.D thesis, Cambridge University, 1995), p.195; Noël Mostert, *Frontiers* (London, 1992), p.386.
18   Ben Maclennan, *A Proper Degree of Terror* (Johannesburg, 1986), p.124.
19   *Ibid.*, p.129.
20   Lester, "Margins of Order", p.642.

territory between the Fish and Kei to white settlement, only to be overruled by the British Colonial Secretary, Lord Glenelg.[21]

The famous Glenelg despatch, reining in an aggressive, expansionist Cape governor, might suggest that the power-holders in the British metropole were more liberal and less racist than their imperial agents in the colonies – an important issue soon to be discussed. Certainly Glenelg's despatch did have the immediate effect of revoking D'Urban's annexation of Xhosa territory, and it ushered in a period of a few years from the mid-1830s when British colonial policy on the eastern Cape frontier was geared less towards subjugation and territorial expansion, and more towards peaceful coexistence with the Xhosa. Lieutenant-Governor Stockenström was entrusted with the task of managing a system of treaties, whereby boundaries and other matters would be agreed upon after negotiation with local chiefs. But this relatively liberal interlude was short-lived. When Sir Peregrine Maitland, another military man, become governor in 1844 he restored the Cradock-D'Urban style and approach. He shared the orthodox colonial view of the Xhosa as uncivilised 'others'. Accordingly he renounced the treaty system, and in 1846, on a trivial pretext, launched an invasion of Xhosa territory.[22]

Of all the British Cape governors of the first half of the nineteenth century Sir Harry Smith (1847-52) perhaps stands out as the most arrogant, expansionist, and racist. Xhosa politics and culture he held in high contempt. He was determined to break the power of chiefs, and to eradicate cultural practices that he despised. His intent was to extend direct colonial control as a means of 'civilising' the Xhosa. He thus went ahead and did what D'Urban had tried to do thirteen years earlier – he annexed the territory between the Keiskamma and Kei Rivers, as the colony of British Kaffraria. While he stopped short of driving all Xhosa beyond the Kei, he did adopt a segregationist policy within the new colony, herding the Xhosa into 'locations' which would supply labour to neighbouring white farming areas. At the same time the power of chiefs was undermined and curtailed with the introduction of white magistrates.[23]

For generations historians underplayed the arrogance and racism that accompanied British imperial expansion in the eastern Cape during the nineteenth century. Numerous writers glossed over the record of successive Cape governors and British high commissioners. The colonial rulers were not

---

21   *Ibid.*, p.645; Crais, *Making of the Colonial Order*, pp.117-19.
22   Crais, *Making of the Colonial Order*, p.143
23   *Ibid.*, p.145; Lester, "Margins of Order", pp.649-50.

deemed to have any responsibility for the emergent racial order.[24] Most liberal accounts up to the 1970s preferred to stress the role of the voortrekkers as the standard-bearers of segregation and apartheid, thereby diverting attention away from the shabby record of British imperialism. According to this historiographical tradition the main fault of the British imperial government was its financial parsimony and its consequent failure to bring stability to the eastern Cape frontier through a more considered and energetic intervention in the region. This emphasis on cost-cutting was self-defeating, because, so the argument goes, the British government ended up waging costly frontier wars that might have been avoided had imperial policy been more effective.

Missing from this kind of analysis is any account of the virulent racism that permeated the British imperial administration from the top down. Successive Cape governors shared a common view of the Xhosa as a people naturally prone to savagery and thieving. Such thinking was widespread among the ranks of the British military and officialdom at the Cape.[25] Moreover, the older orthodox analysis fails to show at all how British imperial policy at the Cape was inherently segregationist. Some recent work has begun to correct this failing. Mostert suggests that the British military onslaught which drove the Xhosa out of the Zuurveld in 1812 set a pattern: 'this military achievement created a new reality by emphasizing separation of the races as a divide between natural enemies and irreconcilable cultures, the only solution for which was complete severance'.[26] Lester provides a useful corrective to the orthodox view, noting how segregationism was evolving by the mid-nineteenth century: 'In the late-1840s segregation as a system of interlocking territories, defined along racially exclusive lines, with labour flows from the black locations to white economic enterprises, was being established along the eastern Cape frontier zone'.[27] This pattern of segregation was evident in two eastern Cape urban areas. Port Elizabeth has been identified by Christopher as 'one of the principal cities where the foundations of ... apartheid ... were laid'.[28] As early as 1834 the London

---

24 See, for instance, Van den Berghe, *South Africa*. His chapter on the historical background to South Africa's racial conflict says virtually nothing about the role of the British colonial administration.
25 Bank, "Liberals and their Enemies", pp.194-95.
26 Mostert, *Frontiers*, p.390.
27 Lester, "Margins of Order", p.650.
28 A.J. Christopher, "Port Elizabeth" in A. Lemon (ed.) *Homes Apart: South Africa's Segregated Cities* (Cape Town, 1991), p.43.

Missionary Society established a formal black settlement on the western edge of the city. In the 1850s the Port Elizabeth municipality created the Native Strangers' Location 'where Hottentots, Fingoes, Kaffirs and other Strangers visiting Port Elizabeth may temporarily reside' – an early colonial expression of the idea, to become dominant for most of the twentieth century, that black people were essentially aliens in urban areas. A century before group areas the Port Elizabeth municipality tried to enforce urban apartheid, issuing regulations in 1855 requiring blacks to live in the Native Strangers' Location if not housed by their employers or not owning a property.[29] East London can also claim to be one of the founders of urban segregation. A government edict of 1849 required 'Fingoes and other coloured natives' to live in 'locations' in East London.[30] Some of the essential features of segregation can be seen, at least in embryonic form, in the eastern Cape by the mid-nineteenth century.

Apologists for British imperialism have sometimes argued that the British imperial government was for the most part honorable and fair, but that imperial officials in the colonies could allow themselves to be swayed by racist white colonists hungry for land and labour. Implicit in this view is a sharply drawn contrast between, on the one hand, an enlightened, rational, metropolitan order embodied in the British government, and, on the other, a rapacious, unenlightened colonial order embodied in a community of white settlers aggressively striving to secure their own material interests. This polarised representation has to be questioned at two levels. First, did the colonial situation at the Cape breed a virulent racism among the colonists? Second, was the metropolitan order a model of enlightenment and non-racialism? Or was the British metropole perhaps the source of Cape colonial racism?

In 1820 about 4000 immigrants from Britain settled in the eastern Cape. Much of the writing on these settlers has been hagiography. It has studiously ignored their racism, highlighting instead their heroic struggles, their vulnerability, and their resilience. Only in recent years have scholars begun to draw out the racist character of settler discourse and practice. Two historians

---

29   A.J. Christopher, "Apartheid Planning in South Africa: The Case of Port Elizabeth", *The Geographical Journal*, 153, 2, 1987, p.197; G. Baines, "The Origins of Urban Segregation: Local Government and the Residence of Africans in Port Elizabeth, c.1835-1865", *South African Historical Journal*, 22, 1990, pp.74-75.

30   R. Fox, E. Nel and C. Reintges, "East London", in Lemon (ed.), *Homes Apart*; E.L. Nel, "Racial segregation in East London, 1836-1948", *South African Geographical Journal*, 73, 1991, pp.60-61; K. Tankard, "Urban Segregation: William Mvalo's 'Celebrated Stick Case'", *South African Historical Journal*, 34, 1996.

who have made significant contributions in this area are Clifton Crais and Andrew Bank. Both share the view that the discourse of the colonists was not, in the early years of their settlement in the eastern Cape, imbued with a virulent racism. According to Crais the settler elite 'initially viewed blacks with positive enthusiasm'.[31] Bank claims that settler race attitudes were relatively liberal until the 1830s. For example, Thomas Pringle, a particularly prominent early settler, offered a positive representation of both the Khoi and the Xhosa in his writings. Another influential settler, Thomas Philipps, criticised the imperial administration for its arbitrary, heavy-handed response to alleged Xhosa misdemeanours. The regular trading conducted at the Fort Willshire fair from 1824 to 1828 seemed to indicate a relatively peaceful coexistence between colonist and Xhosa. The *Graham's Town Journal*, later to purvey brazenly racist views, was mildly humanitarian – supporting the abolition of slavery, for instance – in the first three years of its existence from 1831 to 1834.[32]

Crais and Bank both agree that this outlook was short-lived. It soon gave way to a venomous racism, characterised by widespread negative stereotyping. 'From the end of the 1820s', observes Crais, 'Africans were increasingly represented as libidinous, uncontrolled, lazy and disrespectful of established authority'.[33] Given particular emphasis in this settler discourse was the alleged indolence of the Xhosa and their apparent propensity to thieve. Sharp dichotomies were drawn between the civilised lifestyle of the colonists and the barbarism of the Xhosa, between the fairness and rationality of the British socio-political system and the arbitrary, tyrannical character of the Xhosa polity. Imperial rule and firm control were the only means by which the Xhosa could be redeemed and this great divide bridged.[34] By the 1840s racist writing was becoming commonplace in the eastern Cape. A text by Rev. Niven, entitled *Impartial Analysis of the Kafir Character*, was published in Grahamstown in 1840. In this far from impartial account he denounced Xhosa men as idlers, and dismissed Xhosa society as being 'but a few degrees above zero' in the human scale.[35] Even more virulent was the racist writing of Harriet Ward who published an account of her stay in the eastern Cape during the 1840s. She ranted against the philanthropists '... who romanticise about savages and slavery ... who would leave the savage in

---

31 Crais, *Making of the Colonial Order*, p.128.
32 Bank, "Liberals and their Enemies", pp.200-205.
33 Crais, *Making of the Colonial Order*, p.129.
34 *Ibid.*, pp.132-41.
35 *Ibid.*, p.132.

undisturbed possession of a vast tract of country as much in need of population as England is of the reverse'.³⁶

As Bank points out, it would be wrong to suggest that this racist settler discourse developed as something new, only after the British colonisation of the eastern Cape had been established. Such a suggestion implies that the settlers did not bring racist attitudes with them from their motherland – a patently false assumption, as we shall soon see. However, this settler discourse does seem to have become more virulent from the mid-1820s and 1830s. Crais argues that the discourse became more pronounced from the mid-1820s, while Bank pinpoints the mid-1830s.³⁷ We must now explore the possible reasons for this changing discourse. The different periodisations suggested by Crais and Bank point to different explanations.

Can the developing racism of the British settlers perhaps be explained by applying the old frontier thesis? There is a hint of this in Walker's 1930 essay:

> ... the British settlers in the Eastern Province of the Cape and in Natal ... soon learnt the rules of the game that all men of Western civilization have played if they have been left unchecked by some countervailing authority, whether in their own country or without it, in touch with tribal natives whose land and labour are desirable.³⁸

The suggestion here is that the settlers might have picked up what were deemed to be typical boer attitudes – that the boers somehow infected the settlers with the racist disease. Such a view has no foundation. Indeed, Keegan has recently provided a welcome corrective to this stereotype, arguing that 'it was (very anti-humanitarian) British settlers, and not Boers, who developed a rhetoric of racial and cultural superiority to justify ongoing imperial subversion of the Xhosa'. Keegan goes on to substantiate his claim by quoting from the autobiography of Sir Andries Stockenström, who was to be responsible for implementing a more humane eastern frontier policy in the late 1830s: 'As Stockenström wrote, "The theory which makes the black irreclaimable savages, fit only to be exterminated, like the wolves, was not of

---

36   Quoted in Kenneth Parker, "Fertile land, romantic spaces, uncivilized peoples: English travel-writing about the Cape of Good Hope, 1800-50", in Bill Schwarz (ed.), *The Expansion of England* (London, 1996).
37   Crais, *Making of the Colonial Order*, p.128; Bank, "Liberals and their Enemies", pp.198-99.
38   Walker, *Frontier Tradition*, p.24. Also quoted in Legassick, "Frontier tradition", p.46.

Boer origin" – implying (correctly) that explicitly racist notions about the Xhosa and other African peoples were a British innovation'.[39]

The racism of the British settlers can only be explained if it is situated firmly in an historical context. What were the particular conditions in the eastern Cape that gave rise to a racist discourse? Two considerations seem to be important. First there were the material wants of the settlers, particularly their demand for land and labour. Such interests did much to shape attitudes. Second, successive frontier wars bred insecurity and fear, which in turn converted easily into a racist discourse.

Crais stresses the first factor. 'The rising racism of British settlers', he writes, 'was bound up with the development of rural capitalism and the making of a black working class'.[40] Settler entrepreneurs suffered from a constant labour shortage. In the early stages of the British settlement serious consideration was given to the idea of importing white labour, thereby creating a racially exclusive colonial state. But white workers did not arrive in sufficient numbers. It soon became clear that whites would not make up a colonial working class in the eastern Cape.[41] Therefore settlers increasingly looked to the Khoikhoi and Xhosa as a source of labour. However, the independent Xhosa chiefdoms would not generate a labour supply as long as their territorial base could sustain their rural economy. And the British colonial administration was seemingly doing little to coerce out a supply of Khoikhoi labour. Ordinance 50 of 1828 was not, as we have seen, a liberal non-racial measure. But it certainly appeared as such to settlers at the time. After its enactment there was an outcry from settlers, who demanded more coercive measures that might induce the required labour supply. Indeed, Bank views Ordinance 50 as 'the initial catalyst in crystallising and entrenching settler racism in the decade of emancipations (1828-38)'.[42] He argues that settler frustration over the shortage of labour gained expression in racist stereotyping. In the words of one settler, the Khoikhoi were 'inclined to an unlaborious life, and disposed to roam over their native fields rather than to gain subsistence by their own industry'.[43] The settlers' hostility to missionaries arose in the past from their belief that mission stations provided a haven for idle Khoikhoi and so contributed to the labour shortage.[44]

---

39   Keegan, *Colonial South Africa*, pp.35-36.
40   Crais, *Making of the Colonial Order*, p.139.
41   *Ibid.*, pp.93-94; Keegan, *Colonial South Africa*, p.65.
42   Bank, "Liberals and their Enemies", p.171.
43   *Ibid.*, p.172.
44   Crais, *Making of the Colonial Order*, pp.129-30.

According to settler discourse, indigenous people were not only indolent, but also lacking in respect for private property. Their supposed propensity to thieve thus became another component of this racial discourse. This was attributed particularly to the Xhosa, with whom settlers became embroiled in endless conflicts over the possession of cattle. Land was another material resource that lay at the basis of settler racism. As Fredrickson has observed, 'Land hunger and territorial ambition gave to whites a practical incentive to differentiate between the basic rights and privileges they claimed for themselves and what they considered to be just treatment for the 'savages' who stood in their path ... '.[45] Thus the Xhosa were deemed to be tying up, and wasting, fertile land in the eastern Cape – land which the settlers believed they could utilise far more energetically and productively.

Scratch beneath the surface of settler racism and one can often find some kind of material interest coming into play. Land, labour and cattle were all crucial to the settler economy, and the supply or possession of these key resources was deemed to be obstructed or jeopardised by indigenous communities, Khoikhoi or African. However, it would be an oversimplification to reduce this racism to material factors alone. Such factors are important and have been rightly stressed by writers like Crais. But our second main consideration – the psychological insecurity and fear bred in the context of frontier warfare – must be given careful attention.

The British settlers did not experience a frontier war for the first fifteen years or so of their settlement in the eastern Cape. But the Xhosa invasion of December 1834 aroused fear and panic among the white colonists. The war brought loss of life, cattle and property on both sides in the conflict – and it fuelled racial hatred among the colonial community. Bank, Lester and Mostert view the 1834-35 war as a significant turning-point – as the event that did more than anything to harden racial attitudes among the settlers. Bank argues that 'the outbreak of frontier war prompted an unambiguously negative image of the Xhosa and definitively shattered the early optimism of English settlers regarding the prospects of reforming "savagery"'.[46] A racist tirade against the Xhosa accompanied and followed the war, with the *Graham's Town Journal* leading the assault. One editorial described 'the great mass' of Xhosa as 'sunk in the lowest state of wretchedness'.[47] Robert

---

45 Fredrickson, *White Supremacy*, p.5.
46 Bank, "Liberals and their Enemies", p.217.
47 *Ibid.*, p.219. See also Clifton C. Crais, "The Vacant Land: The Mythology of British Expansion in the Eastern Cape, South Africa", *Journal of Social History*, 25, 1991, p.265.

Godlonton, editor of the *Graham's Town Journal*, after the war wrote of the Xhosa as 'the most barbarous savages, sunk into the lowest abyss of moral degradation'.[48] In an official government proclamation of 1835 the Xhosa were described as 'treacherous and irreclaimable savages'.[49] This discourse rapidly took hold of the settler community, especially in its urban centre, Grahamstown. The British military commander, Harry Smith, reported some months after the war that there was 'a spirit pervading all classes of society at Graham's Town ... to teach everyone to view and treat a Kafir as a beast'.[50] Smith was not merely reporting on the state of feeling – he himself was happy to purvey the discourse, remarking on the Xhosas' 'unconquerable propensity to commit robbery and murder on their neighbours'.[51]

The recent work of Bank, Crais, Mostert and Lester has clearly revealed the growth of a virulent racist discourse among white eastern Cape settlers in the 1820s and 1830s. Racial stereotypes were articulated according to material interests. The demand for labour and land lay beneath the stereotype that characterised indigenous people as indolent and unproductive. And there is little doubt that settler racism became more vituperative, increasingly malignant, during and after the 1834-35 frontier war. The indigenous people were not only failing to serve the settlers' material needs, but were also a threat to life and property. This was fuel for racist outbursts.

This line of analysis implies that racial consciousness emerged in the particular conditions of the eastern Cape in the 1820s and 1830s. Indeed Mostert and Crais see the early nineteenth century eastern Cape as crucial to understanding the development of South Africa's racial order. Mostert states this view unequivocally:

> The wars and the moral struggle on the Cape frontier provided the main formative experience of South Africa and they were a powerful formative influence as well upon the attitudes to colonialism and race that predominated in the later nineteenth century as the British Empire approached its zenith. Their impact is far from over.[52]

---

48 Mostert, *Frontiers*, p.777.
49 Lester, "Margins of Order", p.645.
50 Bank, "Liberals and their Enemies", p.220.
51 A. Lester, "Cultural construction and spatial strategy on the Eastern Cape Frontier, 1806-c.1838", *South African Geographical Journal*, 78, 2, 1996, p.103.
52 Mostert, *Frontiers*, pp.xvii-xviii. See also, Legassick, "The State, Racism and the Rise of Capitalism", pp.329-33.

Crais is also in no doubt that the history of the eastern Cape at this time had major long-term significance:

> White attitudes towards Africans which were forged 'on the ground' ... spread into other areas of white settlement in Southern Africa. So did legislation, imperial policies and agricultural practices. The Eastern Cape witnessed the emergence of colonial Africa's first 'native reserves'. And land and labour policies in what became the Rhodesias and even in the White Highlands of Kenya had many of their historical roots in the Eastern Cape during the first half of the nineteenth century.[53]

This view has plausibility, but requires qualification. The racist discourse of the time was not directed against all Africans, nor indeed against all Xhosa. Some Xhosa chiefs had actually been colonial allies during the war. They were therefore exempted from the planned (and, as we know, abortive) general expulsion of Xhosa beyond the Kei River. Then too there were the 'Fingoes', supposedly displaced, rootless people who were being cultivated and assimilated by the colonial authorities and the missionaries as African allies against the Xhosa.[54] Thus it would seem that settler racism was not rooted in colour difference or a perceived race distinction – rather that this racism was a manifestation of underlying needs and fears on the part of the colonists.

Up till now in this discussion 'settlers' and 'colonists' have been mentioned in a single breath. There is a danger in viewing settler society in monolithic terms – in assuming that it was held together by some presumed common racial identity. Settlerdom was stratified. There had emerged quite rapidly a colonial elite, comprising mainly larger landowners and farmers, and the mercantile class. Crais argues that this elite was mainly responsible for propagating a racist discourse. Capitalist farmers had the greatest interest in securing an adequate supply of indigenous labour and in seizing Xhosa-occupied land. Thus, says Crais, 'it was this very same elite who constructed and disseminated the discourse of the Other'.[55] The *Graham's Town Journal* essentially represented the views of this elite, whose racism, continues Crais, served to shape their identity: 'The settler elite became the opposite of what the African innately was – lazy, thievish, libidinous and so

---

53 Crais, *Making of the Colonial Order*, p.3.
54 Lester, "Cultural construction", p.103.
55 Crais, *Making of the Colonial Order*, p.136.

on – but the central point is that settlers depended on those negative assessments in their definition of self'.[56]

Can one therefore view the eastern Cape colonial elite as a major source of racism in the first half of the nineteenth century – and thus also as a significant contributor to the making of South Africa's racial order? After all, it has been argued, by both Crais and Ross, that this elite exerted a considerable influence over the British colonial administration at the Cape. Successive governors were reluctant to adopt policies that conflicted with the interests of the landowning class.[57] We have seen how Governor D'Urban, in particular, was particularly receptive to settler interests in the 1830s. All this could somehow imply that decent, honorable governors and their officials, imbued with a 'British' sense of justice and fair play, came to be unduly influenced and corrupted by rapacious, self-seeking, racist settlers. This in turn reinforces the commonly held notion that the imperial centre, the British metropole, represented and embodied the ideals of the Enlightenment – rationality, order, respect for fundamental liberties – while the colonial order was in some sense pre-modern, unenlightened, lawless, disdainful of basic human rights. Such a view serves to absolve British imperialism of any real responsibility for the growth of a racial order in South Africa. It rules out the possibility that racist attitudes and assumptions could have been transported from the British metropole to the colonial periphery. It is a view that must be seriously questioned and challenged.

The assumption that British imperialism represented modernity, that imperial agents were the bearers of enlightened ideals and practices, has lain deep in the liberal tradition of South African historiography. The assumption was expressed plainly by De Kiewiet, writing in the early 1940s:

> The spirit of a new age came to perplex the conservative mind of the Colony as well. Even had the English not taken the Cape the new forces of European intellectual and religious life, of humanitarianism and missionary enterprise, would still have come to South Africa. The coming of the English, however, opened the door peculiarly wide to the ideas and the men of the Emancipation movement, the London Missionary Society, and all the others whose purpose it was to improve the lot of slaves, Hottentots, and Kafirs.[58]

---

56   *Ibid.*, p.150.
57   Ross, *Beyond the Pale*, pp.92, 98.
58   De Kiewiet, *History of South Africa*, pp.42-43.

This kind of assumption pervaded liberal writing on South African history for decades. But in more recent years it has come to be challenged. Research is showing that racist thought was widespread in eighteenth century Britain – so much so that the metropole can be viewed as a significant source of colonial racism. As Bank argues, 'Racial ideologies were fashioned not merely through a colonial process of challenge and response, but were constantly reshaped by the transmission of ideas from Europe'.[59] Similarly, Crais points to 'a complex and ongoing dialogue between metropolitan thought and colonial perception, a dialogue whereby settlers employed narrative history and the language of science in the ideological legitimation of a new and racially-divided world'.[60] However, the nature of this dialogue and transmission process remains an under-researched area. Bank does point to the example of the eastern Cape settler farmer, John Mitford Bowker, who drew on the writing of Thomas Carlyle to back his hostile view of Africans.[61] But further information of this kind is not easily found. Instead we have to rely on the growing body of literature that examines racial ideology in Britain in the eighteenth and nineteenth centuries – and assume that this ideology to a considerable degree shaped the outlook of British imperial administrators, military men, and settlers.

Racist discourse was rife in England, at least from the middle of the eighteenth century. Walvin claims that racism 'emerged in a pronounced form' from that time, and that 'the basic tenets of that racialism were inherited by later generations of Englishmen in an uneven, but nonetheless unbroken line'.[62] Barker views the 1770s as a key decade in the history of English racism: 'In this period for the first time men began to argue to the derogatory extreme about the Negro's place in nature'.[63]

What forms did this racism take? How was it expressed? At one extreme some, particularly the defenders of slavery, propagated the idea that black people belonged to a distinct species. Then, too, alarm was often expressed at the supposed horrors of miscegenation, viewed by a large section of English society as a threat to the social structure and to fundamental norms.[64] Racism was most commonly expressed in literary form, through caricature and

---

59 Bank, "Liberals and their Enemies", p.25.
60 Crais, "The vacant land", pp.267-68.
61 Bank, "Liberals and their Enemies", p.28.
62 Walvin, *Black and White*, p.73.
63 Anthony J. Barker, *The African Link: British Attitudes to the Negro in the Era of the Atlantic Slave Trade, 1550-1807* (London, 1978), p.41.
64 Walvin, *Black and White*, pp.55, 73.

stereotyping. This has been emphasised by Walvin: 'Hundreds of books, tracts, newspapers and magazines have dealt with the Negro to produce a cumulative image so absurd, so removed from reality that it belongs more to caricature, calumny and lampoon than it does to descriptive analysis'.[65] A fairly standard set of stereotypes emerged from this kind of writing. Blacks were represented as being innately savage, indolent and stupid; they were deemed to possess a voracious sexual appetite and the prowess to satisfy it. Although blacks were considered to be especially musical, their cultural inferiority was taken for granted among English people by the mid-eighteenth century.[66] David Hume, the famous eighteenth century philosopher, claimed that there were no arts and sciences in black culture – a view that was widely supported. 'There never was a civilized nation of any other complexion than white', wrote Hume, 'nor even any individual eminent either in action or speculation. No ingenious manufacturers amongst them, no arts, no sciences ...'.[67] This kind of thinking was prevalent in England by the early nineteenth century. Its pervasiveness is confirmed by what the *Encyclopaedia Britannica*, that major organ of knowledge and purveyor of authorised information, had to say about black people:

> Vices the most notorious seem to be the portion of this unhappy race; idleness, treachery, revenge, cruelty, impudence, stealing, lying, profanity, debauchery, nastiness, and intemperance, are said to have extinguished the principles of natural law, and to have silenced the reproofs of conscience. They are strangers to every sentiment of compassion, and are an awful example of the corruption of man left to himself.[68]

What was the source of this kind of racist tirade? This question can only be answered if it is addressed in the context of colonialism. Racism in England was most surely bound up with the institution of slavery, the slave trade, and the abolition movement. Some of the most virulent racist propaganda was put forth by the planter class in the West Indies. One of the chief, most notorious, spokesmen for this class was Edward Long. Walvin views his *History of Jamica*, published in 1774, as 'a landmark in the evolution of English racialist thought'. Long purveyed the usual stereotypes

---

65   *Ibid.*, p.159.
66   *Ibid.*, pp.162-71; Barker, *African Link*, pp.100-01, 113, 120-23, 128-30.
67   Quoted in Philip D. Curtin, *The Image of Africa: British Ideas and Action, 1780-1850* (Madison, 1964), p.42.
68   Quoted in Walvin, *Black and White*, p.173.

about black stupidity and backwardness. But he went much further, attributing to blacks a subhuman, bestial character. Throughout his writing Long tried to claim that black people belonged more to the animal world than to humankind.[69]

The connection between slavery and racism has already been examined. In the British mindset slavery and blackness came to be viewed as inseparable. All slaves were black. That colour and status corresponded was obvious.[70] Thus, as Walvin puts it, 'It was logically and legally impossible to maintain on the one hand that Blacks were chattels, and on the other, that they ought to be treated as humans'.[71] It is not surprising, therefore, that defenders of slavery should resort to racist polemic when the abolitionist movement gained momentum in the late eighteenth century. Pro-slavery writers produced even more exaggerated stereotypes of black Africans as a warning that slave emancipation might unleash the savagery that was supposedly so characteristic of blacks. Long's writings gained further prominence during the abolition debate. However, this debate was not entirely centred on the race issue. Some pro-slavery writers relied on economic and legal arguments to support their case.[72] Even the abolitionists themselves were not as free from racist assumptions and practices as they probably imagined themselves to be. When the leading abolitionist, William Wilberforce, held a dinner in 1816 to celebrate the international ban on the slave trade, he invited blacks from the streets of London, but required them to dine in a separate room.[73]

The abolition of the slave trade and slavery itself in the early decades of the nineteenth century may, as has already been argued, have brought in its wake a heightening of racial ideology. The legal, institutionalised subjugation that slavery entailed came to be replaced by enhanced racist propaganda as a means of ensuring the continued subordination of a servile class of black people – a continuation of slavery by more informal means. Whereas once strict legal controls had ensured subordination, now, in the aftermath of abolition, racial ideology would be increasingly deployed to validate the idea that blacks were inferior and so also to legitimate the continuing exploitation of servile black labour.

If the institution of slavery fuelled and reinforced racial ideology one would have expected the abolition of slavery to weaken such ideology. That

---

69 *Ibid.*, pp.163, 168; Barker, *African Link*, pp.41-42.
70 Barker, *African Link*, p.60.
71 Walvin, *Black and White*, p.107.
72 Barker, *African Link*, pp.160-61.
73 Walvin, *Black and White*, p.53.

abolition did not have such an effect is paradoxical. Nancy Stepan opens her book on racial science in Britain by drawing attention to this paradox:

> A fundamental question about the history of racism in the first half of the nineteenth century is why it was that, just as the battle against slavery was being won by abolitionists, the war against racism in European thought was being lost. The Negro was legally freed by the Emancipation Act of 1833, but in the British mind he was still, mentally, morally and physically a slave.[74]

Stepan provides an important clue to this puzzle, showing that from the late eighteenth century ideas about race were no longer just being loosely articulated in literary form, but were increasingly finding a place in the realm of science. In the sixteenth and seventeenth centuries the major scientific advances had been in the fields of physics and astronomy; from the late eighteenth century and into the nineteenth, the biological and human sciences took on much greater significance. Scientists set about investigating different human types around the world with a view to establishing a human typology. Comparative anatomy became an important field. The aim was to discover variations within the human species comparable to the variations between animal species – and to ascertain, perhaps, that humankind did not represent a single species.[75]

Stepan traces the development of racial science in Britain through the nineteenth century. She notes that at the beginning of the century most British scientists were monogenists, believing that all human beings belonged to a single human species, united by a common humanity – a belief reinforced by the accepted Christian view of the time that all humans were descended from Adam and Eve, that all were equal in the eyes of God. However, from the late eighteenth century monogenism was coming to be questioned and challenged, especially by scientists on the continent adopting a polygenist view. According to the polygenists the different human races were marked by sharp mental, moral and physical distinctions – so much so that these races constituted different species of humankind.[76] Only a small minority of British scientists adopted the polygenist position in the first half of the nineteenth century. However, as Stepan argues, a significant shift in thought was occurring, '... from an emphasis on the fundamental physical and moral

---

74 Nancy Stepan, *The Idea of Race in Science: Great Britain 1800-1960* (London, 1982), p.1.
75 *Ibid.*, p.xiii.
76 *Ibid.*, pp.1-2.

homogeneity of man, despite superficial differences, to an emphasis on the essential heterogeneity of mankind, despite superficial similarities'.[77] It was also a shift away from a view of people as social beings, shaped by their environment and therefore capable of improvement, to the idea of people as biological beings, governed by the laws of nature and bound to display the characteristics of their particular race.[78]

A corollary of polygenism was the idea of a racial hierarchy. This notion – that the different races could be graded according to their varying capacities for civilisation and culture – by the 1850s had become, according to Stepan, 'one of the cornerstones of racial science'.[79] Proponents of this 'great chain of being' proclaimed that Europeans were at the top of the hierarchy, and blacks closer to the bottom. In 1799 Charles White, a Manchester physician, introduced the notion of a racial hierarchy in a book in which he made assertions about the inferiority of blacks and their ape-like character. That a racial hierarchy existed became standard thinking in Britain in the first half of the nineteenth century. The idea was central in the developing field of racial science. And it was taken for granted in standard anthropological texts. Not surprisingly the idea appealed to the European public – it was good for their self-image, and it was seemingly endorsed by science.[80]

Another developing branch of science, phrenology, also seemed to confirm the existence of a racial hierarchy. Phrenologists believed that human behaviour was innate, hereditary, and determined by the particular structure of the brain. Not only different individuals, but also different human groups, were deemed to possess different brain structures and therefore different capacities. Human skulls thus became a significant focus of scientific attention. A correlation was drawn between the shape of the head and a person's mental ability. This correlation was extended to racial groups, thereby giving fuel to racial theory. Although phrenology was waning in significance by the 1830s and 1840s, it had served to confirm some of the key ideas of this developing racial science – the idea of a racial hierarchy, and the belief that human behaviour and culture were to a large extent biologically determined.[81]

Two questions arise from this brief examination of racial science in Britain in the early decades of the nineteenth century. First, to what extent did

---

77   *Ibid.*, p.4.
78   *Ibid.*
79   *Ibid.*, p.6.
80   *Ibid.*, pp.8, 18, 46.
81   *Ibid.*, pp.21-28.

this writing in the field of racial science shape and influence a wider, popular racial consciousness in Britain and elsewhere? Did such ideas remain relatively confined to intellectual circles, or were they popularised so as to become part of a public discourse? Second, to what extent did such ideas find their way to the Cape and elsewhere in South Africa?

The first of these questions is a difficult one. Two scholars to have written on the subject, Stepan and Lorimer, are inclined to play down the connection between racial science and more loosely articulated popular racist attitudes. Stepan argues that the views of racial scientists in nineteenth century Britain were shaped more by the dominant scientific thinking and discourse of the time than by common racist assumptions and attitudes:

> Though scientists were people of their times, their scientific ideas gained weight in the scientific community precisely because they were based on the ideas and methods of the sciences of the day, and were expressed in the recognised language and forms of science. Social and political factors, such as the existence of black slavery in the Western world, or race relations in the British Empire ... did not determine directly the specific form scientific arguments took about race. These arguments were instead derived from the procedures and content of the sciences themselves.[82]

While Stepan sees racial theorists being little influenced by popular attitudes towards racial issues, Lorimer takes the separation further by suggesting that Victorian racial science did not have much impact on those popular attitudes. He claims that systematic works on race had a limited readership in nineteenth century England. Rather, he argues, was the emergence of racial science symptomatic of dominant values in English society. And although these values might often gain expression in racist form, they were largely derived from class attitudes, particularly middle-class attitudes of superiority towards those deemed to be inferior, whether they be members of the English lower classes or racial 'others' in the colonies.[83]

It is not easy to map the diffusion of ideas or to measure their impact on a wider popular consciousness. However, it does seem likely that both Stepan and Lorimer have been too readily inclined to separate racial science from popular racist discourse in nineteenth century Britain. Ideas developed by the intelligentsia do have ways of becoming hegemonic, or at least gaining wide

---

82 *Ibid.*, pp.xv-xvi.
83 Douglas A. Lorimer, *Colour, Class and the Victorians* (Leicester, 1978), pp.15, 204-07.

adherence. Just because writings on racial science had a limited readership in the nineteenth century does not mean to say that the pronouncements of racial scientists were not influential. The very fact that racial theory was being propounded by scientists would have given greater validity to such theory. The discourse of science carries weight and authority simply because it is deemed to be 'scientific', supposedly based on thorough observation and expert research. While racial science was almost certainly not the main source of popular racial consciousness, there can be little doubt that the work of racial scientists fuelled, reinforced and validated white attitudes of superiority and contempt towards racial others. After all, as we shall see below, the ideas of racial science found their way to the eastern Cape – how much more likely, therefore, that those ideas would have filtered down through various levels of society in England.

The second question – the extent to which racial theory was diffused from Britain to the white colonial community in South Africa – has thus already been partly answered. It remains, though, a difficult, under-researched question. Little work has been done on the subject, apart from a recent study by Bank. He argues that racial theory was diffused from Britain to the Cape: 'Although it would be misleading to exaggerate the pervasiveness of theoretical racism before 1880, there is evidence to suggest that metropolitan theories of racial difference were already filtering through to the Cape Colony as early as the 1820s'.[84] Bank points to particular individuals to illustrate his case. John Bowker was a prominent eastern Cape colonist who at one time had humanitarian inclinations. But after the 1834-35 frontier war he changed his tune and became prone to vitriolic racist outbursts against the Xhosa. In the late 1840s he went so far as to advocate the genocide of the Xhosa. It is significant that Bowker often drew on the ideas of Thomas Carlyle, the prominent British writer known for his anti-black diatribes.[85]

Bank also links the eastern Cape to the pseudo-science of phrenology. Andrew Smith was a British military doctor on the eastern Cape frontier in the early 1820s. He developed a keen interest in the culture and physiology of the Xhosa – and a tendency to draw correlations between the two, resulting in heavy racial stereotyping. Smith's predecessor as military surgeon in the eastern Cape had been Robert Knox. For Knox the frontier served as a kind of

---

[84] Andrew Bank, "Of 'Native Skulls' and 'Noble Caucasians': Phrenology in Colonial South Africa", *Journal of Southern African Studies*, 22, 3, 1996, p.388.
[85] Bank, "Liberals and their Enemies", pp.230-34.

laboratory where he could develop an understanding of the anatomy 'of the various South African Races'. His book, *Races of Men*, published in 1850, was to become a key text in the field of racial theory. Then there was H.E. Macartney, a London-trained surgeon who came to the Cape in 1829, soon assuming, in Bank's words, 'a leading role as the Cape's most racist phrenological propagandist'. He moved to Grahamstown after the 1834-35 frontier war, and was soon giving public lectures on phrenology, drawing conclusions about the characteristics of race groups based on skull analysis.[86]

Macartney is an interesting figure, and of particular significance for this study. First, he was trained in Britain. Thus he would have brought metropolitan assumptions, scientific and other, with him to the Cape. Second, he applied his 'scientific' knowledge to the anatomical raw materials that he found in the eastern Cape. In this way he would have reinforced and validated the racist thought that was gaining strength in the eastern Cape at the time of the 1834-35 war. And third, Macartney used his 'scientific' findings to support oppressive colonial policies towards the Xhosa: he used negative stereotypes of the Xhosa people in order to recommend the seizure of Xhosa-occupied land and the exercise of firm colonial control over the indigenous people.[87] In the person of Macartney we see the intersection of metropolitan science, colonial racism, and settler land hunger.

Bank also examines the role of Thomas Baines, the famous artist. Baines was another immigrant from Britain, arriving at the Cape in the 1840s, and living on the eastern frontier from 1848 to 1853. Baines, too, was interested in phrenology, an interest that was expressed in his sketches of African skulls. Art and science meshed in a way that reinforced colonial racism – as Baines himself was inclined to hold forth with racial stereotypes that were becoming a standard component of settler discourse.[88]

It is evident that a discourse premised on the idea of white superiority pervaded colonial society at the Cape. But were there not sections of white society who could rise above this discourse? Perhaps the Christian missionaries, for instance? After all, in South African historiography missionaries have often been represented as the humanitarian champions of black rights. Indeed, it was the case that missionaries did at times take up the cause of indigenous people burdened by the excesses of colonialism. However, missionaries were much more part of the colonial world than

---

86 Bank, "Of 'Native Skulls' and 'Noble Caucasians'", pp.392-99.
87 *Ibid.*, p.398.
88 *Ibid.*, pp.399-401.

outside it. It may be too simplistic to argue, as many writers have, that missionaries were often little more than agents of colonialism. There can be no doubt, though, that missionaries imparted the dominant world-view of the colonisers and abetted, more or less wittingly, the colonisation process. The superiority of European civilisation over indigenous culture went unquestioned in missionary discourse; and Christianity was equated with civilisation. Thus Christian evangelisation was not just about spreading the gospel, but also a matter of inculcating western values and behaviour patterns. The assumption of European superiority naturally implied the inferiority of racial others. This was evident in missionary writing, in which, as De Kock puts it, 'difference was swiftly transcoded into idleness, vacuity, degradation (for example, marriage rites, circumcision rites, etc.) and then metaphorically recast as "low" and "fallen" states, or as "spiritual slumber"'.[89] For the most part there was a broad congruence of outlook on the part of missionaries, white settlers and colonial administrators. This is not to say that these three groupings always thought the same way. Indeed, missionaries often aroused settler hostility for being 'too friendly to the natives'. There were also differences of outlook among the missionaries themselves. But more striking were the shared assumptions and the overriding values that informed the missionary endeavour – and these assumptions and values were embedded in colonial racial discourse.

It is thus misleading to draw a distinction between humanitarian missionaries and oppressive, racist colonists. It is equally misleading to differentiate between English colonists and their Dutch/boer counterparts. As we have seen, it is a common myth of South African historiography to attribute to the boers a more intense level of racial thought and practice than existed in English colonial society. An examination of the boer republics in the mid-nineteenth century will show that racial discourse and discriminatory practice were evident in those territories, but not necessarily at a greater level of intensity.

In Afrikaner nationalist historiography the great trek of the boers from the 1830s is viewed as the key formative event in the making of the Afrikaner 'nation'. In much liberal writing, on the other hand, the great trek is often represented as the migration of boer hard-liners away from British rule and the growing racial egalitarianism that accompanied it. In this latter view therefore, the great trek and boer republicanism are assumed to have resulted

---

89 Leon de Kock, *Civilising Barbarians* (Johannesburg, 1996), p.47. See also Willem Saayman, *Christian Mission in South Africa* (Pretoria, 1991).

in a hardening of the racial order – to have brought into being the 'northern tradition' of strict white racial domination, a tradition which Afrikaner nationalist governments strove to perpetuate and perfect after 1948. From the 1930s until the 1960s this was the standard view propounded by liberal South Africanist historians – that frontier boers, having missed out on the Enlightenment and imbued with the Calvinist belief that they were a chosen people, carried their harsh, uncompromising racist outlook into the South African interior, and in so doing laid the foundation for apartheid in the twentieth century.

Underlying this orthodox view is a set of assumptions that have come to be seriously examined and questioned. One assumption is that the great trek was largely driven by boer resentment over the supposedly liberal drift of British race policy at the Cape. This was argued by writers like Brookes and Agar-Hamilton in the 1920s. Brookes was adamant on this: 'That the moving cause of the Great Trek lay in the field of race relations and colour policies cannot be doubted'.[90] Agar-Hamilton drew on the manifestoes of trek leaders and the observations of contemporaries, which all suggested that the trek 'was caused in the end by native policy'. Ordinance 50 was deemed by the boers to have aggravated the problem of vagrancy. The war of 1834-35 had deepened white insecurity on the frontier. And the whole situation was being worsened by the meddlesome interference of missionaries.[91] In his lengthy study of the trek, first published in 1934, Walker took a similar line, noting that '... common to all [the trekkers] was a determination to live no longer in a colony where the divinely appointed colour bar was so flagrantly disregarded'.[92] This assumption that the racial issue lay at the heart of the great trek, both in its causes and its consequences, came to be challenged from the 1970s. But the assumption has lived on, and can still be found in more recent writing on South African history.[93]

One implication of this view is that the trekkers had developed a harsh racist outlook before they embarked on their migration and that they carried the outlook with them on the trek as part of their cultural baggage. However, it is also suggested by some writers that the racism of the trekkers hardened in

---

90   Edgar H. Brookes, *White Rule in South Africa 1830-1910* (Pietermaritzburg, 1974), p.35.
91   J.A.I. Agar-Hamilton, *The Native Policy of the Voortrekkers* (Cape Town, 1928), pp.9-12.
92   E.A. Walker, *The Great Trek* (London, 1965), p.102.
93   See, for instance, Van Aswegen, *History of South Africa*, pp.196-97, and Sparks, *Mind of South Africa*, pp.109-10.

the circumstances in which they found themselves once they had reached their destinations – it was only when the trekkers came into conflict with indigenous African communities in the interior that boer racism became more pronounced. The trekkers became fearful and insecure when they fell victim to what they saw as unprovoked attacks by African neighbours in newly created frontier zones in Natal and north of the Orange River. Surrounded and outnumbered, so the argument goes, the boers developed both a strong sense of out-group hostility, which inevitably took on a racial form, and a laager mentality. Racial boundaries were demarcated as a form of self-protection, and so racial segregation came to be viewed by the trekkers as a means of survival.[94]

The segregationist impulse of trekker communities is seemingly confirmed by the policies and measures adopted by the boer republics. The first such republic was that of Natalia. Under its constitution of 1839 the vote was restricted to adult white men. Davenport has suggested that this racially restrictive franchise was non-negotiable for the trekkers: 'It was a natural precaution, on which group survival depended, at a time when frontiers were still improvised and the institutions of state had not yet settled down'.[95] Further policies and measures adopted in Natalia seemed to underline this segregationist thrust. The apparent aim was to limit the African presence in areas of white occupation without endangering the labour supply (this would become a familiar theme in the era of South Africa's industrialisation). Thus in 1840 the Volksraad passed a measure restricting to five the number of African families that could be retained on white farms. The following year a much more far-reaching proposal, again foreshadowing the population relocation policies of the twentieth century, was passed by the Volksraad: 'surplus' Africans – those surplus to labour needs – would be relocated to a tract of territory to the south of the republic.[96] The measure indicated clearly the segregationist intent of the boer leadership.

The Republic of Natalia rapidly took on the appearance of a white state in which Africans were treated as a subordinate labouring class. A pass system was instituted, requiring African labourers to carry a pass. Africans

---

94 See J.D. Huyser, "Die Naturelle-Politiek van die Suid-Afrikaanse-Republiek" (unpublished thesis, University of Pretoria, 1936), ch.1; Walker, *Great Trek*, p.11; Leo Fouché, "The historical setting of the Great Trek", *Race Relations*, V, 4, November 1938, p.72.
95 Davenport, *South Africa*, pp.70-71.
96 Brookes, *White Rule*, pp.36-38; Fredrickson, *White Supremacy*, p.175; Van Aswegen, *History of South Africa*, p.273.

were forbidden, without the permission of their master, to carry guns, to drink liquor, or even to go for a horse-ride for more than two hours.[97] Then there was a system of apprenticeship. From an early age young people of colour could be indentured – males to the age of twenty-five, females to the age of twenty-one – to white masters. It was a form of bonded labour open to serious abuse.[98]

The British annexation of Natal in the early 1840s prompted a second trek which created a number of scattered boer communities in the interior highveld region. The emergent republics of the interior adopted similar policies and measures for managing indigenous African communities. A set of laws, the Thirty-three Articles, was promulgated in 1844 by the fledgling Potchefstroom Republic, which was later incorporated into the South African Republic. One of these laws precluded any 'half-caste down to the tenth degree' from becoming a volksraad member.[99] This particular law is interesting in that it reflects an early concern with the question of racial demarcation – drawing the line between whites and persons of colour – which would become such a major issue in the twentieth century. However, viewed as a whole the Thirty-three Articles are somewhat surprising in that they generally do not reflect an obsessive concern with matters of race and colour.[100]

In the 1850s constitutions were drawn up for the two independent boer republics, the Orange Free State (OFS) and the South African Republic (SAR). Both constitutions were racially exclusive. The Free State constitution of 1854 limited citizenship to whites, and the franchise to white males.[101] The SAR constitution of 1858 provided for an equally restrictive franchise, and contained a clause that has often been quoted by historians over the years: 'the people desire to permit no equality between coloured people and the white inhabitants of the country, either in Church or State'.[102] The clause has been highlighted by historians because it seemed to provide clear-cut evidence of a rigid racial policy practised by the trekkers. Specific measures adopted in the republics, especially the SAR, seemingly confirmed this picture. For instance, an SAR law of 1858 prohibited the sale of liquor to

---

97   Walker, *Great Trek*, pp.236, 252-53.
98   Agar-Hamilton, *Native Policy*, pp.170-72.
99   Walker, *Great Trek*, p.330.
100 See *ibid.*, pp.330-31.
101 Davenport, *South Africa*, p.74.
102 Agar-Hamilton, *Native Policy*, p.88; Van den Berghe, *South Africa*, p.29; Fredrickson, *White Supremacy*, p.177; L.E. Neame, *The History of Apartheid* (London, 1962), p.23.

any black servant except with the permission of their white employer. A law of 1860 required all African men in the SAR to carry a pass. And a resolution of the SAR Volksraad prohibited Africans from owning land.[103]

The indictment of the SAR also rested on its harsh labour regime. There was a common starting-point to this line of analysis: that the boers saw Africans as naturally inferior and, therefore, rightfully servile. As De Kiewiet put it, 'Literally applying the curse of Ham, the farmers of the Transvaal tended to regard the natives by whom they were surrounded as a people preordained to be the hewers of wood and the drawers of water'.[104] This attitude translated into measures and practices which rested on varying degrees of labour coercion. A law of 1850, for instance, compelled Africans to work for a white master for a maximum of 14 days a year, without wages and with only basic food rations provided.[105] Much more serious was the practice of forced labour, child labour, and slavery. Boer commandos were known to seize African women and children during military excursions and raids, the victims becoming indentured labourers in the service of white masters. Another practice was to take on African orphans as 'apprentices'. Furthermore, although slavery and the slave trade were formally prohibited in the SAR, there is firm evidence that both were carried on, especially in the northern and eastern regions of the republic.[106]

The migration of boers into the South African interior opened up a set of new black-white frontier zones. Many of the issues considered in my earlier discussion of the eastern Cape frontier arise again when these new zones are examined. These new frontiers soon became arenas of conflict between the boers and African neighbours as they jostled and fought over land and other resources. From the 1830s the boers clashed, at one time or another, with Zulu, Ndebele, Basotho, Pedi and Tswana polities. These conflicts would seem to give credence to the view that black-white hostility was inevitable when boers settled in close proximity to African chiefdoms and states. However, as we have already seen, much of the writing on South African frontier history has tended to represent frontier conflict in too starkly racial terms – as a clash between two monolithic racial blocs, the one white, the

---

103 Agar-Hamilton, *Native Policy*, p.87; Neame, *Apartheid*, p.24; Davenport, *South Africa*, p.76.
104 C.W. de Kiewiet, *British Colonial Policy and the South African Republics 1848-1872* (London, 1929), p.244.
105 Van Aswegen, *History of South Africa*, p.295.
106 *Ibid*; De Kiewiet, *British Colonial Policy*, pp.247, 251; Agar-Hamilton, *Native Policy*, pp.192-93.

other black. Just as this representation was too simplified for the eastern Cape frontier, so was it also for the frontier zones of the interior in the mid-nineteenth century. More recent work from the 1970s has shown that both trekker communities and African chiefdoms and states were often riven by internal divisions and factionalism. There were opportunities for particular leaders, boer and African, to exploit these divisions by forging interracial alliances. Boers might intervene in African succession disputes, supporting one claimant against another. Similarly Africans might take advantage of internal divisions in boer communities, building an alliance with one party against another. Cleavages and conflicts in these frontier zones did not necessarily develop along racial lines.[107]

This recent research has forced a re-think of the orthodox, long-held assumption that the voortrekkers were the bearers of a distinct, hard-line racism. It is an assumption that pervades historical writing on South Africa. Back in the 1930s Walker described boer society as 'rigid' and 'unadaptable'.[108] Agar-Hamilton believed that the boers saw the world as

> ... a static universe populated, by a single Act of Creation, with certain immutable types. White and black differed in characteristics which, it seemed, were not matters of degree but of kind. White was white, and black was black, and each would remain in its inviolable category until the end of time.[109]

Later, in the 1960s, Marquard stated that 'the Boers developed a firm conviction that a policy of equal rights for black and white is contrary to the laws of God and the dictates of common sense'. He went further, contrasting the boer republican tradition with the Cape liberal tradition and viewing them as 'two radically different policies with regard to non-Europeans'.[110] Also writing in the 1960s Van den Berghe characterised boer racism in similar terms: 'Towards men of colour outside the boundaries of White settlement, the attitude of the Boers was entirely hostile and predatory'.[111]

One cannot entirely dismiss this conventional wisdom. There is clear evidence that policies of racial exclusion and discrimination were pursued in

---

107 See Giliomee, "Processes in development", pp.91-92; Philip Bonner, "Factions and Fissions: Transvaal/Swazi Politics in the mid-nineteenth century", *Journal of African History*, 19, 2, 1978.
108 Walker, *Great Trek*, p.375.
109 J.A.I. Agar-Hamilton, "The Voortrekkers and the Natives", *Race Relations*, V, 4, November 1938, p.73.
110 Marquard, *Peoples and Policies of South Africa*, p.14.
111 Van den Berghe, *South Africa*, p.24.

the boer republics. It is also clear that highly oppressive labour regimes were established in these territories. But this conventional wisdom is flawed because it rests upon ethnic assumptions – assumptions about the 'boer character', the 'Afrikaner tradition', and so on. It ethnicises racism. It pins the main responsibility for racism on to a particular ethnic or national group. Those like Marquard and Van den Berghe, writing in the 1950s and 1960s, were reading the present back into the past – assuming a continuity between the great trek, the boer republics, and post-1948 apartheid. At a time when the Afrikaner-dominated National Party was strengthening its hold on power and tightening the apartheid system of racial domination and discrimination, it was perhaps hardly surprising that writers should so readily associate Afrikanerdom with racism.

Unsurprising, maybe, but also unhelpful. Explanations of racism have to be de-ethnicised. Racism in South Africa has not arisen from the particular character and outlook of a specific ethnic group. It should rather be seen as a product of colonialism. The Voortrekkers were first and foremost colonisers. They were intruders, not into an empty land (one of many myths in South African history), but into a region populated by many African chiefdoms and states. So they were not only intruders, but also competitors, striving to gain access to and control of resources like land and labour. These boer colonisers were not driven by racial ideology, by a strong sense of white supremacy, nor by any notion of themselves as God's chosen people. It is significant that there is no evidence of boer colonists supporting or identifying with scientific racist thought in the first half of the nineteenth century.[112] Their relations with African communities were not rigid and unadaptable. Such relations were conducted in ways that best ensured the physical and material security of the colonisers. These relations varied over time and place. They could be cooperative – at the military, political or commercial level. Or they could be hostile. But such hostility invariably arose out of competition for resources rather than out of any deep-seated antagonism towards racial 'others'. However, this hostility would become racialised in the minds of the colonisers – hence the strong linkage between colonialism and racism. Keegan puts it well:

> ... the Boers were ... likely to take up accumulative, subjugatory attitudes as and when opportunities arose. They could very easily become violent accumulators at the expense of African communities, especially when settled communities

---

112 Bank, "Of 'Native Skulls' and 'Noble Caucasians'", p.395.

began to throw up elites who controlled the resources of land and labour and the means of warfare.[113]

However, concludes Keegan,

> The origins of the white-supremacist state of the twentieth century ... did not lie particularly in the attitudes spawned on isolated, backward frontiers, where Boers struggled for survival against harsh conditions and hostile indigenes.[114]

Keegan's conclusion certainly holds. And it serves as an antidote to that tendency, common for much of this century, to blame the 'boer mentality' for South Africa's racial order, and to assume a strong continuity and causal link between nineteenth century boer republicanism and twentieth century apartheid.

For those seeking a nineteenth century origin for apartheid the boer republics have not been the only candidates. Commentators have also looked to the 'Natal tradition of native policy' as another root of apartheid. The policies pursued by Theophilus Shepstone, Natal's Secretary for Native Affairs for three decades from the mid-1840s, appeared to contain some of the basic elements which would be integral to apartheid: most importantly, territorial segregation and the utilisation of indigenous authorities as instruments of colonial domination. Van den Berghe described the Shepstone system as 'the first large-scale scheme for the physical segregation of the races in South Africa, and the blueprint for subsequent 'Native Administration' in the rural areas'.[115] And Welsh entitled his book on 'native policy' in colonial Natal *The Roots of Segregation*, believing that 'the segregationist policies of post-Union South African governments owed much to the system of African administration which was created in Natal'.[116] Does this claim hold?

When the British in 1842 decided to annex Natal they laid down some terms to the existing colonists:

> 1. That there shall not be in the eye of the law any distinction of colour, origin, race or creed ...

---

113 Keegan, *Colonial South Africa*, p.203.
114 *Ibid.*, p.292.
115 Van den Berghe, *South Africa*, p.31.
116 David Welsh, *The Roots of Segregation: Native Policy in Colonial Natal, 1845-1910* (Cape Town, 1971), p.1.

> 2. That no aggression shall be sanctioned upon the natives residing beyond the limits of the colony ...
> 3. That slavery in any shape or under any modification is absolutely unlawful ...[117]

These instructions were seemingly deemed necessary to restrain the boers who were prone to predatory, discriminatory behaviour towards indigenous people. The history of British colonialism in Natal over the next forty years shows, however, that the instructions could have been more appropriately directed at the new colonial administration itself. The administration was soon implementing measures that were highly discriminatory. Within four decades an aggressive military campaign was to be launched against the independent Zulu state beyond the borders of the colony. And, while slavery may not have been practised, there were stringent measures to coerce and control African labour. The Refugee Law of 1854 serves to illustrate the point. The measure was wide-ranging and highly discriminatory. Under its terms all black immigrants into Natal were liable to three years of labour service at fixed wages. Africans based in Natal had to carry a pass, signed by a magistrate, before entering a town. Curfews would restrict the movement of Africans after certain hours. Africans were to be prohibited from buying liquor.[118]

At the core of discriminatory policies exercised in South Africa since the mid-nineteenth century have been restrictions on the right to vote in elections, restrictions which have been both racial and gendered. During the period from 1853 to 1994 the general tendency has been for such racial restrictions to be progressively tightened. This tendency was apparent in the early years of colonial Natal. In 1856 the Charter of Natal gave the colony a limited form of representative government. The franchise was initially non-racial, if not non-sexist – all adult males able to fulfil a property qualification were entitled to vote in elections for the newly established Legislative Council. There was not even a prohibition on Africans standing for election to the Council.[119] Although hardly any Africans got on to the voters' roll and exercised their right to vote, the potential electoral power of

---

117 Ibid., pp.9-10.
118 Norman Etherington, "The 'Shepstone system' in the Colony of Natal and beyond the borders", in Andrew Duminy and Bill Guest (eds), *Natal and Zululand from Earliest Times to 1910* (Pietermaritzburg, 1989), p.180.
119 E.H. Brookes and C. de B. Webb, *A History of Natal* (Pietermaritzburg, 1965), p.75; Welsh, *Roots of Segregation*, pp.51-52; S. Trapido, "Natal's non-racial franchise, 1856", *African Studies*, 22, 1963, p.26.

Africans was too much of a threat to Natal's colonists. Within ten years stringent restrictions were introduced to limit this potential. Under a new law of 1865 only 'exempted' Africans retained the right to vote; gaining this right was an uphill battle. To obtain exemption from customary law an African would be required to petition the Lieutenant-Governor, stating personal details and providing proof of the ability to read and write. Once exemption had been granted, the second step was to apply again to the Lieutenant-Governor for the franchise. To qualify an African had to be an adult male, a resident of Natal for at least twelve years, and to have been exempted for seven years. The application required a certificate of recommendation signed by three suitably qualified white residents. After all this the Lieutenant-Governor could still reject the application – which he often did. It was scarcely surprising that there were hardly any African voters in colonial Natal. Between 1864 and 1876 there was not a single application for exemption. By the early 1900s only three Africans had the vote in Natal.[120] The law of 1865 was no more than a poorly disguised electoral colour bar.

Alongside this political segregation in colonial Natal was the territorial, administrative and judicial segregation embodied in the so-called 'Shepstone system of native administration'. For three decades from 1846 Shepstone had the task of administering and controlling Natal's African population at minimal cost to the colonial government. He presided over a system which rested on territorial segregation. Those areas of Natal already occupied predominantly by Africans were marked out as 'locations'. All Africans in Natal, except for the few exempted, were to be governed according to the principles of what later came to be called 'indirect rule'. This administrative structure was headed by Shepstone himself, supported by white magistrates and administrators. Beneath their ultimate authority, roles were accorded to chiefs and headmen, many of whom had to be appointed, as Natal's African population comprised very few structures or hierarchies that could claim traditional legitimacy. These chiefs and headmen were given functions and some power to administer customary law among 'location' residents. In return they enjoyed some financial rewards, receiving portions of the fines that they imposed. But it was only a partial form of judicial segregation. Although Africans were to be subject to customary law, it was ill-defined and uncodified. Moreover, the colonial administration had the power to promulgate measures that could override customary law, and magistrates'

---

120 Brookes, *White Rule*, pp.55-56; Welsh, *Roots of Segregation*, pp.60-66.

courts could become courts of appeal in which the decisions and judgements of chiefs and headmen might be overruled.[121]

Was Shepstonism a kind of embryonic apartheid? Certainly some of the key elements of the later system were to be found in colonial Natal. Political and territorial segregation were fundamental to both. White power overlaid a lower level of authority occupied by African functionaries – another key feature of apartheid. Some might argue that Shepstone himself represented a kind of benevolent paternalism that was missing from the crudely oppressive apartheid order. Shepstone has been viewed as 'a friend of the native' who made himself unpopular with Natal's colonists because of his seemingly soft, lenient approach to 'native policy'. Certainly Shepstone had some sympathy for African culture and tradition, and he disliked the crude racism of many white settlers.[122] But he should not be viewed as an enlightened colonial administrator who was free of the dominant racial attitudes of his time. He did not believe in racial equality, and was sceptical about the idea of a multi-racial society. At worst Shepstone slipped into the racist discourse of his time, describing Natal's Africans variously as 'degraded human beings', as 'savages', as 'a nation of hunters and warriors'.[123] At best he viewed Africans as a distinct category of people who should be governed accordingly. He opposed the Cape's non-racial, qualified franchise, and believed that if there was to be assimilation it should occur gradually.[124]

Though at times critical of white settlers for their racist outlook, Shepstone himself was still party to a broad racist discourse that pervaded colonial Natal in the middle decades of the nineteenth century. White colonists believed firmly in their own superiority over people of colour. And their racism came to be expressed in various ways, through different channels. It is found, for instance, in the 1852 report of a commission of inquiry set up to investigate the situation of Africans in Natal. The report offered a crudely forthright summary of the African character:

> When not effectually restrained and directed by the strong arm of power, the true and universal character of the Kafirs, as framed by their education, habits, and associations, is at once superstitious and warlike. Their estimate of the

---

121 Etherington, "Shepstone system", pp.172-75; Norman Etherington, *Preachers, Peasants and Politics in Southeast Africa, 1835-1880* (London, 1978), pp.9-17; Welsh, *Roots of Segregation*, pp.111-31.
122 Welsh, *Roots of Segregation*, pp.210-12.
123 *Ibid.*, pp.19, 32.
124 *Ibid.*, pp.202-10.

value of human life is very low; plunder and bloodshed are engagements with which their circumstances have rendered them familiar from their childhood; they are crafty and cunning; at once indolent and excitable; averse to labour; but bloodthirsty and cruel when their passions are inflamed. They pretend to no individual opinion of their own, but show the most servile compliance to the rule of a despotic chief when it is characterised by vigour and efficiency. Cupidity is another strongly developed feature in the Kafir character; their general habits, like those of other savages, debased and sensual to the last degree; possessing but a confused, indistinct idea of a future state, and of the existence of a Supreme Being, they cherish a belief in the most degrading system of witchcraft.[125]

Encapsulated in this passage are many of the standard stereotypes of colonial racist thinking. The report emanated from a commission that mainly comprised white officials and colonists, and so reflected the predominant outlook among white colonists at the time. The report also expressed colonial political and economic interests, stating unequivocally that the firm hand of white rule had to be maintained, that the power of chiefs should be curbed, that the size of locations be reduced, and that servile labour was the proper function of Africans.[126]

Settler racism in colonial Natal was pervasive. Although the above passage from the 1852 commission report represents a single illustration of the tendency, there are many other examples to be found. As Welsh has observed, '... most [colonists] would have agreed with an editorial comment in the *Natal Mercury* in 1858: "We believe in the divinely purposed supremacy of the white over the black race; and all history interprets and illustrates this belief"'.[127] Settler racism was pervasive, but also ambiguous and contradictory. According to the typical colonial discourse Natal Africans were trapped in a state of savagery, ruled by superstition and primitive custom. There was thus a strong hostility towards Africans who adhered to 'traditional' cultural beliefs and practices. And yet at the same time settlers commonly displayed a distaste for assimilated Africans. Christian Africans might be distrusted, as tending to 'act above themselves'. Assimilated Africans undermined notions of white racial superiority. Hence the

---

125 Quoted in *ibid.*, pp.33-34; see also Julian Riekert, "Race, Sex and the Law in Colonial Natal", *Journal of Natal and Zulu History*, 6, 1983, p.83.
126 B.A. Le Cordeur, "The Relations between the Cape and Natal, 1846-1879", *Archives Year Book for South African History*, i, 1965, pp.50-52.
127 Welsh, *Roots of Segregation*, p.41.

contradiction – settlers often criticised the Shepstone system for its failure to 'civilise' Africans, but would also oppose measures that might have hastened the assimilation process.[128]

There are further ironies and contradictions. Settlers in Natal originally voiced strong opposition to the Shepstone system, believing that the locations tied up land and labour, thereby restricting the material advancement of the colonists. However, the more that African social and political structures broke down over time, the more the settlers came to support Shepstonism, which depended on such structures being preserved to some extent.[129] These ambiguities and shifts arose out of contradictory concerns on the part of the colonists. On the one hand their material interests required that the territorial base and socio-political system of African communities be undermined, so that the settler demand for labour and land could be satisfied. On the other hand, the colonists' fears and insecurity were heightened by the growing number of rootless, proletarianised Africans no longer under the controlling hands of chiefs and elders.

Settler racism in colonial Natal probably arose largely out of fear, what Shula Marks has called 'fear of the savage and unpredictable tribesman, fear of the newly emerging educated African ...'.[130] Fear could occasionally turn into panic. In Durban and Pietermaritzburg in 1851 colonists were terrified that a black uprising was imminent and set about fortifying their properties.[131] These colonists viewed Africans living close to towns as threatening and bothersome. Swanson has put it well:

> The urban experience began to demand its price from the whites for the service of men so determinedly sought ... Complaints and rumours of nuisances, thievery, squatting, depredations, drunkenness and indecent assaults upon citizens, especially their wives and children, became frequent fare in the press and council chamber.[132]

Here one sees the contradiction between the white demand for African labour and the white insistence that people of colour be kept at a distance from areas of white residence. This would be a familiar, central theme in the

---

128 *Ibid.*, pp.53-54, 66.
129 *Ibid.*, p.319.
130 Shula Marks, *Reluctant Rebellion* (Oxford, 1970), p.26.
131 Maynard W. Swanson, "The urban factor in Natal native policy, 1843-1873", *Journal of Natal and Zulu History*, 3, 1980, p.5.
132 *Ibid.*, p.11.

twentieth century as South Africa became more and more industrialised and urbanised.

The similarities between Shepstonism and twentieth century segregationist policies have suggested a continuity between the two. Welsh argues that apartheid's 'antecedents are to be found in Natal rather than in any of the other provinces'. He notes that 'policies and institutions originating in Natal found favour with later policy-makers. The Supreme Chieftainship, demarcation of reserves, the use of chiefs and the recognition of customary law all became embedded in "native" policy'.[133] Cell, on the other hand, is critical of this view. He argues that Shepstone was a pragmatist rather than a segregationist ideologue – Shepstone was compelled by circumstances and fiscal constraints to adopt the policies that he did. Moreover, Cell warns against searching the past for '... harbingers, superficial similarities, and fictitious lineages'.[134] Postmodernists would share Cell's scepticism. The teleological quest for origins, evolutionary patterns, and continuities is generally considered unhelpful by those who, following Foucault, prefer to stress rupture and discontinuity. It would certainly be an oversimplification to suggest that twentieth century policy-makers merely borrowed their ideas from colonial Natal. However, it is fair to say that both Shepstone and the formulators of segregationism and apartheid were guided by similar concerns. They were all striving to secure the interests of the white colonial or capitalist elite, while at the same time maintaining social stability so as to alleviate white insecurity and fear of racial others deemed to be dangerous or threatening.

While the conventional wisdom has it that Shepstonism was a forerunner of apartheid, another common assumption has been that the 'native policy' pursued in colonial Natal was distinctly different from patterns developing in the Cape in the mid-nineteenth century. The difference was deemed to be essentially twofold. First, Natal's discriminatory policies, with a restrictive franchise, were not dissimilar to those of the boer republics and stood in sharp contrast to the developing Cape liberal tradition. Second, while Shepstonism rested on the preservation of a 'traditional' African 'tribal' order, at the Cape in the 1850s the Governor, Sir George Grey, was pursuing assimilationist policies designed to break up indigenous African social and political structures.

---

133 Welsh, *Roots of Segregation*, p.322.
134 John W. Cell, *The Highest Stage of White Supremacy* (Cambridge, 1982), pp.54-55.

The mid-nineteenth century Cape has been described as 'an experimental station for more liberal ideas'.[135] The strength of this claim has rested largely on the Cape's non-racial franchise. Defenders of the idea that there was a Cape liberal tradition suggest that a tendency towards constitutional non-racialism was developing at the Cape from the 1830s. They point to the absence of any qualifications based on race or colour for elections to various bodies, such as municipal boards set up in the Cape in 1836, the Cape Town municipality (1839), road boards (1843), and divisional councils (1855).[136] But it is the Cape's representative government constitution of 1853 that has long been held forth as a beacon of non-racialism. This constitution provided for a franchise qualification based on sex, income and property, but not on colour. The vote was granted to any adult male who earned £50 a year, or occupied property worth £25, and could sign his name and write his address and occupation.[137] White men who did not meet these qualifications were denied the right to vote.

Clearly the Cape constitution of 1853 was more liberal in its franchise provisions than were the constitutions of Natal and the boer republics. However, it would be a mistake to view the Cape constitution as an expression of some kind of liberal spirit guiding policy-makers and power-holders. As Fredrickson has rightly noted, 'The colonists accepted a political arrangement that gave former slaves and indigenous dependants a potential voice in government not so much from egalitarian conviction as because they saw no threat to their social and political dominance from a color-blind franchise'.[138] The qualification was set high enough to ensure white dominance. The black vote did not assume all that much significance during the two decades or so of representative government at the Cape. And when the collective voting power of people of colour gradually increased, so did the Cape parliament stiffen the franchise qualifications. Moreover, a survey of legislation passed by the Cape parliament in the second half of the nineteenth century belies the notion that there was a Cape liberal tradition. Some of this legislation will be examined in a later chapter. But we should note that the Cape parliament, after only two years of its existence, passed the Masters and Servants Act of 1856. It laid down penalties to be imposed upon

---

135 Neame, *History of Apartheid*, p.21.
136 Phyllis Lewsen, "The Cape Liberal Tradition - Myth or Reality?", *Race*, 13, 1, 1971, p.71.
137 Stanley Trapido, "The origins of the Cape franchise qualifications of 1853", *Journal of African History*, V, 1, 1964, p.37.
138 Fredrickson, *White Supremacy*, pp.183-84.

the labouring class for a whole set of offences, ranging from desertion to drunkenness and the use of abusive language. Although the measure was in theory colour-blind, in practice it was only ever brought into operation against people of colour. As Sachs has argued, 'the effect of this apparently race-free law was to consolidate rather than weaken race domination'.[139]

Those who commonly contrast Natal and the Cape in the mid-nineteenth century also point to the different approaches of Shepstone and Sir George Grey, High Commissioner and Governor of the Cape from 1854 to 1862. While Shepstone's policy was accommodationist, centred on the preservation of African political and legal systems, Grey's was assimilationist. Grey believed that Africans must adapt to western cultural norms and to western political and economic behaviour. He would use various instruments to hasten this process of 'civilisation', labour being the most important of these. Grey expected Africans to acquire 'habits of industry'; so he promoted public works schemes to create work opportunities. Education was another key instrument – schools were opened, entrusted with the task of instilling new cultural norms in African pupils. At the same time Grey strove to break the power of chiefs. They were to become agents of the colonial state, forced to operate alongside white magistrates.[140]

Welsh has pointed to some reasons for this difference between the Natal and Cape 'traditions'. The cultural gap between whites and people of colour was narrower in the Cape, with its large 'coloured' population, than it was in Natal. In the Cape there had been a longer history of missionary enterprise, so important an agent of assimilation, than was the case in Natal. And in the eastern Cape the Mfengu had already shown themselves to be amenable to assimilation in a way that Africans in Natal had generally not been.

However, in terms of analysing the emergence of a racial order in South Africa can one say that these differences between Natal and the Cape were all that significant? Policies adopted in both colonies rested firmly on an unquestioned belief in white supremacy. Grey's assimilationist approach was predicated upon the assumed absolute superiority of European culture, institutions, and laws. He was not guided by some noble concern to bring advancement to the indigenous people of the Cape – part of Grey's assimilationist agenda was to pursue policies which would generate a labour supply for the colonists. Shepstone's beliefs were not fundamentally different

---

139   Quoted in *ibid.*, p.182. See also H.J. & R.E. Simons, *Class and Colour in South Africa 1850-1950* (Harmondsworth, 1969), pp.23-24.

140   Crais, *Making of the Colonial Order*, pp.199-203; Wilson, "Co-operation and Conflict", pp.261-63.

from Grey's. Shepstone's initial plan was assimilationist. He was forced by the particular circumstances of Natal, and by cost constraints, to adopt the accommodationist, 'indirect rule' approach.

Historicising and periodising South Africa's racial order is proving to be a problematic exercise. Notwithstanding the richness of much historical writing on South Africa, there are surprising gaps in the historiography. The connection between slavery and racism, as we have already seen, has not been analysed thoroughly. So too is the contribution of British imperialism to the South African racial order a theme that is not as well developed as one might expect. Ideological battles between apologists for British imperialism and its critics, whether they be Afrikaner nationalists or Marxists, have tended to obscure the historical connection between imperialism and racism in the South African context. Moreover, the early phase of British colonialism in South Africa also became a subject of historical debate between colonial nationalists, whose sympathies lay with the white colonists, and those who distinguished between a benevolent metropolitan imperialism emanating from London, and a predatory colonialism epitomised by the misdeeds of land-grabbing, labour-exploiting settlers.

Each of these positions has its shortcomings. Afrikaner nationalist historians, guided by their own particular agenda, wrongly assumed that British imperialism was a force that liberalised the racial order. Both the liberal defenders of the British imperial record and colonial nationalist writers made the same false assumption, albeit for different reasons. While the defenders of the imperial record wanted to represent metropolitan British imperialism as an agent of progressive, enlightened development, colonial nationalists saw the British government in London making misguided decisions, unaware of local realities in the colonies. Marxist historians, on the other hand, have viewed British imperialism as essentially an exploitative system geared to the promotion of capitalist interests. In such an analysis the connection between imperialism and racism would always be secondary.

In terms of my four-dimensional conceptualisation of racism what kind of picture can be drawn for this colonial phase, the first two-thirds of the nineteenth century? Some excellent recent research on particular regions provides clues. Racial discourse became more virulent in this phase. It still remained largely at the level of loosely articulated racial ideology – the first dimension of racism. But Bank's work shows that racial theory, formulated by intellectuals and scientists in Europe, began to find its way to the Cape. The second dimension was becoming evident under the auspices of British imperialism.

There were also signs that the racial order was becoming more formalised and institutionalised during this phase. Far from British imperialism being an agent of deracialisation the opposite seems to have been the case. Labour measures promulgated at the Cape from the 1820s, often presented as evidence of liberalisation, were directed at specific racial categories, and therefore marked the growth of an institutionalised racial order. And, as Lester shows, there was a strong segregationist element in British colonial policy in the eastern Cape by the 1830s and 1840s.

By the middle decades of the nineteenth century the racial order may have been more pronounced in the British colonies of the Cape and Natal than in the boer republics of the interior. Critics of this view will at once point to the difference between the 1853 Cape constitution, with its non-racial franchise, and the strict racial exclusion built into the constitutions of the boer republics in the late 1850s. Certainly there was racial differentiation and discrimination in the boer republics, but these communities do not seem to have generated the kind of virulent racist discourse that was found in the Cape and Natal. Those who have drawn a sharp distinction between the supposedly more liberal 'southern tradition' of the Cape and the racist 'northern tradition' of the boer republics have rested their case too much on the contrast between the Cape and republican constitutions. Other aspects of racism have been obscured in drawing this contrast.

There is still a need for further research on the developing racial order at this time, particularly in relation to the boer republics. However, it is becoming clear that the middle decades of the nineteenth century, from the 1830s, represent an important formative phase in the making of South Africa's racial order, and that a British colony, the Cape, was a significant arena in which this order was evolving. As Worden and Crais argue,

> The early and mid nineteenth-century Cape is rising from its historiographical slumber to emerge as a formative juncture in the modern history of South Africa. Here was created a labour-repressive economy where workers may not have been slaves, but where they were certainly not free. Modern racism arose in this complex reworking of domination at Africa's southern tip.[141]

Such a view overturns the conventional idea of a Cape liberal tradition. Elsewhere Crais states the revisionist position even more forcefully arguing

---

141 N. Worden and C. Crais, "Introduction", in N. Worden & C. Crais (eds), *Breaking the Chains* (Johannesburg, 1994), p.6.

that '... these quite fundamental developments ... – the creation of a modern disciplinary state, the emergence of capitalist relations of production, the genesis of racism – unfolded during the hey-day of liberalism in the Cape ...'.[142] He states his case perhaps too boldly – the mid-nineteenth century hardly marks the emergence of capitalism, nor the genesis of racism. But the point is well taken that this is a crucial formative phase. However, white supremacism had not yet come to be fully expressed or institutionalised. It was to be during the era of industrialisation that the country's racial order took on a more developed, rigid form. And it is to this era that we must now turn our attention.

---

142 Craise, "Race, the State, and the Silence of History", p.17.

PART II:

THE RACIAL ORDER HARDENS: THE INDUSTRIAL ERA

PART II.

4 Diamonds, Gold and the Colour Bar

Until about thirty years ago few scholars saw any special or necessary connection between industrialisation and racism in South Africa. Indeed the dominant view was that racism and discrimination were essentially products of the preindustrial order, and that industrialisation would tend to erode those supposedly archaic beliefs and values that produced racial discrimination. However, from the 1970s the relationship between industrialisation and racism in South Africa came to be rethought, reevaluated, and reconceptualised. If industrialisation had the effect of eroding a racial order, it was asked, why did racial discrimination come to be so firmly entrenched and institutionalised in South Africa precisely during the industrial era? Materialist analysis seemed to provide an answer to this question: the racial oppression of people of colour served the interests of the country's emergent capitalist class. This line of analysis had far-reaching implications for the wider consideration of the history of racism in South Africa. One corollary was to play down the significance of racism in the preindustrial era – thereby nullifying many of the findings and conclusions that have been discussed in the previous chapters of this book. Another was to minimise the importance of the political, psychological, ideological and cultural dimensions of racism, stressing rather the material forces that gave rise to the a racial order.

This question, and other related questions, requires careful examination. What was the role of the main capitalist sectors – mining, manufacturing and farming – in the making of segregation and apartheid in the twentieth century? To what extent were white workers key players in promoting discriminatory measures that were to their benefit? Has the materialist line of analysis oversimplified the issues? What weight can be attached to non-material forces in explaining the South African racial order in the twentieth century? How have different writers approached these questions? And what factors have shaped their answers to these questions at particular times? These are the issues that will be at the forefront in the ensuing pages.

South Africa's industrialisation is taken to begin with the development of capitalist mining operations in the modern era. And so our exploration of these questions starts logically at the development of diamond mining in and around Kimberley from the late 1860s. As the focus continues to be on the growth of a racial order, three questions will be addressed. How did a racial pattern of ownership and control develop in the diamond mining industry? How did the work-force come to be divided along racial lines? And did any other discriminatory policies and practices accompany the development of diamond mining?

There soon emerged in the diamond industry a pattern of white ownership and control. That this would be the case had not been clear-cut from the outset. In the first years of the industry, up till 1869, Griqua, Kora and Tlhaping producers had dominated the supply of diamonds, selling stones found on the surface to white traders. But this pattern did not persist. Few persons of colour became claimholders. It is true that by 1874 120 out of 130 claimholders in the Bultfontein mines were persons of colour; but these were mines that had been largely abandoned by white diggers. By 1879 there were only about twenty black diggers running their own operations at the Dutoitspan and Bultfontein mines.[1] In the early 1870s the white diggers had campaigned vigorously, sometimes violently, and with considerable success, to establish a white monopoly of claim ownership. In 1872 the white diggers issued a set of demands to the commissioners who were administering the diamond fields on behalf of the British government who had annexed Griqualand West in 1871. The first demand was stated plainly: 'No "Kafir or other coloured person" to hold a digging licence unless supported by fifty white claim holders'. The diggers followed up this demand with violent action, burning the tents of black claimholders.[2] The Cape Governor would not permit overt discrimination against black claimholders. Instead diggers were required to hold 'a certificate of good character' from a justice of the peace or the resident magistrate.[3] In effect, though, the Cape Governor's veto did not prevent a pattern of white ownership and control becoming entrenched in the industry.

There also developed in the diamond mining industry a *de facto*, if not total, racial division of labour, whereby unskilled jobs were performed almost entirely by black workers and more skilled and supervisory jobs largely by whites. It is true that some whites became unskilled labourers, and that some mining companies in an effort to reduce costs employed blacks as engine-drivers and overseers.[4] But for the most part the working-class at the

---

1 William H. Worger, *South Africa's City of Diamonds: Mine Workers and Monopoly Capitalism in Kimberley, 1867-1895* (Johannesburg, 1987), pp.71-72, 80.
2 *Ibid.*, pp.114-15.
3 R.V. Turrell, *Capital and Labour on the Kimberley Diamond Fields 1871-1890* (Cambridge, 1987), p.30.
4 *Ibid.*, p.131.

diamond fields was divided along racial lines. Who should bear the main responsibility for this – the mining capitalists or the white workers?

That the ranks of unskilled labour were filled almost entirely by blacks was clearly in the interests of the mineowners. At some point consideration was given to the possibility of employing a predominantly white labour force. This was strongly opposed by the mineowners who knew that white unskilled labour would be more expensive and more difficult to control than black unskilled labour.[5] Indeed a rigid racial division of labour was not in the interests of the mineowners who strove at times to substitute black for white labour in more skilled positions at cheaper rates of pay. Does this therefore mean that the white workers themselves were the main agents in bringing about this racial division of labour?

The amalgamation process in the diamond industry advanced during the 1870s and 1880s, with larger companies buying out the many individual owners of small claims. And so these former independent white diggers came to be employed by the larger companies as paid overseers, skilled miners, and artisans.[6] By holding these relatively elevated positions in the labour hierarchy white workers came to see themselves as belonging to the managerial sector and identified themselves with the middle class. This sense of class superiority was reinforced by racial ideology: blacks were viewed as different and inferior.[7]

Seeing themselves as superior to black workers, white workers demanded differential status and rejected any moves to treat them the same as their black counterparts. This attitude came out strongly during the struggle over searching. Diamond theft had long been a problem in the industry. Mine management was keen to implement a system of searching, which would apply to most workers directly involved in mining operations, regardless of colour. In 1880 an ordinance was introduced providing for such a system. The white overseers fiercely opposed the measure – or, rather, the application of the measure to themselves. They asserted their own trustworthiness, and expressed their fear of degradation – of being forced down and reduced to the status of blacks if all were subjected to the same treatment under the ordinance. In the event the measure was not implemented in 1880 – partly because white workers had the vote.[8] But the issue arose again in 1883, when another search measure, similar to the 1880

---

5   *Ibid.*, p.126.
6   *Ibid.*, p.87; Worger, *City of Diamonds*, p.148.
7   Turrell, *Capital and Labour*, p.56; Worger, *City of Diamonds*, pp.161, 186.
8   Worger, *City of Diamonds*, pp.158-161; Turrell, *Capital and Labour*, pp.87-89.

ordinance, was introduced. The white overseers agreed to submit to the measure as long as they were not searched in the presence of black workers – revealing their fear that their sense of superiority might be undermined. Later in the year the measure was extended to all workers who came into the mining areas, including workers previously exempted. White artisans and engine-drivers protested vigorously, again arguing that searching would reduce white workers to the status of blacks. As Turrell put it, 'The public struggle over "stripping" was conducted in terms of "white degradation" as opposed to Africans whose "state of nature" was one of nudity'.[9] White workers went on strike over the issue, and only a compromise agreement brought the strike to a halt. A few months later, in March 1884, mine management reneged on this agreement and reinstituted a full search of all workers. Again there was a strike, and a bloody confrontation in which six white miners were killed.[10]

One fear of the mineowners – and a reason why the racial division of labour partly served their interests – was that black and white workers would show solidarity and resort to joint militant action. In 1883 and 1884 there were signs that this might indeed have been happening. African workers joined the 1883 strike, and there was evidence of even greater African participation in the 1884 strike.[11] However, it is doubtful whether this cooperation was any real expression of solidarity, but rather a short-term collaboration based on expediency. The participation of black workers in the strikes helped the cause of the white workers by maximisir˜ the damage to the mining companies. In turn, the black workers themsel˙ ₅s gained an opportunity to express their discontent without drawing the combined wrath of mine management and the white overseers.

These moments of interracial worker cooperation did little to undermine the racial division of labour which was steadily becoming entrenched at the diamond fields. A government measure of 1872 had required all 'servants' at the diamond fields to carry a pass. Although the wording of the measure was colour-blind, the terms applied in effect only to black workers; and the measure was policed accordingly. As Worger shows, black workers at the diamond fields were subjected to vigorous surveillance by police on the look-out for black workers who had deserted their work-place or were not carrying a pass.[12] In the 1880s legislation became more explicitly racial. The

---

9   Turrell, *Capital and Labour*, pp.135-36; Worger, *City of Diamonds*, pp.172-75.
10 Turrell, *Capital and Labour*, pp.139-42; Worger, *City of Diamonds*, pp.179-83.
11 Worger, *City of Diamonds*, p.174; Turrell, *Capital and Labour*, pp.143-45.
12 Worger, *City of Diamonds*, pp.115-17, 123, 135-37.

the labour hierarchy was a class of more skilled workers, artisans and overseers who were drawn almost entirely from the ranks of the white population. This racial division of labour was not simply the continuation of a pre-existing pattern, as some have argued. It was not the result of a 'traditional' white prejudice against doing menial, 'kaffir' work. It was rather the product of economic forces and class interests. The large-scale employment of cheap African migrant labour was clearly in the interests of the mineowners who were concerned to minimise their costs. In the early years of mining, market forces allocated the more skilled jobs to whites simply because whites, many of whom were immigrants with previous mining experience, enjoyed a monopoly of the required skills. In time, however, black workers acquired skills, thereby providing an incentive to the mineowners to employ more black workers in skilled positions at lower rates of pay. It was when the racial division of labour threatened to break down that the white workers fought to defend their class position – their relatively privileged status in the labour hierarchy. In this struggle they used various weapons. One was strike action. Another was racial ideology. But this racism was not a straightforward colour prejudice or distaste for menial work. Rather was it an expression of a class interest – a means to protect their relatively privileged position against competition from cheaper black workers.

Patterns of ownership and labour division that first developed in diamond mining came to be perpetuated in the gold mining industry from the 1880s. So Johnstone is not quite correct to say that it was in gold mining 'that occurred the first and most extensive industrial institutionalisation of racial discrimination in South Africa'.[15] It may not have been the first instance of such discrimination, but it certainly was extensive. An examination of this discrimination in the gold mining industry raises similar questions to those just addressed in relation to diamond mining – and produces similar answers.

Gold was discovered on the Witwatersrand in 1886. Within a few years ownership of the industry was highly centralised, firmly in the hands of a few companies heavily dependent on foreign capital. And, as at the diamond fields, the labour force was also soon divided between an upper stratum of skilled white workers and a lower but much larger stratum of unskilled African migrant workers. The latter were subjected to forms of exploitation and domination that did not affect white workers. And a job colour bar restricted upward mobility for Africans in the labour market.

---

15 Frederick A. Johnstone, *Class, Race and Gold* (London, 1976), p.3.

1883 Mining Act imposed restrictions on black workers in the handling of explosives. In 1889 another racial exclusion was written into a regulation legislated at the Cape (into which Griqualand West had been incorporated in 1880): 'No native shall work or be allowed to work in any mine, whether in open or underground workings, excepting under the responsible charge of some particular white man as his master or "baas"'.[13]

The working-class at the diamond fields was also internally divided by residential segregation. There was no official policy of racial residential segregation at the diamond fields before the late 1870s. But *de facto* segregation occurred from the early years of mining. Many white diggers lived close to their claims, while others tended to live in their own areas; African workers occupied diggers' compounds. Africans not living in compounds came to be housed in separate locations during the 1870s. From 1879 there were moves to regulate and formalise residential segregation in Kimberley as the Cape Location Acts were applied to Griqualand West, but the law did not enforce residential segregation. During the 1880s the racial, residential segregation of mineworkers came to be firmly established. Tightly controlled, gaol-like, closed compounds came into existence from 1885. These accommodated only African workers, and their purpose was both to prevent diamond theft and to impose strict discipline on workers. In 1889 De Beers, by then a monopoly company, began constructing a model village for its white employees.[14]

So was the beginning of the industrialisation process in southern Africa marked by any significant hardening – or weakening, perhaps – of the racial order? We have seen that ownership and control of diamond mining came to be firmly in the hands of white capitalists. This was hardly surprising as the amalgamation process, culminating in the De Beers monopoly, required large injections of capital. Moreover the pattern of white control represented a continuation of pre-existing trends – we have already seen in an earlier chapter that by the end of the eighteenth century the dominant economic class at the Cape was almost entirely white. Early industrialisation did, though, bring one new element into the racial order – the racial division of labour. The diamond mining industry, like the gold mining industry later, came to depend on the exploitation of thousands of low-paid, tightly controlled African migrant labourers performing predominantly unskilled tasks. Above them in

---

13 Turrell, *Capital and Labour*, pp.153-54.
14 *Ibid.*, pp.94-100, 154-58; Worger, *City of Diamonds*, pp.141-44; Alan Mabin, "Labour, capital, class struggle and the origins of residential segregation in Kimberley, 1880-1920", *Journal of Historical Geography*, 12, 1, 1986, pp.11-22.

An attempt to explain these patterns must begin, not with an emphasis on primordial white race attitudes, but with an examination of the fundamental nature of the gold-mining industry in its early years – an examination informed by Johnstone's excellent analysis of the 1970s. Johnstone showed that the industry operated under severe constraints in its initial phase. The grade of the ore was generally low, and much of it could only be mined at very deep levels. This meant that high levels of capital investment were required to finance the machinery and equipment needed for mining operations. Production costs were therefore high, but these costs could not be passed on to the buyers of gold, because the gold price was fixed in the international market. Therefore the only way that the industry could become profitable was by maximising output and minimising production costs. And the only way to minimise production costs was to keep down the price of labour to as low a level as possible.[16]

This was absolutely imperative for the industry. The mineowners met the requirement by employing thousands of African migrant workers in unskilled jobs at minimal rates of pay. The labour had to be cheap for the industry to survive. That the labour was cheap was partly because it was migrant. The mining companies paid a migrant worker a single man's wage on the grounds that his family, left behind in rural areas, could obtain their subsistence from the land. The ultra-cheapness of African labour was also secured by forms of racial discrimination. African workers were subjected to measures and practices that did not apply to white mineworkers. People of colour could not acquire mining licences or trade in minerals; and they could only work on the gold mines in the service of whites. Masters and servants laws were applied to black workers with the main purpose of binding them to their labour contracts. The 1911 Native Labour Regulation Act made breach of contract by black workers a criminal offence. Pass laws were applied only to black workers, again with the purpose of restricting their mobility and tying them to their employers. Only black workers were accommodated in tightly controlled mine compounds.[17] Black workers were thus subjected to extreme structural subordination which took on a racial form. In Johnstone's view this racial discrimination and subordination amounted to a system of class exploitation. The profitability of the gold mining companies, he argues, depended on the whole apparatus of racial discrimination.[18]

---

16   *Ibid.*, pp.17-20.
17   *Ibid.*, pp.23, 34-40.
18   *Ibid.*, pp.23, 45-46, 48-49.

Although Johnstone's analysis has been criticised its general thrust has come to be broadly accepted over the last twenty years or so. There can be little doubt that the development of mining, in particular gold mining, brought in its wake significant changes in the social, political and economic order – and that forms of racial discrimination and oppression became ever more prominent features of that order. Moreover the racial division of the working class became more pronounced in the era of gold mining. This again becomes a fundamental issue as we attempt to unravel the evolution and dynamics of the racial order in South Africa.

A striking feature of the job colour bar in the early years of gold mining on the Rand is that it was consistently legislated and enforced by three different kinds of government – Kruger's republican government in the 1890s, the British colonial administration after the South African War, and the Union government after 1910. Measures were instituted by Kruger's government in the 1890s, laying the foundation for the job colour bar. No person of colour could hold an engine driver's certificate. Only whites could hold a blasting certificate. And a number of supervisory jobs were restricted to whites on a *de facto* basis. This latter restriction came to be entrenched in law by the post-war Milner administration, with the enactment of Ordinance 54 in 1903. And the new Union government, established in 1910, was quick to entrench the job colour bar in the mining industry. It was prescribed in Mining Regulations instituted by the government in 1911, restricting the most skilled jobs to whites. The Mines and Works Act of the same year confirmed that only white miners could hold blasting certificates. Through these measures about two-thirds of white mineworkers had the legal protection of the job colour bar. The remaining one-third of white miners in less skilled jobs were in effect protected by *de facto* discrimination.[19]

The racial division of labour has been a noticeable feature of South Africa's racial order. It has also been the subject of considerable debate. Although we have already discussed the subject in relation to diamond mining, the issue requires further consideration in the context of gold mining. Was the job colour bar in the gold mining industry simply a continuation of a pattern established in diamond mining? Was it the product of white worker racism and militancy? What was the role of the state and mining capital in bringing about and perpetuating this racial division?

---

19   *Ibid.*, pp.67-70; Alan H. Jeeves, *Migrant Labour in South Africa's Mining Economy* (Johannesburg, 1985), p.30.

A book by G.V. Doxey on the industrial colour bar appeared in the early 1960s. Although Doxey recognised the mining industry's need to minimise costs as a factor behind the job colour bar, he preferred to lay greater stress on white racism as the root cause of the racial division of labour. He argued that the 'racial, group approach to the South African dilemma' lay beneath 'the evolution and maintenance of the colour bar in industry'.[20] Thus the racial division of labour was an expression of traditional white prejudice – a prejudice that took two related forms: in part a prejudice against people of colour, but it was also a prejudice against performing 'kaffir work'. Indeed, Doxey assumed that poor whites would rather face starvation than suffer the indignity of manual labour.[21]

Johnstone not surprisingly played down the significance of race prejudice in shaping the racial division of labour. He stressed the class position of white mineworkers: while they occupied a relatively privileged, protected level in the labour hierarchy, they were also structurally insecure, always vulnerable to being undercut by cheaper black labour. So white mineworkers used their bargaining-power – the vote, and their capacity to organise and strike – to secure measures that would safeguard their position as a 'labour aristocracy'. This brought the white workers into direct conflict with the mining companies, for whom the job colour bar had contradictory implications. While it allowed for the ultra-exploitation of black unskilled labour, it also prevented the companies from further reducing costs by employing cheaper black labour in more skilled positions. When the cost minimisation imperative became more pressing, during profitability crises for instance, the mining companies strove to tamper with the colour bar by promoting more black workers into skilled positions. This drew resistance from the white miners, culminating in the major strike of 1922 – the so-called 'Rand Revolt'.[22]

One of Johnstone's key arguments is that white mineworkers bore a major responsibility for the implementation of the job colour bar. They promoted the racial division of labour, not because they harboured race prejudice, but because they wished to defend their class position. Underlying this argument is the assumption that the white mineworkers somehow had it in their power to secure their interests, even if those ran counter to the interests of mining capital. Johnstone states this quite explicitly: 'The white

---

20 G.V. Doxey, *The Industrial Colour Bar in South Africa* (London, 1961), p.3.
21 *Ibid.*, pp.58, 77, 80-81, 196.
22 Johnstone, *Class, Race and Gold*, pp.57-71, 77-86, 119-38.

mine workers thus came to institute and operate a system of racial discrimination in the form of a job colour bar in skilled work ...'.[23] This clearly implies that the white workers were the main actors in bringing about the colour bar.

It is on this point that Johnstone's analysis differs from that of Davies. Although both writers share a strict materialist approach to the issue, Davies argues that the main responsibility for the racial division of labour lay with the mineowners rather than with the white mineworkers. For Davies the racial division of labour on the mines was necessary to mining capital not only because it provided for the exploitation of African migrant labour, but also because it divided the working-class. Mineowners were afraid that black and white workers would develop a sense of solidarity and engage in common struggles against capital. This was why the 'poor white' issue was deemed to be such a problem – not because mineowners were particularly concerned about the plight of fellow whites, but because the white lumpenproleteriat might well have identified and associated more closely with oppressed blacks. This association 'was seen as a factor undermining the efficacy of the ideology of racism as a means of exerting social control over Africans'.[24] Thus, in Davies' view, racism was essentially an instrument of social control, used in this instance to divide the working class on the mines and so limit the threat of united class action against mining capital. He claims that 'institutionalising white trade unions on a racially discriminatory basis served to weaken any possible identification which white wage-earners might have had with even the economic class struggles of the black dominated classes thus depriving the latter of support ...'.[25] The racial division of labour also served a further function. Many white mineworkers performed supervisory roles. Davies argues that racial ideology and ideas of white superiority reinforced the authority of these mineworkers as overseers of black labour.[26]

Davies' instrumentalist, functionalist analysis – not atypical of the radical historiography of the 1970s – was shared by other writers at that time. Magubane, for instance, stated the position quite starkly: 'Racism as an ideological system had to be cultivated by the politically conscious classes to subvert class unity between black and white labour'.[27] But during

---

23   Ibid., p.71.
24   Davies, *Capital, State and White Labour*, p.78. See also pp.80, 100, 228.
25   Ibid., p.131.
26   Ibid., p.67.
27   Bernard Magubane, *The Political Economy of Race and Class in South Africa* (New York, 1979), p.16.

the 1980s this line of analysis came to be viewed by many as too rigid and mechanistic, as too simply reducing racism to material interests. Jeeves argued that 'The colour bar cannot be seen either as the exclusive product of racial prejudice in the white labour unions or as a necessary result of the pursuit of profit by mining capital'.[28] However Jeeves' research into the records of the mining industry in the late nineteenth and early twentieth century did reveal that 'most of the owners preferred a racially based society with the whites clearly on top'.[29]

What might be called a modified materialist position was put forward by Greenberg. He shares Johnstone's view that serious structural constraints in the gold-mining industry forced the mineowners to opt for a policy of labour repression, whereby thousands of African migrant workers were subjected to extreme coercion, exploitation and discrimination.[30] But Greenberg is more uncertain in his explanation of the job colour bar. He suggests that the racial division of labour was fashioned by businessmen, the state and white workers, and that white racism was a probable factor bringing it about.[31] He stops short of attributing the primary responsibility for the job colour bar to either the mineowners or the white workers. But in his final analysis he does stress the bargaining power of white workers – their capacity to organise in trade unions and engage in strike action, and their right to vote – as crucial in securing their position in the labour hierarchy.[32]

While Greenberg represents a modified radical position in this debate, Lipton is best viewed as offering a modified liberal position. One of Lipton's concerns is to lessen the responsibility of the capitalist sector in bringing about a racial order in modern South Africa. She accepts that mining capital supported some aspects of the racial order, 'particularly measures which enlarged the supply of cheap, unskilled, black labour and ensured its docility'.[33] However, she goes on to say that the mineowners 'could not escape the job colour bar', and that over the years they generally opposed it.[34]

---

28 Jeeves, *Migrant Labour*, p.31.
29 *Ibid.*, p.70.
30 Stanley B. Greenberg, *Race and State in Capitalist Development* (Johannesburg, 1980), p.161.
31 *Ibid.*, p.290.
32 *Ibid.*, pp.313-15.
33 Merle Lipton, *Capitalism and Apartheid* (Cape Town, 1985), p.110.
34 *Ibid.*, pp.110-19.

South Africa's Racial Past

For her there is no doubt that white workers must bear the prime responsibility for the racial division of labour, as they were the main beneficiaries of this particular kind of discrimination. Lipton avoids Doxey's position – that the white workers were driven by race prejudice – accepting that the racism of white workers was 'reinforced' by their material interests and quest for job security.[35]

A recent intervention from Katz has given a rather different slant to this debate. In tracing the origins of the job colour bar in the gold mining industry she stresses the role of the SAR State Mining Engineer in the 1890s rather than any pressure emanating from white mineworkers or mine management. This state official, Joseph Klimke, was primarily responsible for introducing the job colour bar into mining regulations on the Witwatersrand in the early 1890s. His justification for the colour bar was racist – that whites were superior and that dangerous tasks, like handling dynamite, should therefore rest solely in their hands. Katz goes on to say that both mine management and the white mineworkers broadly supported the job colour bar, but definitely did not instigate it.[36]

Who, then, bears the prime responsibility for institutionalising the racial division of labour in this early phase of industrialisation? Mineowners intent on dividing the working-class? White workers determined to preserve their relatively privileged position in the labour hierarchy? Or were both capitalists and workers driven by a deep-seated racism? The latter view carries little weight. Mineowners were not committed to maintaining the racial division of labour. It is difficult to accept Davies' argument that they foisted the job colour bar on the white mineworkers, duping them into betraying their class solidarity with black workers. The mineowners occasionally attempted to break the rigid job colour bar so as to reduce their labour costs. Profitability took clear precedence over racial separation in their thinking. Mining capitalists came to live with the racial division of labour as long as it did not endanger profitability.

Nor were white mineowners driven by racism – notwithstanding the crudeness of their slogan, 'Workers of the World, Fight and Unite for a White South Africa', proclaimed during the 1922 strike. Rather did white workers use racial discourse to protect their class position. But culpability for the job

---

35 *Ibid.*, p.184.
36 Elaine Katz, "Revisiting the Origins of the Industrial Colour Bar in the Witwatersrand Gold Mining Industry, 1891-1899", *Journal of Southern African Studies*, 25, 1, 1999, pp.83-97.

colour bar cannot be readily pinned on to the white workers. Certainly they had bargaining-power – the vote and trade union rights – but this was hardly sufficient to secure their interests against the state and capital. After all, when white mineworkers resorted to strike action in 1907, 1913 and 1922 – against the mineowners' attempts to erode the job colour bar – on each occasion the strikes were crushed by the coercive power of the state.

As South Africa industrialised the racial order took a clearer shape. That can hardly be disputed. Ownership of the means of production came to be more firmly concentrated in the hands of the white middle class. The racial division of labour became more pronounced. Other segregatory patterns followed, such as residential segregation. But was there a straightforward causal connection between industrialisation and racialisation? This question gave rise to a rather stark, unhelpful polarisation in the historiography.[37] Marxist analysis offered a clear-cut answer to that question – the racial order grew out of underlying material forces. In a sense this analysis provided sharp insight into the history of the racial order, forcing a re-think of old assumptions. But it also sidelined and marginalised the phenomenon of racism in the historical record, dismissing it as a superstructural element. This deflected attention away from other forces, outside the industrial arena, that were making for the consolidation of the racial order. Racism cannot be separated from class interests, but nor can it be viewed as a straightforward expression of those interests. Those other forces giving rise to racial discrimination and segregation require attention.

We have already examined the growth of racial discourse and discriminatory practice up till the mid-nineteenth century in the Cape, Natal and boer republics. Did this discourse and practice intensify during the last three decades of the nineteenth century? If it did, was this intensification connected to, or simply parallel to, the emergence of the mining industry?

In the earlier discussion of the Cape it was suggested that the 'Cape liberal tradition' rested on thin foundations, that notions of white superiority and the reality of white supremacy were more pronounced in the mid-nineteenth century Cape than was any spirit of non-racialism or egalitarianism. In the later decades of the century the liberal tradition, as insubstantial as it was, came to be further eroded. In the 1850s Grey's assimilationist approach had won support in sectors of colonial society. But from the 1870s there was a shift away from assimilationist thought. This shift

---

37 See below, ch.5, for a discussion of this debate.

was probably not connected to the development of diamond mining, but was more likely a response to colonial wars – on the eastern frontier, in Zululand and Basutoland – between 1877 and 1881. Colonial wars invariably aroused the colonial psyche, provoking racial consciousness. They undermined assimilation by seemingly confirming that Africans were essentially barbaric and war-like.[38]

Apologists for the 'Cape liberal tradition' have pointed to the Cape's non-racial franchise as evidence that the assimilationist ideal was firmly held. The shift away from this ideal is therefore reflected in the gradual erosion of the non-racial franchise in the last two decades of the nineteenth century. As it was the black vote had never been of great significance at the Cape. The qualifications were set sufficiently high to ensure white political dominance. But there did appear to be more of a threat to this dominance from the 1880s with the annexation of the Transkeian territories, and with more black voters registering.[39] The threat was sufficient to draw a legal and legislative response. First, there was a successful settler challenge in court against attempts by headmen to register African voters *en bloc*.[40] There followed the 1887 Parliamentary Voters Registration Act which denied the vote to those who held property under communal tenure. The reasoning behind the measure was stated bluntly by the Cape premier, Sprigg: if tribal and communal tenure was allowed to count for registration 'you would hand over this noble colony to the barbarous Native population'.[41] The 1892 Franchise and Ballot Act further eroded the black vote by raising the property qualification for the franchise from fifty pounds to seventy-five pounds, and by imposing a basic literacy test.[42] Both measures had the effect of disfranchising a few thousand black voters.

From where did the assault on the Cape non-racial franchise emanate? The eastern Cape settler community was consistently hostile – in keeping with attitudes examined in the previous chapter. In 1852 there had been a huge public meeting of colonists in Grahamstown to oppose the impending enactment of the Cape constitution with its non-racial franchise. Thereafter

---

38 See Vivian Bickford-Smith, *Ethnic Pride and Racial Prejudice in Victorian Cape Town* (Cambridge, 1995), pp.87-89; and Richard Parry, "'In a sense citizens, but not altogether citizens ..'.: Rhodes, race, and the ideology of segregation at the Cape in the late nineteenth century", *Canadian Journal of African Studies*, 17, 3, 1983, pp.381-84.
39 J.L. McCracken, *The Cape Parliament 1854-1910* (Oxford, 1967), p.80.
40 Les Switzer, *Power and Resistance in an African Society* (Madison, 1993), p.141.
41 McCracken, *Cape Parliament*, pp.90-91.
42 *Ibid.*, pp.93-95.

there were regular expressions of opposition to the franchise coming from the eastern Cape.[43] The franchise was also strongly opposed by the Afrikaner Bond, a body founded in 1879 to represent the interests of Dutch and Afrikaans-speakers. It was the avowed policy of the Bond to raise the franchise.[44] Its position on this began to carry some weight when Cecil Rhodes, as part of his own political manoeuvring, tried to build an alliance with the Bond in the 1880s. No liberal himself, Rhodes was happy to push for restrictions on the franchise as a way of cementing this alliance.[45]

Rhodes was also the key figure behind another significant measure, the Glen Grey Act of 1894, passed by the Cape parliament when he was prime minister. The bill, drawn up by Rhodes and his private secretary, applied to the Glen Grey District, near Queenstown in the eastern Cape. The measure divided the district into locations, which were in turn carved up into individual allotments to be held by their African occupants under individual tenure. The idea was to fix a proportion of the existing population on the land and force the surplus into the labour market. As Rhodes put it, it was the government's duty 'to remove these poor children out of their state of sloth and laziness, and give them some gentle stimulants to go forth and find out something of the dignity of labour'.[46] The act also had political implications. Although tenure was to be individual in practice, it was viewed as communal, thereby denying African landholders the vote under the 1887 act. A limited form of local government was also to be established in the area, with the creation of a district council and location boards. These would be effectively controlled by the colonial administration and traditional African leaders. The Glen Grey Act represented another important step away from assimilationism. It provided for a differential political system for Africans, albeit in a particular area, and was designed to confine, as far as possible, African political participation to the local level, restricting their voice at higher levels. The measure was a prototype of the political segregationism that would gather momentum from the first decade of the twentieth century.[47]

---

43 *Ibid.*, pp.68, 84-89.
44 *Ibid.*, p.89.
45 *Ibid.*, p.88.
46 William Beinart and Colin Bundy, *Hidden Struggles in Rural South Africa* (Johannesburg, 1987), p.140.
47 Switzer, *Power and Resistance*, pp.101-105; Parry, "'In a sense citizens'", pp.384-86; Ruth Edgecombe, "The Glen Grey Act: Local origins of an abortive 'Bill for Africa'", in J.A. Benyon *et al* (eds), *Studies in Local History* (Cape Town, 1976), pp.91-94.

The Glen Grey Act and the moves to erode the non-racial franchise were just part of a bundle of measures passed by the Cape parliament in the last three decades or so of the nineteenth century – measures which specifically discriminated against Africans. Attempts were made through a series of Location Acts, passed in 1869, 1876, 1884, 1892 and 1899, to curb Africans' independent access to land by restricting African sharecroppers and cash tenants with a view to forcing them to become labourers.[48] The 1875 Cape Mounted Yeomanry Act confined membership of this cavalry force to whites only.[49] A curfew act of 1895 permitted any city or town in the Cape to impose night-time curfews on Africans.[50]

Racial segregation at the Cape in the late nineteenth century was coming into force not just through legislation. In the best study of segregation in nineteenth century southern Africa, Bickford-Smith has examined in detail the growth of segregationist practice and thought in Cape Town in the last quarter of the nineteenth century. At the beginning of this period, the 1870s, there was segregation in Cape Town, but it was yet to become entrenched. Bickford-Smith notes that segregation was being practised in some spheres – in the church, for instance. By 1857 the Dutch Reformed Church had officially sanctioned segregation in all its churches; and by the mid-1870s separate services for whites and blacks were being held in Anglican churches in some western Cape towns. However, among the lower classes in Cape Town there was still much integration between poorer whites and people of colour. In lower class areas like District Six and Woodstock black and white lived in the same residential area, cohabited and intermarried, socialised with each other in unsegregated bars, or played together on the sports field.[51]

In the last two decades of the nineteenth century Cape Town increasingly became a segregated city. The more upmarket residential areas were almost exclusively white-occupied. At the turn of the century the Cape Town municipality was moving towards the creation of a segregated township for Africans.[52] By the 1890s prisons and hospitals were becoming more segregated (that is, separate sections or wards within the same institution). So too were trains – by 1896 first and second-class carriages were largely white, if not exclusively so, and third-class meant black. By the end of

---

48   Switzer, *Power and Resistance*, p.107.
49   Bickford-Smith, *Ethnic Pride and Racial Prejudice*, p.63.
50   Robert I. Rotberg, *The Founder: Cecil Rhodes and the Pursuit of Power* (Johannesburg, 1988), p.477.
51   Bickford-Smith, *Ethnic Pride and Racial Prejudice*, pp.25, 28, 90, 150, 176-77.
52   *Ibid.*, pp.150-51, 159-60.

the century segregated sport had become the norm; segregation was practised at the theatre and the circus; and by 1904 blacks could not stay at Cape peninsula hotels. Not all of Cape Town's schools were segregated by the 1890s. But from 1893 the top public schools became exclusively white, as were most industrial schools and night schools; and coloured children were increasingly being turned away from certain schools.[53] Under the School Boards Act of 1905 public schools at the Cape were formally segregated.[54]

There also developed an informal racial division of labour, in line with the pattern at the diamond fields. Before the 1880s this pattern had not been established in Cape Town where white unskilled labour was employed in some sectors. However, by the mid-1880s something like a racial division of labour had developed in the western Cape, especially on farms and the railways. Employers preferred to hire black unskilled labour, which was cheaper and considered more controllable than white labour. Barriers limiting the upward mobility of black workers were also introduced. In 1894 the Cape government restricted artisanal apprenticeship to whites. And white artisans came to organise more and more along racial lines to protect themselves against undercutting by cheaper black workers[55] – a tendency already noted in the mining industry.

All of this was accompanied by a growing racial discourse and unashamed expressions of racist thought, emanating especially from the dominant class of Cape colonial society. This discourse took different forms, but always rested on the presumed superiority of European culture. One strand of the discourse was assimilationist. This was the tradition of the British High Commissioner and Cape Governor in the 1850s, Sir George Grey. It was an outlook that still informed some British administrators and frontier officials at the Cape in the late nineteenth century. These officials shared, in Schreuder's words, 'faith in British customary morality, cultural values and the new political economy'. With this went contempt for African traditionalism and custom which were deemed to be 'static' and 'unprogressive'. Idleness, immorality and heathenism were seen as the essential characteristics of African society; and Christianity and education were thought to be the necessary remedies. Only by instilling the Victorian

---

53 *Ibid.*, pp.104-06, 138-39, 142-43, 147, 149-50; see also Harriet Deacon, "Racial Segregation and Medical Discourse in Nineteenth-Century Cape Town", *Journal of Southern African Studies*, 22, 2, 1996, pp.287-308.
54 Davenport, *South Africa*, p.107.
55 Bickford-Smith, *Ethnic Pride and Racial Prejudice*, pp.64-66, 138, 166, 172 ff.

values of hard work, enterprise and self-reliance could improvement and progress be brought to African society.[56]

Another strand of this racial discourse was distinctly anti-assimilationist, and gained ground in late nineteenth century Cape colonial society. This discourse was personified in the figure of Cecil Rhodes, prime minister of the Cape from 1890 to 1896. Rhodes was an avowed white supremacist. He stated his views in the debate on the 1887 Parliamentary Voters Registration Bill: 'We have got to treat natives, where they are in a state of barbarism in a different way to ourselves. We are to be lords over them'. He went on to say, 'The native is to be treated as a child and denied the franchise'.[57] While Rhodes viewed Africans as children, he also viewed them as labourers, and believed that policies should be geared to preparing Africans for that role. There were, in his view, too many schools which specialised in 'turning out a peculiar class of human beings – the Kafir parson' – people who became agitators, and constituted 'a dangerous class'.[58] Rhodes was contemptuous of assimilationism. Indeed, Rotberg argues that 'Rhodes' disregard of ... the human and political value of Africans foreshadowed, indeed, prepared the path for the segregationist attitudes and legislation that were so prevalent during the decades of actual union'.[59]

Rhodes was not alone in expounding such views. The shift away from assimilationism to segregationism had been reflected in the 1883 report of the Cape Native Laws and Customs Commission. Produced by an all-white, all-male commission, the report embodied the approach long since adopted by Shepstone in Natal, recommending that whites and Africans be subjected to different political and legal systems, at least temporarily.[60] There was also a more benevolent, paternalist strand to this developing segregationist thought – a strand that was to gain fuller expression in the early decades of the twentieth century. Some Cape politicians, for instance, were uneasy at the crude white supremacism of somebody like Rhodes, and believed that segregation might best serve the interests of African people by offering them protection against rapid social dislocation and cultural alienation. But the cruder version of segregation generally prevailed. This was widely

---

56 D.M. Schreuder, "The Cultural Factor in Victorian Imperialism: a case-study of the British 'civilising mission'", *Journal of Imperial and Commonwealth History*, 4, 3, 1976, pp.289-96, 310.
57 Rotberg, *The Founder*, p.225.
58 *Ibid.*, p.471.
59 *Ibid.*, p.362.
60 *Ibid.*, p.362.

propounded by English-speaking politicians and journalists in Cape Town. It was an ideology that rested on negative stereotypes of black people, particularly on the idea that blacks represented a dangerous class. There was also the assumption that Africans were unassimilable – an assumption seemingly confirmed by the findings of racial science which was having an increasing influence on racial discourse in the late nineteenth century.[61]

Why this shift away from assimilationism at the Cape in the last quarter of the nineteenth century? Three possible reasons must be considered. First, was it a consequence of the mineral revolution? The development of mining required measures that would generate a supply of cheap wage labour. This rendered inappropriate the older liberal strategy of promoting a free African peasantry who could serve as suppliers for the colonial merchant class and be incorporated politically. Mining required labourers rather than peasants, and the political incorporation of labourers was out of the question.[62] Hence the erosion of the non-racial franchise, so the argument goes. That Rhodes was both the foremost mining capitalist and a leading anti-assimilationist politician would seem to lend weight to this view. However, the argument is not that convincing. There is little evidence to suggest that there was an immediate and direct connection between diamond mining and the shift away from assimilationism at the Cape from the 1870s. Certainly mining, especially gold mining, brought in its wake significant economic, social and political change. But this impact was to become more apparent from the 1890s, by which time the shift away from assimilationism at the Cape was quite well advanced. This is not to rule out any connection between mining and the anti-assimilationist tendency, but to suggest rather that the connection was more indirect, and of lesser significance than the other two factors.

Second, of greater importance, were the processes of colonial annexation and warfare from the early 1870s to the early 1880s. In the 1870s the demographic make-up of the Cape came to be altered with the annexation of African territories in the Transkeian region. This had implications both for the Cape franchise and for the colonial administration of indigenous people. The exercise of racial power, previously unthreatened by the non-racial franchise, appeared less secure. The Shepstone system, which operated in similar conditions in Natal, now seemed more appropriate for the eastern

---

61 *Ibid.*, pp.68-70, 77-80, 98-99, 115-16.
62 See Stanley Trapido, "'The friends of the natives': merchants, peasants and the political and ideological structure of liberalism in the Cape, 1854-1910", in Marks and Atmore (eds), *Economy and Society in Pre-Industrial South Africa*; and Parry, "'In a sense citizens'", p.379.

Cape. On top of this, the late 1870s and early 1880s were years of conflict and warfare between the colonial powers and indigenous African polities – the last Cape-Xhosa war of 1877-78, the Anglo-Zulu War of 1879, the Transkeian rebellions of 1880, the Basotho rebellion of 1880-81. These wars and rebellions raised the fear and insecurity of white colonists, and fuelled racist discourse. In the colonial mindset these conflicts were racialised; and racial thought became a justification for the conquest and subjugation of Africans.[63]

The third factor, at least in the western Cape, was urbanisation. As Bickford-Smith's work shows, racial stereotyping increased with the growing presence of people of colour in Cape Town in the last quarter of the nineteenth century. The colonial mentality equated whiteness with respectability, blackness with filth, immorality and decadence. Such thinking was fuelled particularly by the 1882 smallpox epidemic in Cape Town. People of colour were seen as contaminated, as a source of infection. The epidemic was followed by growing calls for segregation – racial separation becoming a form of immunisation for whites.[64]

Thus, in this analysis, the rising racism evident in the Cape in the 1880s and 1890s was more a product of fear than self-interest. It was less the product of capital's demand for cheap labour – although the industrialisation process cannot be taken out of the picture. More significant were the images and stereotypes that became embedded in the consciousness of whites – images of blacks engaged in violent rebellion or resistance, notions of black people as contaminated and a threat to the health of the white elite, the idea of black people being a dangerous class.

From the mid-nineteenth century policies and practices evolved differently in Natal from the Cape, as we have already seen. While the Cape moved away from assimilationism in the last quarter of the century, Natal's policies had been anti-assimilationist from the outset. There was to be no significant change of direction in Natal towards the end of the century, but one does see an intensification of racial domination and oppression in the colony. This was manifested in a variety of measures, many of which were concerned with labour, land and taxation. The tightening of control over African labour became a consistent theme in colonial Natal. A system of forced labour (*isibhalo*) had been introduced as early as 1848, whereby chiefs

---

63 Bickford-Smith, *Ethnic Pride and Racial Prejudice*, p.78.
64 *Ibid.*, pp.91-92, 100-06, 110-11.

were required to supply labourers to work on Natal's roads each year.[65] Regulations were introduced in 1873 to bring about greater control over African casual labour in Durban.[66] A Master and Servants Act of 1877 legalised corporal punishment for worker infractions, reinforcing the authority of employers, especially farmers.[67] From the 1880s pass regulations were introduced and steadily tightened, restricting African mobility.[68] Labour coercion was closely connected to taxation. Colonial taxation of Africans was in part a revenue-raising device, but it was also a means of forcing Africans into the labour market to earn a cash wage to pay the tax. In Natal an annual hut-tax was introduced from 1849, to be supplemented by other taxes and levies in the ensuing decades.[69]

White colonial domination in Natal was further entrenched with the steady undermining of chiefly power. The Native Administration Act of 1875 deprived chiefs of jurisdiction in all criminal cases. From the 1890s chiefs could not allocate land without the permission of a white magistrate. An act of 1896 empowered the colonial government to draw up regulations for the administration of reserves. Much greater power was being given to colonial officials, and chiefs themselves were becoming little more than agents of the colonial government rather than indigenous authorities in their own right.[70] While the authority of the traditional elite, the chiefly class, was being steadily undermined, so too was the position of the emerging assimilated elite, the *kholwa*. There had been provision, albeit stringent, for such persons to obtain exemption from customary law, and the right to apply for the franchise. But from the 1890s exemption became even more difficult to obtain, and the *kholwa* were increasingly subject to discriminatory measures.[71] Even Natal's sop to assimilation was being abandoned.

---

65 John Lambert, *Betrayed Trust: Africans and the State in Colonial Natal* (Pietermaritzburg, 1995), pp.30-31.
66 David Hemson, "Class Consciousness and Migrant Workers: Dock Workers of Durban" (unpublished Ph.D thesis, University of Warwick, 1989), pp.23-25.
67 Robert Morrell *et al*, "Colonisation and the establishment of white domination 1840-1890" in Robert Morrell (ed.), *Political Economy and Identities in KwaZulu-Natal* (Durban, 1996), p.40.
68 Lambert, *Betrayed Trust*, p.96; J. Lambert and R. Morrell, "Domination and subordination in Natal 1890-1920", in Morrell (ed.), *Political Economy and Identities*, p.72.
69 Lambert, *Betrayed Trust*, pp.19-20.
70 *Ibid.*, pp.124, 168; John Lambert, "From independence to rebellion: African society in crisis, c.1880-1910", in Duminy and Guest (eds), *Natal and Zululand*, p.379.
71 Lambert and Morrell, "Domination and Subordination", pp.69-72; Welsh, *Roots of Segregation*, pp.241-47.

Africans were not the only victims of racial oppression in colonial Natal. From 1860 the colony imported indentured labourers from India to work on the sugar plantations. They were followed by free, 'passenger', Indian immigrants who would form the basis of a trading class. Although Indians in Natal were divided by class, caste and religion, all would in time become subjected to racial discrimination. This discrimination took various forms – residential segregation, political exclusion, commercial suppression, and fiscal coercion. Residential segregation was to be more a twentieth century phenomenon – the Durban municipality before 1879 tried without success to establish a separate residential area for Indians.[72] Political exclusion was achieved more easily. An act of 1896 effectively disfranchised the vast majority of Indians in Natal, although the municipal vote was retained. Thereafter Indians would not enjoy any electoral power for almost a hundred years. Fiscal coercion took the form of a £3 tax imposed, under the 1895 Immigration Law Amendment Act, on Indian adult males who failed either to renew their indentures or return to India. In 1903 the tax was extended to women, girls over the age of 13, and boys over 16. The message to Indians was clear – become labourers, or get out. In 1897 the Natal legislature gave local authorities the power to grant or refuse traders' licences – in effect enabling the local white elite to eliminate Indian commercial competition.[73]

Most of these measures were passed after 1893, the year when Natal obtained responsible government. The colony's *de facto* racially exclusive franchise meant that power was now firmly in the hands of the white settler minority. And such was the delimitation of constituencies that farmers represented the most powerful bloc in the legislature. So the demands of farmers came to have a considerable influence on Natal government policy. White farmers, especially the inland stock-farmers, also happened to be leading exponents of racist thought and practice in the colony. They viewed Africans as units of labour, there to serve the needs of their white masters. They demanded government measures to ensure a ready supply of labour and to secure control over that labour. This meant limiting African access to land and administering stiff punishments for desertion, pass infringements and other offences committed by workers. Successive governments duly obliged,

---

72   M.W. Swanson, "'The Asiatic Menace': Creating Segregation in Durban, 1870-1900", *International Journal of African Historical Studies*, 16, 3, 1983, p.405.
73   *Ibid.*, pp.415-17; Joy Brain, "Natal's Indians, 1860-1910: From co-operation through competition, to conflict", in Duminy and Guest (eds) *Natal and Zululand*, pp.261-62, 267.

tightening restrictive measures to control Natal's African population. Even so, farmers still felt able to by-pass the legal system, quite prepared to take the law into their own hands in disciplining workers. Natal's farmers were notorious for their ill-treatment of African labourers.[74]

Racist thought and practice in colonial Natal was not always as crude or oppressive as this. Colonial discourse contained a paternalist strand drawing on the Shepstonist tradition. It gained expression in the report of the 1906-07 Natal Native Affairs Commission. The commissioners, in their report, regarded 'the native', at least until the more distant future, as 'a minor who had to be safeguarded against things which he otherwise might think right'. This meant that the administration of Africans should be characterised by firm control – but at the same time the government should be 'a benevolent and sympathetic father', as Shepstone had been. Sharing this outlook was James Stuart, a magistrate who was well versed in Zulu language and culture.[75]

Generally officialdom in colonial Natal was crudely supremacist, lacking some of the benevolence of the paternalists. Two men epitomising this cruder style were Leuchars and Winter who served as successive ministers responsible for 'native affairs' in the Natal government between 1904 and 1906. Both were stock-farmers who commonly expressed the prejudices of their class. Winter told the 1903-05 South African Native Affairs Commission that the African 'has no wants ... As long as a Native can amuse himself by going to dances, courting girls, and generally drinking beer; as long as he can have his little amusements, he is not going out to work. That is, really, the life of the Natal Kaffir'.[76] Both were uncompromising, autocratic ministers who showed scant regard for African interests. More junior agents of the colonial state seem to have acted in similar vein. Magistrates invariably identified with the interests and attitudes of white farmers. Some magistrates were notorious for imposing harsh sentences on black offenders. By the early twentieth century sentences were becoming even harsher – excessive fines, flogging, and lengthy gaol sentences commonly being imposed.[77]

The racial order in colonial Natal became intensified during the last three decades of the nineteenth century. But as already argued in relation to

---

74   Lambert, *Betrayed Trust*, pp.67, 94, 97, 159, 166; Marks, *Reluctant Rebellion*, pp.14-15.
75   Marks, *Reluctant Rebellion*, pp.13; Welsh, *Roots of Segregation*, pp.231-32.
76   Welsh, *Roots of Segregation*, p.322.
77   Lambert, *Betrayed Trust*, pp.60-62, 165-66, 170.

the Cape, there is no firm evidence to connect this trend with the development of mining. Certainly material interests have to be taken into account when explaining the hardening of this racial order. However, these were not the material interests of industrial capital, but rather the interests of colonial farmers and the white commercial class. Colonial farmers were particularly concerned to secure their land and labour needs. Their racist discourse and the accompanying legislation emanating from a colonial parliament that they dominated, developed in ways that served to meet these needs. Similarly, white merchants in Durban, resentful of the competition from Indian traders selling goods at lower prices, fomented anti-Indian feeling. Again this was accompanied by legislation designed, in part at least, to suppress this competition. Marks has suggested that in Natal in the 1890s prejudice 'tended to be expressed more openly and violently against the Asians than the Africans'.[78]

It is, though, too simplistic and reductionist to explain racism in colonial Natal in straightforward materialist terms. As in the Cape, there was a considerable element of fear underlying racial consciousness in Natal. There was the fear of racialised 'others' who seemed to threaten the security of white colonists. Africans posed a collective threat with their potential for rebellion and resistance. When this was actualised in the 1870s, with the Langalibalele rebellion of 1873 and the Anglo-Zulu War of 1879, this fear could grow into panic, and images of Africans as war-like and savage flooded the colonial mind. It was not just this collective physical threat that fuelled racist thinking. People of colour, African and Indian, also represented an individual threat, particularly as criminals and carriers of disease.[79] All such fears fed into colonial discourse and discriminatory policy. This brief study of the Cape and Natal in the last decades of the nineteenth century invites a comparative examination of the situation in the boer republics during the same era. Again we need to ask whether there were signs at this time of a more pronounced 'northern tradition' of racial oppression developing in contrast to the supposed Cape 'liberal tradition'. The political order of the SAR and the OFS rested firmly on the principle of white domination. There was no question of power being shared. This principle was laid down in the 1859 constitution of the SAR, and reaffirmed in a *Volksraad* resolution of 1873. And in 1894 a judge in the SAR ruled that political exclusion and differentiation applied to all persons of colour – to Indians and coloureds as

---

78 Marks, *Reluctant Rebellion*, p.10.
79 Lambert, *Betrayed Trust*, pp.137-38.

well as Africans.[80] The African inhabitants of the SAR were also subjected to administrative differentiation, entrenched in law with the passing of an act in 1885. This measure brought Africans under the direct control of the SAR government. The SAR president was deemed to be paramount chief over all Africans in the republic, with powers to depose chiefs and replace them with appointees. The Superintendent of Natives was to be the chief executive officer responsible for African administration. He would be assisted by native commissioners stationed as administrative officials in areas with sizeable African populations.[81]

From the 1850s the boer authorities in the SAR supported the principle of territorial segregation. But in the ensuing decades little attempt was made to implement such a policy in a systematic way. Instead the governments of the SAR and OFS concentrated their efforts on limiting and controlling African squatters – occupants of state land or privately owned land. Measures were enacted with this end in mind from the late 1850s.[82] But the aim was never the total removal of African squatters, many of whom supplied labour or paid rent to white landowners. A policy of territorial segregation would not be implemented wholesale if it conflicted with the economic interests of boer landowners. But the measures that were implemented were highly discriminatory – prohibiting Africans from owning land, as well as placing tough restrictions on African squatters.

That racial discrimination in the boer republics was closely tied to economic interests is further underlined by the regular enactment of pass legislation. Pass laws were first enacted in the SAR from 1858, and amended several times subsequently. Their main purpose was to restrict African mobility within and away from the republics so as to bind African farm workers to their employers. An SAR measure of 1870 was designed to prevent farm labourers from seeking work on the diamond mines. Laws enacted in the SAR in 1895 further tightened white farmers' control over their labour by requiring African servants to obtain a pass from their employer before moving within their district or to another region. A second law was designed to regulate the flow of labour to the Rand gold mines.[83] Labour oppression in the SAR did not only take the form of pass controls. The

---

80   Rhoodie and Venter, *Apartheid*, p.90; G.D. Scholtz, *Die Ontwikkeling van die Politieke Denke van die Afrikaner: Deel III 1854-1881* (Johannesburg, 1974), pp.227-28.
81   Brookes, *White Rule*, pp.101-02; Rhoodie and Venter, *Apartheid*, p.95.
82   Brookes, *White Rule*, p.103; Rhoodie and Venter, *Apartheid*, pp.92-95.
83   Doug Hindson, *Pass Controls and the Urban African Proletariat* (Johannesburg, 1987), pp.22-23.

republic was to become notorious for its exploitation of African child labour. Children captured in warfare were often handed over to white farmers as *inboekselings* – 'apprentices'; or else the farmers might obtain the children through barter.[84] If the so-called 'northern tradition' of racial oppression did have a distinctive feature this might have been it.

In the later decades of the nineteenth century there was in the boer republics a trend towards segregation in the social sphere. But this was not rigid, and certainly no more pronounced than it was in the supposedly liberal Cape. The governments of the republics supported a policy of residential segregation, but lacked the means to enforce it in practice. There was no legal prohibition on mixed marriages, but an SAR act of 1871 made legal provision only for marriage between whites, thereby making it impossible for persons of colour to contract legal marriages with whites.[85] The Dutch Reformed Church (DRC) also moved towards the practice of strict racial segregation. In the 1850s a DRC synod accepted by a large majority a proposal that people of colour use separate church buildings. In the republics Africans were not allowed to visit white churches.[86]

The republics also adopted discriminatory measures against people of Asian origin. According to laws passed in the SAR in 1885 and 1886 such persons could not own fixed property, were obliged to pay a fee of three pounds to engage in trade, and were expected to reside in segregated areas – although the government lacked the means to enforce these measures fully.[87] The OFS government pursued even more severe discriminatory policies against Asians/Indians, even though the Asian population of the OFS was minimal. An ordinance of 1885 classified Asians as 'non-whites' and barred them from owning or renting fixed property, thereby effectively preventing any trading operation. In 1890 an even more far-reaching ordinance was enacted – no Asian could remain in the OFS for a period of more than two months without the permission of the state president.[88]

This survey of discriminatory practice in the last decades of the nineteenth century suggests a few conclusions. One is that the supposed difference between the so-called 'northern' and 'southern' traditions of race

---

84 Peter Delius, *The Land Belongs to Us* (Johannesburg, 1983), pp.137-42.
85 Rhoodie and Venter, *Apartheid*, pp.97, 100-01; Fredrickson, *White Supremacy*, p.178.
86 Scholtz, *Die Politieke Denke van die Afrikaner*, iii, pp.148-49; Rhoodie and Venter, *Apartheid*, p.97.
87 G.B. Pyrah, *Imperial Policy and South Africa 1902-10* (Oxford, 1955), p.97.
88 H.J. Van Aswegen, "The Orange Free State Experience", in B. Pachai (ed) *South Africa's Indians* (Washington, 1979), pp.186-87, 195.

relations should be played down. In both the boer republics and in the Cape and Natal whites took it for granted that a system of white domination should operate. Any idea of power-sharing was out of the question. The political exclusion of people of colour and their differential treatment at the administrative level was the norm in all four territories, although the Cape's constitution did allow for a degree of political incorporation. So too was segregatory practice developing in all four regions. Racial thought and racist discourse was probably more fully developed and more explicitly articulated among white English-speakers than it was among the Dutch/boers. In the OFS, for instance, it was English traders who led the agitation against Asians.[89] This is not to say that racism was less a feature of boer society – it may just be that racial discourse in the boer republics is an under-researched theme. Or it may be that white domination was taken more for granted – something that was accepted as natural and normal, and not requiring justification.

Colonialism in South Africa took different forms in the second half of the nineteenth century. Shepstonism, for instance, was unique to Natal. In the eastern Cape and the SAR Africans came under more direct forms of white domination and control. The varying racial demography of different regions also did much to shape the particular forms of discriminatory practice that developed south of the Limpopo. Furthermore, economic considerations always weighed heavily in the exercise of white power. Anti-Indian discourse was shaped largely but not solely, by the resentment of white traders against Indian competitors. Measures to control African land occupation and to regulate the movement of Africans were implemented mainly to satisfy the labour needs of farmers and mining companies. At the end of the nineteenth century such measures were steadily being introduced. In the twentieth century they were to be tightened considerably, coming to form part of an expanding gamut of discriminatory policies and exploitative practices. It is to the twentieth century that we must now turn our attention.

---

89   *Ibid.*, pp.188-89.

5 The Segregation Era

The first two decades or so of the twentieth century were crucial in the development of South Africa's racial order.[1] This was the beginning of what came to be called the 'segregation era' – a time when not only were legislative measures enacted by the new unified government of South Africa, but also a time when the issue of segregation found its way more and more into the realm of intellectual and scientific discourse. Writers have focused specifically on the first decade of the century. These were years when British imperial rule was established across what would soon become South Africa – and years when, it is assumed, the imperial government had it in its power to impose a more liberal order on the region, to reverse discriminatory policies, and so to lay the foundation for a less racialised society.[2] So, as we take this discussion into the twentieth century, many questions arise. Would British imperialism be a force that might curb the racist inclinations and practices of the region's white population? What would be the impact of South African unification after 1910? Would the racial order be hardened or eroded by the processes of industrialisation, capital accumulation, and urbanisation? Would key figures emerge in the domain of white politics to play a central role in further promoting racial discrimination? How significant would Afrikaner nationalism be as a factor? Were segregation and apartheid designed mainly to secure white domination, to achieve racial separation, or to further capital accumulation? These are large questions already given considerable attention by scholars from many disciplines for the past few decades. Some might say that they have been given too much attention, that the issues are now 'old hat'. It is my view that there is value in revisiting these questions in the hope of developing a synthesis of existing scholarship, perhaps a useful overview.

The twentieth century began with much of the country embroiled in the South African War. But for this discussion of the racial order the years after the war are of much greater significance than the actual war itself. From 1902 until 1910 the four territories that would form the South African union fell

---

[1] See, for instance, Martin Legassick, "British hegemony and the origins of segregation in South Africa, 1901-14", in William Beinart and Saul Dubow (eds), *Segregation and Apartheid in Twentieth-Century South Africa* (London and New York, 1995).

[2] See, for instance, Nicholas Mansergh, *South Africa 1906-1961: The Price of Magnanimity* (London, 1962).

under British suzerainty. Far from reversing the growth of the racial order British imperial authority served to promote segregationism. Milner, British High Commissioner for South Africa until 1905, was an avowed white supremacist. He made his views plain in a speech in 1903: 'A political equality of white and black is impossible. The white man must rule, because he is elevated by many, many steps above the black man; steps which it will take the latter centuries to climb ...'. A few years earlier, in 1899, he had stated his overall objective: 'The *ultimate* end is a self-governing white Community, supported by *well-treated* and *justly governed* black labour from Cape Town to Zambesi'.[3] Milner's thinking made some concession to the notion of trusteeship – whites were under an obligation to 'raise the natives, coloureds, and Asiatics to a higher level of civilization'. And in any union parliament black interests should be represented by whites.[4] Milner's successor as high commissioner, Selborne, shared similar views. Selborne was determined to secure white rule and the capitalist order, in which the primary role for Africans would be to serve as labourers. Although he believed that there was some scope for the black elite to be incorporated into white society, Selborne was essentially segregationist in outlook, advocating territorial segregation and a separate administrative system for Africans.[5]

One of Milner's objectives was the creation of a common 'native policy' across South Africa. With a view to the formulation of such a policy his administration established the South African Native Affairs Commission (SANAC) in 1903. The commission comprised eight white English-speaking men, and one Dutch-speaker. It was chaired by Sir Godfrey Lagden who was firmly caught up in the racist discourse of the time: 'A study of the physiognomy of the masses', he wrote in a memorandum to Selborne, 'shows plainly the lack of intellect ... [and gives] the impression of being not unlike baboons'.[6] The commission heard a great deal of evidence that was unashamedly racist. Leonard Thompson's reading of this evidence led him to suggest that race attitudes were harsher in Natal and the former boer republics. But among the vast majority of whites who gave evidence the dominant overall view was that people of colour were inferior socially, must remain subjugated politically, and should function as a labouring class.[7]

---

3 L.M. Thompson, *The Unification of South Africa 1902-1910* (Oxford, 1960), p.6.
4 Pyrah, *Imperial Policy and South Africa*, p.95.
5 David E. Torrance, *The Strange Death of the Liberal Empire: Lord Selborne in South Africa* (Montreal and Kingston, 1996), pp.103, 115, 120-25.
6 Donald Denoon, *A Grand Illusion* (London, 1973), p.100.
7 Thompson, *Unification*, pp.112-15.

The Commission's report and recommendations reflected this prevailing discourse. It was assumed that white supremacy and authority were sacrosanct. The report did not recommend the extension of the Cape franchise. Instead it proposed that persons of colour be granted separate representation in the legislatures of self-governing colonies on the basis of one or more representatives being elected on a separate voters' role.[8] The principle of political exclusion and differentiation was confirmed. The report also advocated territorial separation. African access to white-owned land, either through tenancy or purchase, should be curtailed – the Commission recognised the 'repugnance' of whites 'to the invasion of the neighbourhood by Natives for residential purposes'.[9] Foreseeing the 1913 Land Act the report recommended a system of reserves for Africans. Labour issues also featured. Measures were proposed 'with a view to stimulate industry among the Natives' – proposals included laws against vagrancy, the expulsion of 'idle persons' from urban areas, and gearing black education towards practical, manual training.[10]

The SANAC report was highly significant. Legassick has described it as 'an important landmark in the evolution of the "native policy" of the South African state', and as 'a guidebook for future reference'.[11] It was the first attempt to provide an overall policy framework for administering and controlling Africans. It reflected the ideas and discourse that prevailed within white elite circles. And it foreshadowed measures and policies that would be implemented in the ensuing decades – policies that would go under the name of 'segregation'.

There was an essential continuity between the discriminatory policies of the former boer republics and the British-controlled territories of the Transvaal and Orange River Colony in the early 1900s. There was no attempt by the British colonial administration to reform or reverse older republican policies. The new administration continued to apply the pass laws, for instance.[12] An ordinance of 1902 confirmed the old SAR structure of differentiated 'native administration'.[13] The Milner administration acted against African tenants on white-owned land, determined to convert them into

---

8   Brookes, *White Rule*, p.106;   D.R. Burton, "Sir Godfrey Lagden: Colonial Administrator" (unpublished Ph.D thesis, Rhodes University, 1989), pp.440-41.
9   Burton, "Lagden", p.409.
10 Brookes, *White Rule*, pp.105-106.
11 Legassick, "Origins of segregation in South Africa, 1901-14", p.49.
12 André Odendaal, *Vukani Bantu!* (Cape Town, 1984), p.38.
13 Brookes, *White Rule*, p.102.

wage labourers.[14] And the discriminatory drive against Indians in the Transvaal was continued. Laws of the former SAR were applied to curb Indian trading, in spite of the reservations of the Colonial Office in London. In 1907 two further measures were introduced – the first requiring Indians to go through an oppressive registration process, and the second restricting Indian immigration.[15] The constitutional foundation of white male power was the racial, gender-exclusive franchise. The question of who should qualify for voting rights aroused considerable debate in the years 1902 to 1910. At the end of the South African War the British government had it in its power to deracialise the franchise, perhaps extending the Cape's colour-blind, qualified franchise to the other three colonies. Milner, though, argued that this would be unacceptable to the majority of white colonists, who should be allowed to settle the matter themselves. And so it was laid down in the Treaty of Vereeniging that the question of granting the franchise to persons of colour would be held over until after self-government was granted to the Transvaal and Orange River Colony. When self-government was conceded to the Transvaal in 1906, and the Orange River Colony in 1907, their respective constitutions provided only for white manhood suffrage.[16] The issue arose again in 1908 and 1909 when the new union constitution was being debated and drafted. Among the all-white delegates at the national convention where the constitution was drawn up, there was some division. Most delegates from the Transvaal, Orange River Colony and Natal wanted a racially exclusive franchise to apply throughout the country. Some Cape delegates wanted a uniform, colour-blind franchise to apply nationally. The outcome was a compromise – the existing franchise laws of the four colonies would continue to operate under the new union constitution, with the Cape retaining its qualified, colour-blind franchise, and with white manhood suffrage continuing in the other three provinces.[17]

It has often been argued that this failure to extend the non-racial franchise in the first decade of the twentieth century marked the triumph of white racism in South Africa. The British government, it is claimed, sacrificed black political rights so as to secure Anglo-Afrikaner reconciliation

---

14 Shula Marks and Stanley Trapido, "Lord Milner and the South African State", in P. Bonner (ed.), *Working Papers in Southern African Studies* (Johannesburg, 1981), ii, p.77.
15 Denoon, *Grand Illusion*, pp.113-16; Pyrah, *Imperial Policy and South Africa*, pp.104-106.
16 Thompson, *Unification*, pp.11, 26, 29.
17 *Ibid.*, pp.213-25.

The Segregation Era

in the aftermath of the South Africa War – in other words, the British shelved one 'race question' in order to help solve another (Anglo-Afrikaner relations being deemed to be the major 'race problem' of the day).[18] Does this interpretation hold? Certainly there can be no doubting that a firm belief in white supremacy, and in the absolute necessity of preserving it, was held almost universally among whites in the four colonies. It is also evident that white opinion may also have been hardening in the early years of the twentieth century, especially in the aftermath of the 1906 Bambatha Rebellion in Natal. Less convincing is the notion that this racist white community forced the hand of an essentially liberal imperial government, so much so that black political rights were sacrificed. It is difficult, for instance, to support Thompson's view that Milner 'caused Britain to yield to the Boers on the franchise question'. The demand for a racially exclusive franchise was coming from English-speakers as well as from 'the Boers'. And there is little evidence to suggest that the key figures in the British imperial government – neither those at the centre of power in London nor their chief agents in South Africa – cared much about black political rights. The Colonial Secretary, Chamberlain, may have intended that the Cape franchise be extended to the other colonies after the South African War.[19] But in the early twentieth century the general drift of British imperial policy in Africa was away from assimilationism and towards a system of colonial rule that provided for the differential political treatment of African people. And in the South African case the paramount concern of the imperial authorities was to establish a stable, self-governing, unified, white-controlled regime that would be loyal to Britain at a time of looming international crisis and would provide a secure basis for capitalist development.

Segregationist policies and measures soon began to emanate from the new union government, especially in four main areas – land, labour, political differentiation, and urban control. Within six months of South African unification the new union government addressed the land question. It appointed a parliamentary select committee to investigate African land occupation with special reference to squatting. The committee recommended a uniform policy for regulating the settlement of Africans on private property. It also proposed the enactment of legislation based on the principle of territorial separation, as earlier recommended by the SANAC in 1905. The

---

18 See, for instance, Mansergh, *South Africa 1906-1961*, pp.63-78.
19 Thompson, *Unification*, p.11.

eventual outcome was what Keegan calls the 'most closely studied law in South Africa's history'[20] – the 1913 Natives Land Act. According to its terms, Africans were prohibited from occupying land outside the reserves, except as labour tenants – cash tenants and sharecroppers were the targets. Nor could Africans purchase land outside the reserves, while the reserves themselves were set aside for exclusive African occupation. The act also defined scheduled areas which would form the basis of these reserves.[21]

The overall significance of the 1913 Land Act is somewhat ambiguous. On the one hand its short-term impact should not be exaggerated. Certainly the measure was followed by large-scale evictions of African tenants from white-owned land. However the state was in no position to implement the provisions of the act. There is evidence, for instance, that sharecropping continued for at least three decades after the passing of the act. The greater immediate significance of the measure was that it enabled white farmers to increase the work burden on their labour tenants.[22] On the other hand, the 1913 act was crucially important in the wider political economy of segregation and apartheid in South Africa. It provided for a system of territorial segregation which would shape the economic geography of South African farming in the twentieth century. It also formalised the reserves – which were vital to the migrant labour system and would provide the territorial basis for the future bantustans of the apartheid era.

The process of racial differentiation at the political and constitutional level was also advanced in the first decade of union. The principle of political segregation was embodied in the 1920 Native Affairs Act. This measure followed in the tradition of the Glen Grey Act in that it provided for the establishment of local councils in the African reserves. In other words, a degree of self-government was conceded to Africans, but only in the reserves, implying that the central government and urban areas would be exclusively under white control. There was also a tinge of paternalism to the measure: an extra-parliamentary Native Affairs Commission – all-white and all-male – was set up to advise the government on policy and legislation affecting Africans; and the African voice would be heard at an annual 'native

---

20   Timothy Keegan, "Crisis and catharsis in the development of capitalism in South African agriculture", *African Affairs*, 84, 1985, p.373.
21   *Ibid.*, p.387; C.M. Tatz, *Shadow and Substance in South Africa* (Pietermaritzburg, 1962), pp.13, 22.
22   Keegan, "Crisis and catharsis", pp.387-96.

The Segregation Era

conference'.²³ Dubow believes that the act represented 'the highpoint of liberal segregation in both its ideological and administrative forms'.²⁴ In the short term the act had little impact – few councils were established, and the commission and the conference did little to represent African interests. In the longer term, however, the act did set a firm trend towards political segregation – a trend that was to continue for seventy years.

Territorial separation had been at the top of the union government's segregationist agenda. Urban segregation was to follow somewhat later, in the shape of the 1923 Natives (Urban Areas) Act – the first major intervention by the central state in the business of attempting to manage and control the urban African population. The act empowered municipalities to establish segregated locations for Africans, to implement a rudimentary system of influx control, and to set up advisory boards, bodies which would contain African elected representatives with the right to discuss local issues affecting Africans, but without any power to change policy. The measure also required municipalities to institute 'native revenue accounts', separate municipal funds into which all income derived from local Africans would be paid.²⁵

As with the Native Affairs Act the short-term significance of the 1923 Act was limited. Municipalities were not compelled to establish separate African townships, and few did, lacking the necessary financial means. Few local authorities instituted influx controls, and many did not establish advisory boards. However, the act did provide an overall framework for urban segregation by laying down the principles of residential segregation, influx control, fiscal segregation, and segregated local government. These would be the key components of urban segregation and apartheid for most of the century.²⁶

The fourth main arm of this early segregationist programme was labour legislation. Acts passed in 1911 made breach of contract a criminal offence, but only for black workers, and entrenched in law the job colour bar in the mining industry. An act of 1922 laid down minimum qualifications for apprenticeship, effectively restricting access to skilled trades to whites only.

---

23 Saul Dubow, *Racial Segregation and the Origins of Apartheid in South Africa 1919-36* (London, 1989), pp.107-11; Tatz, *Shadow and Substance*, pp.34-36; Nicholas Cope, *To Bind the Nation* (Pietermaritzburg, 1993), p.100.
24 Dubow, *Racial Segregation*, p. 108.
25 Rodney Davenport, "African Townsmen? South African Natives (Urban Areas) Legislation through the Years", *African Affairs*, 68, 1969, p.99; Paul Maylam, "The rise and decline of urban apartheid in South Africa", *African Affairs*, 89, 1990, p.66.
26 Maylam, "Urban apartheid", pp.66-67.

The 1924 Industrial Conciliation Act created new collective bargaining machinery which was accessible only to unionised white and coloured workers.

Between 1910 and 1924 the foundations were laid for a far-reaching policy of segregation. But at that time the state, both at the central and local levels, lacked the means to implement the policy to any significant degree. As Dubow has observed the government's Native Affairs Department was in the post-union era 'politically weak and administratively fragmented'.[27] A more vigorous pursuit of segregationist policy, and its more forceful implementation, is usually associated with the person and government of General Hertzog. The Nationalist-Labour Pact government, headed by Hertzog, came to power in 1924 after the alliance's election victory.

Hertzog has been viewed as the 'father' of segregation, just as Verwoerd later came to be seen as the key figure in the making of apartheid. In both cases the picture is misleading – perhaps in line with that tendency to blame Afrikaners for the country's racial order. To blame an individual is to miss the broader political, social and economic forces – industrialisation, urbanisation, black protest, among others – that gave rise to segregationism. However, there is no denying that Hertzog was a key figure over a period of nearly three decades. He was the first Afrikaner leader to take seriously the question of 'native policy'. In 1912 he had held the position of Minister of Native Affairs for six months in Louis Botha's government. He studied race relations in other countries. His thinking was that of a convinced segregationist who saw Africans as a danger to 'white civilisation'.[28] Hertzog set out his views in a speech at Smithfield in the OFS in 1925, denouncing the Cape African franchise as a threat to white supremacy. The vote should be taken away from Africans, and alternative forms of African political representation be considered. As compensation for the loss of the vote, the size of the African reserves ought to be enlarged. These ideas were soon embodied in Hertzog's segregation bills, first presented to parliament in 1926. Their passage through parliament was to be stalled at various points, and Hertzog's *quid pro quo* – trading land for the vote – only materialised in 1936.[29]

While Hertzog's greater segregationist agenda took time to be realised, his government was in the meantime pushing through other measures. The job colour bar was tightened with the passing of the 1926 Mines and Works

---

27 Dubow, *Racial Segregation*, p.125.
28 Tatz, *Shadow and Substance*, pp.14-16.
29 Dubow, *Racial Segregation*, pp.136-37.

The Segregation Era

Amendment Act which restricted many skilled trades only to whites and coloureds. This was in line with Hertzog's 'civilised labour policy', designed to create full white employment and preserve the better jobs for whites (although the 1926 Act did not exclude coloureds). Social segregation was advanced in 1927 with the passing of the Immorality Act which prohibited sexual relations between whites and persons of colour. The most significant measure of this time was the 1927 Native Administration Act, described by Dubow as 'a decisive moment in the state's attempt to reconstitute and embalm tribal authority'.[30] The aim of the act was to curb or reverse any trend towards assimilationism, and to establish a more uniform policy and structure for administering Africans throughout the country. The act contained elements of both direct and indirect rule. It tended towards direct rule in that the Governor-General became, under the terms of the act, the nominal supreme chief over all Africans – with the power to govern by decree, to create, divide or amalgamate tribes, and to prescribe regulations controlling the movement of Africans. These were *de jure* powers – in effect the Native Affairs Department (NAD) and its officials would exercise real authority. The 1927 act was also a type of indirect rule measure in that it created separate courts to administer customary law for Africans. Chiefs and headmen would be invested with some judicial authority in these courts.[31] The measure confirmed the direction of state policy towards a differentiated political and administrative system for Africans – and so presaged the later bantustan system of the apartheid era.

It was ten years from the time that his bills first appeared in 1926 before Hertzog's greater segregationist measures were passed through parliament. The passage of the measures was made possible by the merger of Hertzog's National Party and Smuts' South African Party in 1934, to form the United Party (UP), which would enjoy a huge parliamentary majority over the Purified National Party (NP), consisting of those nationalist hardliners who had rejected the merger. The first of the two acts of 1936 confirmed the trend towards political exclusion and differentiation. The Representation of Natives Act abolished the Cape African franchise. In its place Africans were to be granted indirect representation, in the shape of four white senators, each to be elected by Africans in four electoral areas. Under the act a Natives' Representative Council (NRC) would also be established, comprising six

---

30 *Ibid.*, p.115.
31 *Ibid.*, pp.96-98, 115-16; Marian Lacey *Working for Boroko* (Johannesburg, 1981), pp.84-85, 97-99; Mahmood Mamdani, *Citizen and Subject* (Princeton, 1996), pp.71-72, 94-95.

NAD officials, four members nominated by the government, and twelve elected African members. It would, though, be no more than a powerless advisory body – as it turned out, in the years of its existence its advice was largely ignored. The second key measure was the Native Trust and Land Act. This confirmed the policy of territorial segregation. More land was to be allocated to the African reserves; there were also clauses designed to curb African tenancy on white-owned land with a view to restricting African occupancy only to those whose labour was required.[32] A similar principle was applied to urban areas the following year with the passing of the Native Laws Amendment Act, the aim of which was to tighten influx control so as to limit, as far as possible, the African urban presence to the labour needs of the particular urban area.

By the late 1930s a more uniform approach to the government of Africans was being adopted, an approach broadly informed by segregationist ideology. Moreover policy implementation had become more centralised in the hands of the NAD which had gained in strength since the late 1920s. However, it would be wrong to view segregationism at this time as some kind of systematic programme being vigorously implemented by the state. Far from being systematic it was a policy marked by ambiguity. As Shula Marks has observed, segregation

> ... was a many-faceted policy made up of varying components which could be and were subtly shifted in response to circumstance and to the needs of different interests of the dominant white group in South Africa. Indeed its great strength as an ideology was its very elasticity, its ability to serve the needs of very many different interests ...[33]

Segregation in South Africa has been interpreted in various ways. There is a particular historiographical tradition that gives special explanatory weight to political factors and lays stress on the roles of leading political actors. Those working in this tradition emphasise the role of Hertzog in the development of segregationist policy. Such an emphasis is misleading. Hertzog certainly initiated the segregation bills, but he was swimming with a strong tide behind him. In the white political arena opposition to the broad principles of segregation was insignificant. There may have been opposition in parliament to Hertzog's bills on points of detail. But before 1934 there were

---

32 Dubow, *Racial Segregation*, pp.133-35.
33 Shula Marks, "Natal, the Zulu Royal Family and the Ideology of Segregation", *Journal of Southern African Studies*, 4, 1978, p.177.

no fundamental differences between Hertzog's NP and Smuts' SAP over the basic principle of segregation.

Smuts himself was an ardent segregationist. He made his position clear in a famous lecture delivered at Oxford in 1929, spelling out his rejection of assimilationism. The process of African urbanisation and detribalisation had to be stemmed: segregation – institutional and territorial – was the ideal solution, although Smuts recognised that the accelerating pace of African urbanisation would make this difficult to achieve.[34]

Some Cape MPs opposed the abolition of the Cape African franchise. But in Natal there was strong support for political segregation along the lines of 'the Natal tradition'.[35] One Natal MP, Heaton Nicholls, was a particularly forceful advocate of segregation. His concern was to bolster indigenous African social and political structures so as to counter what he saw as the danger of black proletarianisation: 'If we do not get back to communalism', he wrote in 1929, 'we will certainly arrive very soon at communism'. Nicholls argued that the government should give some official recognition to the Zulu king, Solomon.[36] The proposal did not come to fruition, but it was a clear indication that the segregationist tradition of white Natal politics was still very much alive.

Much of the focus of this section up till now has been on segregationist government policy and legislation in the early decades of the twentieth century. Clearly one must move beyond such a focus if a fuller picture of the racial order is to be obtained. Racial differentiation and division come to be manifested in a variety of spheres at this time – in the countryside, in cities and towns, in educational institutions, in the work-place, on the sports fields, in the judicial sector, in different social sectors. Moreover segregationism gains greater expression at the ideological level during these decades – in political thought, in scientific theory, in medical discourse, and in literature. It is to these various manifestations and expressions of segregation in South Africa between 1910 and 1948 that we must now turn our attention.

The possibility that South Africa's racial order was firmly rooted in the preindustrial era has already been considered. Many writers have argued that it was – that white racial domination evolved over the centuries, and that it

---

34 Mamdani, *Citizen and Subject*, pp.3-6.
35 Dubow, *Racial Segregation*, pp.14-15.
36 Marks, "Ideology of Segregation", pp.179-81.

came to be most rigidly established in the countryside. As one writer put it over twenty-five years ago,

> The roots of apartheid are not to be found in the white cities, or even in the endless tunnels of the gold mines of the Rand. They are buried deep in the red soil of the white owned farms, where for some 200 years, before ever South Africa became an urban industrial economy and the word apartheid was thought of, relationships were being forged between white master and black serfs.[37]

This view is an offshoot of the South African frontier thesis, already considered in an earlier chapter. It is also an assumption implicit in modernisation theory – that racism is essentially an archaic, premodern phenomenon which is eroded with the growth of a modern, industrial, urban order. In South Africa the opposite happened, with racial oppression becoming intensified during the industrial era.

The assumptions of modernisation theory do not hold in the South African case. But it is still necessary to examine racial domination in the countryside during the segregation era. To what extent did the rural racial order become intensified at a time when white capitalist farming was enjoying rapid growth? Is there evidence that racism was deeply entrenched in the white farming community? Did white farmers have a significant voice in the making of segregation policy? There is no doubt that white farmers have enjoyed substantial political clout for most of the twentieth century. Under the 1910 constitution the electoral system was weighted heavily in favour of rural constituencies. Successive ruling parties depended significantly on the electoral support of white rural voters. Farmers featured prominently among the ranks of MPs and enjoyed considerable access to state power and patronage. Not surprisingly successive governments, especially in the five decades or so after 1924, acted in ways that were favourable to white farming interests.

What were those interests? Not, it seems, segregation as an end in itself. As Dubow has observed, 'Perhaps more than any other natural constituency ... farmers were by and large uninterested in segregation as an abstract idea'.[38]

---

37 R. Ainslie, *Master and Serfs* (London, 1973), p.7 - quoted in Charles van Onselen, "Race and Class in the South African Countryside: Cultural Osmosis and Social Relations in the Sharecropping Economy of the South-Western Transvaal, 1900-1950", *American Historical Review*, 95, 1, 1990, p.101.

38 Dubow, *Racial Segregation*, p.60.

The main concerns of white farmers were land and labour – both of which, of course, were issues that had significant implications for the racial order. On the land question white farmers rarely spoke with a single voice. Attitudes differed according to the particular interests of farmers – interests which varied from region to region and depended on the specific nature of a farming enterprise. White farmers would generally have agreed that some land should be set aside for exclusive African occupation, but might well have disagreed about the extent of that land. Lacey argues that at times of labour shortage, such as the 1920s, white farmers voiced opposition to the reserve policy, believing that reserves tied up African labour.[39] White farmers might also disagree among themselves over the desirability of black tenancy on white farms. Keegan argues that there was among such farmers a dominant ideology which opposed the practice of independent black farming on white-owned land. He also suggests that there was a strong racial, cultural dimension to this stance – especially in the early twentieth century at a time when black tenant farmers were occupying land while a growing number of landless, unemployed whites were becoming more and more impoverished.[40] However, not all farmers opposed black tenancy arrangements. Those who owned larger landholdings, and so had land to spare for such arrangements, favoured tenancy – particularly labour tenancy which better ensured that the farmer's labour needs could be met. It was often the farmers without tenants who wanted tenancy abolished.[41]

Both these sets of farming interests gained some satisfaction from the passing of the 1913 Natives Land Act. Those concerned to curb African tenancy approved of the actual terms of the act, which sought to prohibit all forms of tenancy on white-owned land other than labour tenancy. In the immediate aftermath of the act tenant evictions occurred on a wide scale.[42] But in practice the act failed to destroy the semi-independent African tenant class. In some regions of the country, especially the highveld, sharecropping continued to be practised as late as the 1950s.[43] Indeed, it was never the purpose of the act to impose a rigid racial order in the South African

---

39 Lacey, *Working for Boroko*, pp.120, 302.
40 Timothy Keegan, "The Dynamics of Rural Accumulation in South Africa: Comparative and Historical Perspectives", *Comparative Studies in Society and History*, 28, 4, 1986, pp.639-40, 644-45; Keegan, "Crisis and Catharsis", p.386.
41 Lipton, *Capitalism and Apartheid*, pp.89-90; Lacey *Working for Boroko*, pp.145-46.
42 Keegan, "Crisis and catharsis", pp.387-90.
43 *Ibid.*, p.393; Keegan, "Dynamics of Rural Accumulation", p.645; Van Onselen, "Race and Class in the South African Countryside", pp.118, 121-22.

countryside. This was made clear in the 1916 report of the Natives Land (Beaumont) Commission. The report reflected upon the 1913 act: 'A very general impression prevails that the Act contemplates a segregation – complete or partial – of the Native races throughout the Union. The impracticality of such an idea makes it difficult to understand how it has come to be entertained'.[44] Clearly rural segregation could only be enacted and implemented insofar as it did not conflict with the interests of white farmers, whose labour needs had always to be taken into account.

White farmers wanted, and regularly clamoured for, a supply of black labour that was abundant, cheap, and tightly controlled. As Lipton has noted, 'The pages of SA history books resound with the cries of white farmers for more cheap labour'.[45] To secure a sufficient supply of such labour farmers demanded strict controls over Africans in white-owned rural areas. In particular they called for measures to restrict African mobility so as to tie African workers to farms and to offset the competition for labour from the urban sector.[46] Generally farmers got what they wanted from the state, especially from the mid-1920s. For instance, the Master and Servants' Law (Transvaal and Natal) Amendment Act of 1926 imposed on labour tenants six months compulsory service a year, and empowered magistrates to have labour tenants flogged for breach of contract.[47] The control over labour tenants was tightened even further by the 1932 Native Service Contract Act. This measure reinforced the compulsory service requirement, allowing farmers to evict whole families if one member of the family failed to meet that requirement.[48] These two measures, together with the tightening of pass controls in 1929 and 1930, have been described by Lacey as 'forced labour laws introduced and passed by the Hertzog regime in a mere seven years to meet the demands of farming capital'.[49]

All this might seem to confirm the idea that the racial order was indeed more sharply delineated, more harshly manifested, in the South African countryside. One could reasonably presume, too, that white farmers, so insistent on strict control over their workers, would be among the foremost

---

44 Quoted in Greenberg, *Race and State*, p.80.
45 Lipton, *Capitalism and Apartheid*, p.88.
46 *Ibid.*, pp.86, 91-92; Greenberg, *Race and State*, pp.83-85; Lacey, *Working for Boroko*, p.149.
47 Lacey, *Working for Boroko*, pp.158-59, 170.
48 *Ibid.*, pp.120-21; Lipton, *Capitalism and Apartheid*, p.91; Greenberg, *Race and State*, p.83.
49 Lacey, *Working for Boroko*, p.165.

practitioners of racial oppression. There is plenty of evidence to support such a view. That farmers could take the law into their own hands and inflict brutal treatment on their workers is well known. Bradford has remarked that '... fists, whips and guns were central in maintaining master-servant relationships on farms'. And she points to some of the more heinous cases of brutality: 'Labourers were murdered for refusing to say "good day, *baas*", and were shot for demanding withheld wages. They were killed by being hung upside down on a tree and thrashed to a pulp, or by being tied to galloping horses which dragged their mutilated bodies long after life had expired'.[50] The cruelty of rural masters could also take less violent forms: refusing to allow their workers to attend social gatherings, denying children schooling, or barring visitors entry to the property. All this was buttressed by a virulent racism, expressed perhaps in a language of contempt directed freely at workers and their families.[51]

This has become a fairly standard picture in some literature. But the picture has come to be qualified, most particularly by Van Onselen in his work on the south-western Transvaal *platteland* during the first half of the twentieth century. Van Onselen tries to show that '... the behaviour of significant numbers of blacks and whites on the *platteland* often transcended the stark and restrictive code of race relations as it is generally understood and reached a surprising measure of accommodation in a sadly divided society'.[52] Lower-class, landless, white Afrikaners often enjoyed close social relations with African sharecroppers. Even white landlords might socialise with their tenants, in a benevolent sort of way. Patterns of interaction were more flexible than is often assumed, even if relations, particularly where middle-class whites were involved, were governed by certain codes of behaviour and racial etiquette.[53]

Notwithstanding these more flexible patterns of human interaction, in the first half of the twentieth century the South African rural order (outside the reserves) was characterised by racial differentiation and by white domination and privilege. The South African state consistently pursued policies and implemented measures that favoured the emergence of a class of white capitalist farmers. Black farmers were denied any such benefits or advantages. Instead they lived an increasingly precarious existence on land

---

50 Helen Bradford, *A Taste of Freedom: The ICU in Rural South Africa 1924-1930* (New Haven and London, 1987), p.55.
51 *Ibid.*, pp.41-42.
52 Van Onselen, "Race and Class in the South African Countryside", p.102.
53 *Ibid.*, pp.109-12, 114-17.

that they did not own, ever more at the mercy of their white landlords, ever liable to render more onerous labour service to their masters. There may not have been a rigid pattern of territorial segregation in the South African countryside before the mid-twentieth century. The persistence of tenancy arrangements, most notably sharecropping, is testimony to a degree of spatial integration. However the political economy of rural South Africa was marked by a significant level of racial differentiation, best seen in two related trends – the rising prosperity of white capitalist farmers and the growing insecurity, exploitability and poverty of black tenants and workers.

The idea that the countryside provided the most fertile ground for white racism is implicit in much historical writing on South Africa. This is an underlying assumption of, for instance, the South African frontier thesis. It also complements the further notion that urban areas represent more 'modern' environments in which racism dissolves. Some historians have drawn a contrast between the crude racism of early white frontier communities and the more urbane, open-minded outlook of those living in South Africa's first urban area, Cape Town. It has been said that Cape Town enjoyed throughout its history a 'special tradition of multi-racialism'.[54] Just a cursory examination of South African urban history in the twentieth century shows that this 'special tradition' (if it ever existed) was not extended to other towns and cities.

The racial order in South Africa's urban areas came to take on specific forms and was driven by a complex dynamic. In the twentieth century urban segregation and apartheid in South Africa have taken three main forms: the segregation of space – residential, commercial, recreational – along racial lines; the restriction of access to urban areas according to racial (and other) criteria; and the racial differentiation of local government. Each of these requires consideration, for the first half of the twentieth century.

The origins of urban racial segregation in South Africa cannot be easily pinpointed. The earliest instances of separate living areas being created for African people are to be found in Port Elizabeth and East London in the 1830s and 1840s. But it was only during the twentieth century that urban segregation came to be extended and systematised. The key moment in this process was the passing of the Group Areas Act in 1950. But urban segregation had been proceeding apace long before then, implemented through various legislative measures and other mechanisms. At the turn of the century there were early attempts to create whites-only residential areas by writing racial restrictions

---

54 Fredrickson, *White Supremacy*, p.260.

into title deeds. The Pietermaritzburg City Council inserted anti-Asiatic clauses in title deeds from 1898.[55] The same mechanism was used in Port Elizabeth where from about 1900 newly established suburbs were racially segregated.[56] The 1923 Natives (Urban Areas) Act is often identified as a key measure in the development of urban segregation. In a sense it was – it provided an overall framework for a policy of urban segregation and laid the basis for later measures. The act empowered municipalities to establish separate townships for African residents, and recommended that they do so. But there was no compulsion, and the measure did not bring about rapid segregation in urban areas. Some municipalities did begin to proclaim certain sections of their cities as segregated areas for exclusive white occupation – Johannesburg and Kimberley did this in 1924, Cape Town in 1926, and Durban in the early 1930s. But this segregationist drive could not be carried through unless alternative accommodation was provided for those black people forced out of the proclaimed areas. Generally municipalities lacked the will or the financial means to construct such accommodation. So the building of townships, as recommended in the 1923 act, proceeded slowly.[57]

Urban segregation was also promoted in other more indirect ways. From the 1910s the discourse of public health, expressed in the 1919 Public Health Act, increasingly viewed disease in racial terms and promoted segregation as one solution to urban health problems – problems that were perceived to arise out of the overcrowded and insanitary living conditions of urban Africans.[58] The 1934 Slums Act sought to extend residential segregation under the guise of public health care, aiming to bring about the removal of black slum communities so as to create space for white working-class housing schemes and business development.[59] Town planning regulations could also be utilised to further urban residential segregation. The overt purpose of such regulations was to improve the administration of urban areas and to enhance living conditions (at least, for the middle-class), but there was often a racial sub-text to such regulations, and the agencies created to administer town planning had

---

55 T.M. Wills, "Pietermaritzburg", in A. Lemon (ed.), *Homes Apart: South Africa's Segregated Cities* (Cape Town, 1991), p.92.
56 Christopher, "Apartheid Planning in South Africa", pp.45-56.
57 Maylam, "Rise and decline of urban apartheid", p.66.
58 A. Mabin, "Origins of Segregatory Urban Planning in South Africa, c.1900-1940", *Planning History*, 13, 3, 1991, p.9.
59 S. Parnell, "Racial Segregation in Johannesburg: The Slums Act, 1934-39", *South African Geographical Journal*, 70, 2, 1988, pp.112, 116-17, 123-24.

racial zoning on their agenda.[60] This agenda became even more pronounced during the 1940s, a decade of rapidly increasing black urbanisation. Local authorities in the major cities became more and more disturbed by the growth of uncontrolled black settlement in their midst. So urban planners became increasingly committed to racial zoning and the demolition of uncontrolled settlements. The Johannesburg City Council in 1944 approved a scheme for the removal of the black freehold townships of Sophiatown, Martindale and Newclare – over ten years before the removals were eventually carried through by the National Party government.[61] Similarly, the Cape Town City Council proposed the elimination of District Six as early as 1940.[62] And the Durban City Council was eagerly advocating group areas principles in the 1940s.[63]

By the time that the National Party came to power in 1948 the idea that residential and commercial space in urban areas should be segregated along racial lines was well entrenched among state policy-makers, local authorities and urban planners. However, the implementation of this policy had not been carried through to nearly the extent that it would be after 1950. Although separate black townships had been built in many areas, the more rigid racialisation of residential space was still to come, in the apartheid era.

A second feature of urban segregation was the racial restriction imposed on movement into urban areas. Passes came to be one of the most hated features of apartheid, but their history went back long before apartheid. In the nineteenth century passes were primarily used to tie black farm labourers to their white employers. After the development of mining passes served another purpose, the maintenance of the migrant labour system.[64] During the course of the twentieth century pass controls were directed more and more at regulating the access of Africans to urban areas – what came to be known as 'influx control'. The 1923 Natives (Urban Areas) Act provided for a rudimentary system of influx control, but, like the provision for segregation,

---

60 Mabin, "Segregatory Urban Planning", pp.10-12; Susan Parnell and Alan Mabin, "Rethinking Urban South Africa", *Journal of Southern African Studies*, 21, 1, 1995, p.48.
61 Deon van Tonder, "'First Win the War, Then Clear the Slums?': The Genesis of the Western Areas Removal Scheme, 1940-1949", in P. Bonner, P. Delius and D. Posel (eds), *Apartheid's Genesis 1935-1962* (Johannesburg, 1993).
62 C. Saunders, "District Six and Urban History in South Africa", *South African Historical Journal*, 26, 1992, p.203.
63 Paul Maylam, "Explaining the Apartheid City: 20 Years of South African Urban Historiography", *Journal of Southern African Studies*, 21, 1, 1995, p.28.
64 Hindson, *Pass Controls*, pp.25-26.

municipalities were not obliged to implement it. By 1937 only eleven urban areas had systematically operated such controls.[65] Much more significant was the 1937 Native Laws Amendment Act. This provided for the removal to rural areas of Africans deemed surplus to labour requirements in any particular urban area; it made it more difficult for African women to enter an urban area and for work-seekers to remain in one.[66] Passed at a time when the urban African population was growing, the measure reflected a concern on the part of policy-makers to limit the size of that population to labour needs. It was a tougher measure, with more teeth – local authorities could be compelled to implement it – foreshadowing the even more rigorous legislation that was to follow in the 1950s and 1960s.

A third dimension of urban segregation was white domination of local government and the development of a differential administrative system for Africans. In the first half of the twentieth century the structures of local government came firmly under white control. In the Cape there was a non-racial municipal franchise, and coloureds could qualify for the municipal vote in Natal. Outside the Cape persons of colour had no municipal voting rights at all. The 1923 Natives (Urban Areas) Act provided for alternative structures for Africans in urban areas. These were the advisory boards, which municipalities could establish, without being obliged to do so. Although elected bodies, voted in by African township residents, the boards were utterly powerless. They could only make recommendations to municipal councils, and such recommendations were generally ignored. Moreover the advisory boards were normally chaired by a white councillor well positioned to control proceedings.[67] Advisory boards were just one feature of a differentiated system of local government. During the course of the twentieth century persons of colour in urban areas came to fall under differentiated administrative arrangements and structures. Durban was one municipality that pioneered this approach, setting up a separate native administration department in 1916. A whole local state apparatus was created to oversee and control African urban life. This also involved the practice of fiscal segregation, whereby 'native revenue accounts' were created as separate municipal sub-accounts. These derived much of their income from the sale of liquor in municipal beer-halls which, in some municipalities, enjoyed a monopoly, at least in theory, over the production and sale of liquor to

---

65 Michael Savage, "The imposition of pass laws on the African population in South Africa 1916-1984", *African Affairs*, 85, 1986, p.194.
66 Maylam, "Urban apartheid", p.67; Hindson, *Pass Controls*, pp.45-46.
67 Maylam, "Explaining the Apartheid City", p.32.

Africans. This monopoly required strict policing which in itself epitomised the control, not always achieved, and racial differentiation that so characterised urban segregation.[68]

What were the essential aims and dynamics of urban segregation? This question has given rise to a typical materialist-idealist debate. According to a materialist approach urban segregation is explained in the broader context of urban political economy, and is viewed as serving, at different times, a variety of material interests. In Natal, for instance, there was for long a strong segregationist drive directed against Indians, resulting in a number of discriminatory measures and practices. It is apparent that white merchants' resentment of Indian commercial competition was a key factor behind this drive.[69]

Residential racial segregation could be in the interests of capital, for two main reasons: first, in facilitating labour control and, second, in releasing land for industrial purposes. Segregation as a means of labour control is well attested. Mabin claims that the roots of urban segregation can be traced to Kimberley and that in Kimberley segregation was all about labour control. It is well known that industrial compounds originated in Kimberley and that their obvious purpose was labour control. It is less well known that the further residential segregation of black and white workers in Kimberley was instituted – in the form of a company 'village' for whites and 'locations' for blacks – during the 1880s in order to divide the working class at a time when labour struggles were manifesting signs of non-racial working-class solidarity. Parnell extends this argument into the twentieth century by arguing that urban segregation was necessary to disunite the working class and maintain the racial division of labour.[70]

Urban segregation, and the relocation of communities that accompanied that process, could serve capitalist interests by releasing prime land for business activities. As cities have industrialised during the twentieth century, so have inner-city pockets of proletarian or lumpenproletarian settlement, tying up land, become more and more anathema to local power-holders. In Port Elizabeth industry expanded northwards, taking over areas of black settlement. African and Indian communities were removed from scarce flat land to the south of Durban to make way for industrial development.

---

68 *Ibid.*, pp.30-31.
69 *Ibid.*, p.25.
70 *Ibid.*, p.26; Mabin, "Labour, Capital, Class Struggle", pp.5, 11-13, 21-22; S. Parnell, "Creating Racial Privilege: The Origins of South African Public Health and Town Planning Legislation", *Journal of Southern African Studies*, 19, 1993, pp.473-76.

Inner-city black communities in Johannesburg were similarly destroyed to release land for business projects.[71]

Other writers have played down the significance of economic factors as an explanation for urban segregation. Robinson, for instance, tries to demonstrate 'the significance of the African location as a strategy for building state power'.[72] Hart, too, stresses the role of the state in promoting urban segregation in pursuit of political goals, even if it went against the logic of capital accumulation.[73] Even greater emphasis has been placed on psycho-social factors. In most case-studies of urban segregation in South Africa one comes across references to the 'sanitation syndrome'. First emphasised by Swanson,[74] it explains urban segregation in terms of moral panic and racial hysteria, as whites increasingly came to associate the black urban presence with squalor, disease and crime. For a while, in the late 1970s and early 1980s, the 'sanitation syndrome' was dismissed by Marxists as a superficial, idealist explanation. More recent work has given due acknowledgement to Swanson's line of analysis. There is indeed plenty of evidence to indicate a strong connection between, on the one hand, perceived threats to white health and safety and, on the other, the drive to urban segregation. Especially conspicuous is the causal link between epidemics and urban removals. The spread of bubonic plague around South Africa from 1901 to 1904 was always followed by white ratepayer demands for greater racial segregation. The plague first hit Cape Town in 1901. Its popular name, the 'black death', had unfortunate connotations in South Africa, as the plague was blamed more on the black urban presence than on the rats that were the carriers. Within a few weeks of the outbreak some six to seven thousand Africans were removed from central Cape Town to temporary accommodation on the city periphery.[75] It was the same story in Port Elizabeth, Durban and Johannesburg as the plague spread around the country – the same white hysteria, and moves to segregate Africans in separate 'locations'.[76]

---

71 Maylam, "Explaining the Apartheid City", p.26.
72 J. Robinson, "The Power of Apartheid: Territoriality and State Power in South African Cities – Port Elizabeth 1923-1972" (unpublished Ph.D thesis, Cambridge University, 1990), p.323.
73 D. Hart, "Master Plans: The South African Government's Razing of Sophiatown, Cato Manor and District Six" (unpublished Ph.D thesis, Syracuse University, 1990), pp.267-68.
74 M.W. Swanson, "The Sanitation Syndrome: Bubonic Plague and Urban Native Policy in the Cape Colony, 1900-1909", *Journal of African History*, 18, 1977.
75 *Ibid.*, p.392.
76 Maylam, "Explaining the Apartheid City", pp.24-25.

The 'sanitation syndrome' should not be viewed as the major imperative towards segregation. Even Swanson himself stresses rather the metaphorical significance of the syndrome, suggesting that 'urban race relations came to be widely conceived and dealt with in the imagery of infection and epidemic disease'.[77] One should also be wary of privileging material forces in explaining urban segregation. But there is, too, a danger in the postmodernist tendency to dismiss materialist explanations. The continuing salience of materialist analysis in the field of urban history must be stressed. One cannot begin to understand South African urban policy if it is set apart from material forces.[78]

During the course of the twentieth century the practice of racial differentiation and discrimination impinged upon all aspects of South African society. We have already seen how it pervaded rural and urban life. Racial segregation also came to be institutionalised in the educational system, in sport and recreation, and in other arenas of South African society. Segregation in the education field took two main forms in the first half of the twentieth century. There was institutional segregation, and there was differentiation, along racial lines, in the type of education provided.

Long before the twentieth century there had been a distinct tendency towards segregated education in the various regions of South Africa. In the twentieth century this tendency became rigid practice. In 1905 a system of state schools, exclusively for white children, was established in the Cape – as was already the practice in the other three territories.[79] There were separate schools for persons of colour. As Hunt Davis put it, 'Africans attended segregated and sadly under-funded schools often run under a different set of regulations from white schools'.[80] Individual schools for Africans were generally controlled by missionary societies and managed by whites. Only in Natal did the provincial administration, in 1918, set up state schools for Africans. By 1923 the Cape, Natal and Orange Free State provincial governments had set up separate administrative sub-departments for African education, taking further the process of institutional segregation.[81]

---

77   Swanson, "The Sanitation Syndrome", p.387.
78   Maylam, "Explaining the Apartheid City", pp.25, 37.
79   R. Archer and A. Bouillon, *The South African Game: Sport and Racism* (London, 1982), p.26.
80   R. Hunt Davis, "The Administration and Financing of African Education in South Africa 1910-1953", in Peter Kallaway (ed.), *Apartheid and Education* (Johannesburg, 1984), p.128.
81   *Ibid.*, pp.130-32.

Accompanying this institutional segregation was racial differentiation in the type of education provided. In official government circles the idea gained ground, especially from the 1920s, that Africans were inherently unsuited to a bookish, academic type of education and that they should rather be trained to perform manual work. A 1936 government report put it in a nutshell: 'The education of the white child prepares him for life in a dominant society and the education of the black child for a subordinate society'.[82] The educational system should thus be geared to underpinning white domination and reinforcing existent social, economic and political relations. In the education of Africans special attention should be paid to the inculcation of moral values – obedience, punctuality, honesty, respect, industry – the qualities that employers demand of workers.[83] In 1922 differentiated school curricula were introduced for whites and Africans at the Cape. In 1921 the Cape had even established a special syllabus for coloured primary schools. This was to be a cross between the syllabi for white and African schools, illustrating just how the notion of a racial hierarchy, in which coloureds occupied an intermediate position, influenced educational policy at the time.[84]

Educational segregation extended into the tertiary sector. In 1916 the South African Native College (later the University of Fort Hare) was founded, to provide higher education for Africans. While the University of Cape Town and the University of the Witwatersrand were open to all students in the pre-apartheid era, the University of Natal in Durban ran special, separate classes for 'Non-Europeans'. Similarly technical colleges which were set up primarily to serve white interests either ran special classes for persons of colour or organised separate branches.[85]

Segregated sport and recreation also became the norm in South Africa during the first half of the twentieth century. Theatres and cinemas in white areas usually did not admit persons of colour who could only watch films in separate facilities. There were even attempts to control the content of films screened, with the 1931 Entertainment Act calling for the censorship of 'scenes of intermingling of Europeans and non-Europeans'.[86] There was no

---

82 Frank Molteno, "The Historical Foundations of the Schooling of Black South Africans", in Kallaway (ed.), *Apartheid and Education*, pp.63-64.
83 *Ibid.*, pp.67-68.
84 P.A.W. Cook, "Non-European Education", in Ellen Hellmann (ed.), *Handbook on Race Relations in South Africa* (Cape Town, 1949), pp.351, 359.
85 *Ibid.*, pp.371-74.
86 Keyan Tomaselli, *The Cinema of Apartheid* (London, 1989), p.14.

formal law preventing blacks and whites competing on the sports fields, but in practice there was little integration. Horse racing was an exception – blacks could become jockeys. And at race meetings and soccer matches there was little to stop black and white spectators intermingling. For the most part, though, sport was segregated. Most white clubs had membership conditions which were racially exclusive.[87] Federal sporting bodies and associations were largely racialised. Because white bodies were racially exclusive, a set of separate black associations were established – such as the South African Bantu Rugby Board, set up in 1935.[88] By the 1940s many such associations had been formed; these were not bodies catering for persons of colour in general, there mostly being separate associations for Africans, coloureds and Indians.[89]

During the pre-apartheid era of the twentieth century the practice of racial segregation was ever more embedded in South African society. It pervaded the social, economic and political spheres. It is therefore not surprising that the race question – racial difference, race policy – became a matter of ideological significance. Intellectuals, scientists, political thinkers, writers, all devoted more and more attention to the issue. Their ideas found a way into the public domain, generating a discourse that became hegemonic in white society and underpinned discriminatory policies and practices. Until the last ten years or so scholars have tended to pay little attention to racial thought. There have been reasons for this, as Dubow has observed:

> In the struggle to create a common society the non-racial political tradition of opposition to apartheid – which has drawn heavily on the universalist claims of Christianity, liberalism and Marxism – has deliberately downplayed the issue of race. On account of its divisiveness, the salience of race has at times almost been wished away.[90]

Moreover materialist analysis, prominent from the 1970s, played down the ideological dimension of segregation and apartheid.

---

87 Archer and Bouillon, *The South African Game*, pp.39-41.
88 Albert Grundlingh, André Odendaal and Burridge Spies, *Beyond the Tryline: Rugby and South African Society* (Johannesburg, 1995), p.46.
89 E. Jokl, "Physical Education, Sport, and Recreation", in Hellmann (ed), *Handbook on Race Relations*, pp.445-47.
90 Saul Dubow, *Illicit Union: Scientific Racism in Modern South Africa* (Johannesburg, 1995), p.4.

Any exploration of the history of South African racial thought raises some fundamental questions. What was the relationship between racial thought and racial policy? What was the connection between racial thought, as propounded by intellectuals and scientists, and popular racism and race consciousness? Dubow is perhaps foremost among historians to have examined South African racial theory. He refrains from attempting to establish a causal link between racial thought and racial policy, seeking rather to explore the 'correlations and connections' in an effort to enhance 'understanding of the ideological context in which segregation and apartheid were developed'.[91] On the second question Dubow rejects both 'top-down' and 'bottom-up' assumptions about the development and circulation of racist ideas. Rather is it necessary to place such ideas in a social context and see how it is that they gain wider resonance at particular times.[92]

For much of the twentieth century it was taken for granted in South Africa, and elsewhere, that the population of Africa could be broken down into a set of distinct racial categories. There was the further assumption that different race groups displayed specific cultural and linguistic traits. Such assumptions were widely held in the first three decades of the twentieth century, and persisted in some circles into the second half of the century. In South Africa physical anthropologists played a significant role in promoting racial typology, which rested on these assumptions. One of South Africa's best known scientists of the twentieth century, Raymond Dart, worked in the typological tradition. In 1937 he produced a paper in which he argued that Africa's population comprised three basic racial types.[93] The typological tradition of physical anthropology gave scientific authority to popular beliefs about race. These beliefs were held across the ideological spectrum – by progressive thinkers like Olive Schreiner at the turn of the century, by African writers like Silas Molema, and by Afrikaner nationalists like Gustav Preller from the 1930s.[94] Dubow suggests that 'racial history and typological models' had a 'tenacious hold' well into the 1960s, and that in South Africa 'Physical anthropology did more than any other discipline to generate and sustain the racial paradigm'.[95]

While physical anthropology firmly established ideas about racial types and racial difference, it was Social Darwinist thought and the eugenics

---

91 *Ibid.*, p.10.
92 *Ibid.*, pp.7-8.
93 *Ibid.*, pp.45, 94-95; Leonard Thompson, *The Political Mythology of Apartheid* (New Haven, 1985), p.99.
94 Dubow, *Illicit Union*, pp.72-74.
95 *Ibid.*, pp.106, 117.

movement that more explicitly propounded notions of racial superiority and inferiority. Social Darwinist ideas were propagated in South Africa from the 1870s, and the discourse took on among the white community – for whom the idea of the survival of the fittest had an obvious appeal, as justification for white supremacy.[96] The eugenics movement, which gained some prominence in the western world in the early twentieth century, had a less broad appeal in South Africa, being confined more to a small circle of intellectuals, scientists and doctors. Eugenicists envisaged a programme whereby genetic pools could be manipulated so as to achieve a wider spread of desirable human characteristics among the population and to eradicate weaker strains. Such views were propounded in South Africa during the first three decades of the twentieth century. Darley-Hartley promoted discussion of the ideas in the pages of the medical journal, the *South African Medical Record*, after 1909.[97] A more ardent proponent of eugenics was H.B. Fantham, professor of zoology and comparative anatomy at the University of the Witwatersrand from 1917. In South Africa eugenics inevitably took on racial overtones. Fantham in particular warned against miscegenation, fearing that it would bring racial degeneration. The advocates of eugenics were firm supporters of segregationist policy.[98] However, the influence of eugenicist ideas in South Africa was limited. This may have been because eugenicist theory did not always match up with ideas of white superiority, especially during the early twentieth century when the growth of a 'poor white' class suggested that the European stock comprised many who were genetically ill-equipped. Eugenicist discourse faded in the 1930s, discredited by its association with Nazism.[99]

What was the significance of racial theory and scientific racism in the making of South Africa's racial order? As Dubow came to realise in writing his book, to gauge the impact of ideas on society is 'one of the most intractable problems in intellectual history'.[100] One can write about the production of ideas, but to research their consumption is so much more difficult. We do not know who read what, let alone how the content influenced the outlook

---

96 *Ibid.*, pp.117-18, 128.
97 Susanne Klausen, "'For the Sake of the Race': Eugenic Discourses of Feeblemindedness and Motherhood in the *South African Medical Record*, 1903-1926", *Journal of Southern African Studies*, 23, 1, 1997, pp.33-35.
98 Dubow, *Illicit Union*, pp.134-35; Paul Rich, "Race, Science, and the Legitimization of White Supremacy in South Africa, 1902-1940", *International Journal of African Historical Studies*, 23, 4, 1990, p.677.
99 Dubow, *Illicit Union*, pp.170-80, 196.
100 *Ibid.*, p.286.

of the reader. However, it is evident that some of the ideas emanating from the field of racial theory did take root and become embedded in popular discourse. Foremost among these was the notion that race groups constituted real, distinct entities. It was a short step from this belief to the idea of a racial hierarchy – that the different races could be ordered in a league table. Such ideas have been subjected to intellectual demolition in the past four decades, but they still live on in popular racist discourse in South Africa. That such ideas resonated among South African whites in the earlier part of the century is hardly surprising, given the socio-economic context of the time. It was a period of trauma and dislocation brought about by the twin processes of industrialisation and urbanisation. As Dubow puts it,

> The concerns of racial science spoke directly to these anxieties. Its findings helped to rationalise social strictures against racial and cultural intermixture, and its warnings of pollution, defilement and degeneration served as powerful justifications of the need for statutory segregation along lines of colour. In so doing, racial science helped to facilitate the realisation and ideological maintenance of white power and authority.[101]

White racism in South Africa has intersected with two fundamental human concerns – sex and health. Hyam has remarked that 'Sex is at the very heart of racism'. He sees 'the white man's formal objection to intimacy between black men and white women' as 'the quintessential taboo'. And this was not merely a rationalisation of political and economic fears – 'white men were genuinely apprehensive of the erotic competition', an apprehension perhaps aggravated by the popular supposition that black men were particularly well-equipped for sexual encounters.[102] In South African history white racism has often been at its most virulent at times of 'black peril' scares. The fear of black men raping white women has fuelled these panics. Etherington has recounted how in the late 1860s and early 1870s white Natalians in Durban and Pietermaritzburg were gripped by a fear of black rape, even though the fear was not derived from actual events – '... everyone was scared and practically no one was raped'.[103] The white hysteria surfaced at a time of insecurity – when the neighbouring Zulu state appeared threatening in the years before the Anglo-Zulu War, and with single male

---

101   Ibid.
102   Ronald Hyam, *Empire and Sexuality* (Manchester, 1990), pp.203-205.
103   Norman Etherington, "Natal's Black Rape Scare of the 1870s", *Journal of Southern African Studies*, 15, 1, 1988, p.36.

migrant workers seeming to represent a dangerous floating population in the towns.[104] Van Onselen has also documented a series of rape scares in early Johannesburg. In 1897 a white woman was raped by her black male domestic worker, giving rise to widespread white hysteria, and calls for public hangings. 'Black peril' scares blew up again in Johannesburg between 1905 and 1908. In 1911 and 1912 there were two more cases of white women being raped by black men. Both were followed by a white backlash. After the second 'revolver-brandishing southern suburbs residents organised themselves into vigilante groups'; the local press further fuelled the rising racial hatred. Van Onselen notes that these scares occurred at times of economic recession – when white employers might have been reducing their servants' wages. So, he concludes, 'In several cases these economic pressures manifested themselves openly in "black peril" conflict between mistresses and "houseboys"'.[105]

The psycho-sexual dimension of white racism was not only manifested during 'black peril' scares, it also extended to an abhorrence of consensual relations between black and white, especially between black men and white women. At the turn of the century there was an upsurge of white prostitution. Many of the prostitutes, especially those who were recent immigrants from Europe, were prepared to receive black clients. This aroused a moral panic among whites. It resulted in measures being passed in the Cape, Orange River Colony, Natal and the Transvaal in 1902 and 1903, whereby sexual relations between black males and white prostitutes were outlawed.[106]

Not dissimilar was a concern that surfaced in the nursing profession in the early years of the twentieth century – a white repulsion against the practice of white female nurses tending black male patients. There was a groundswell of opposition to the practice from, among others, members of the Natal colonial legislature in the early 1900s and from Afrikaner nationalist organisations in the 1930s – but, it seems, interestingly, not from the nurses themselves. The proposed solution was the training of black nurses who could treat black patients.[107] Again this racial fear needs to be viewed in the socio-economic context of the time. As Marks has remarked,

---

104   *Ibid.*, pp.45, 53. See also Pamela Scully, *Liberating the Family?* (Portsmouth, Oxford, and Cape Town, 1997), pp.153-75, for a discussion of rape and race in the western Cape during the first half of the nineteenth century.

105   Charles van Onselen, *Studies in the Social and Economic History of the Witwatersrand 1886-1914: Volume 2: New Nineveh* (Johannesburg, 1982), pp.49-52.

106   Van Onselen, *Studies: Volume 1: New Babylon*, pp.136-40.

107   Shula Marks, *Divided Sisterhood* (Johannesburg, 1994), pp.48-61.

The Segregation Era

... the very process of industrialisation and urbanisation around the turn of the century that created the need for hospital services for blacks fuelled the fears around white female sexuality and racial purity and the angst that the vision of white (female) hands on black (male) bodies and black (female) hands on white (male) bodies roused in the white population.[108]

This kind of repulsion clearly had a psycho-sexual dimension, especially where it involved physical intimacy and closeness between black men and white women. But there was more to it than this. In the twentieth century there developed among whites an especially strong abhorrence of white-black sexual relations. This must be viewed in the context of racial theory and a particular horror of racial degeneration resulting from miscegenation. If races were distinct entities, almost sub-species, as they were widely deemed to be in the early decades of the twentieth century, then it was vitally important that their distinctive character be preserved. Interracial sex would destroy this race purity. This abhorrence was fed by eugenic theory, according to which the children of mixed partners suffered from inherent physical and moral flaws. It was also reinforced by popular stereotypes of South African coloureds whose supposed degeneracy was manifested in criminal, drunken behaviour.[109]

Miscegenation became an official issue in South Africa during the twentieth century. We have already seen that measures were passed in 1902 and 1903 banning relations between white prostitutes and African men. The 1927 Immorality Act prohibited sexual relations outside marriage between white women and African men. The clamour for tougher legislation increased during the 1930s, with Afrikaner churches in the forefront of the campaign. Two bills outlawing mixed marriages failed to pass through parliament in 1936 and 1937. During the debate on the 1936 bill a United Party MP applauded Hitler's views on mixed marriages and race purity. In 1939 a government commission set up to investigate mixed marriages issued a report opposing such marriages and expressing dismay at the 'infiltration of non-European blood into the European population'.[110] But it was not until the National Party came to power that this thinking was entrenched in law.

Just as a fear of black sexuality and racial degeneration has been integral to racism, so too has a white suspicion that black bodies have been the sources and carriers of disease. As Swanson has observed,

---

108 *Ibid.*, p.82.
109 Dubow, *Illicit Union*, pp.180-83, 186-87.
110 Patrick Furlong, *The Mixed Marriages Act* (Cape Town, 1983), pp.1-10.

> ... medical officials and other public authorities in South Africa at the turn of this century were imbued with the imagery of infectious disease as a societal metaphor, and ... this metaphor powerfully interacted with British and South African racial attitudes to influence the policies and shape the institutions of segregation.[111]

From the 1870s, especially in Natal and the Transvaal, fear of epidemics lay behind moves to segregate Africans and Indians in municipal locations.[112] We have already seen how the spread of bubonic plague in the early 1900s prompted the removal of Africans from central urban areas to segregated townships. In the 1920s and 1930s attempts to control the spread of tuberculosis centred on segregation and slum clearance. These were the means deemed necessary to keep the disease away from whites – they had little to do with aiding African victims of the disease.[113] Gradually further assumptions about health and disease crept into white racial discourse. There developed, for instance, what Packard calls 'a more generalized association of unsanitary behaviour with race'. Africans were deemed to be particularly susceptible to disease because of their lifestyle – their overcrowded living conditions and their 'habits of inebriety and depravity'. The sociological explanation was accompanied by a biological one – that physiological differences made Africans more susceptible to disease, especially tuberculosis.[114]

Ideas about race and racial difference pervaded not only the discourse of science and medicine, but also that of political thought, anthropology, history and literature during the early decades of the twentieth century. As Dubow points out, it was in the early 1900s that 'concerted efforts were made to define the significance of race within South Africa's future social and political system'.[115] The 1905 report of the South African Native Affairs Commission had put forward a rudimentary programme based on segregationist principles. But it was a small group of writers and thinkers, later known as 'liberal segregationists', who elaborated upon these principles and propounded them with some conviction. One such thinker was J. Howard Pim who put forward segregationist ideas in the first decade of the century. Informed by Social Darwinist thought Pim carried with him those

---

111 Swanson, "The Sanitation Syndrome", p.387.
112 *Ibid.*, p.390.
113 Randall M. Packard, *White Plague, Black Labor* (London, 1989), p.194.
114 *Ibid.*, pp.50,195,196.
115 Dubow, *Illicit Union*, p.129.

The Segregation Era

assumptions about race that were dominant at the time – that, for instance, physical differences between human groups correlated with mental and cultural differences. Segregation was, for him, necessary to prevent both racial degeneration and social dislocation. Africans should as far as possible be confined to rural reserves where the tribal system could function to maintain order, discipline and social cohesion.[116] Similar views were expressed by Maurice Evans in his book, *Black and White in South East Africa* (1911) – one of the first books ever to be published on the theme of black-white relations in South Africa. Evans insisted that control of government should remain firmly in white hands, and that 'The main line of policy must be the separation of the races as far as possible, our aim being to prevent race deterioration, to preserve race integrity, and to give both opportunity to build up and develop their race life'.[117] There were other liberal segregationists. C.T. Loram propounded the idea that a differential type of education should be provided for Africans – again an idea firmly predicated on notions of race and racial difference. Edgar Brookes in the 1920s advocated segregation, proceeding from the premise that African social systems were naturally rooted in the countryside.[118]

These segregationists have been labelled 'liberal' because their ideas were tinged with benevolent paternalism. They themselves saw their policies as moderate – as a middle course between unrestrained assimilation on the one hand, and total white domination on the other. And segregation seemed to be a programme for social stability – a policy that would offset the destabilising consequences of urbanisation and proletarianisation.[119] This was one reason why segregationism won increasing support among government policy-makers and officials in the years after 1910.[120] However, by the 1930s some of these liberal segregationists were changing their tune and turning away from segregationism. At a time of growing industrialisation and urbanisation the reality of black-white integration was becoming ever more apparent – and segregation ever more a pipe-dream. Moreover, some of the older assumptions about race and racial difference were coming to be challenged by a younger generation of liberal thinkers concerned to promote interracial cooperation and harmony.[121]

---

116   *Ibid.*, pp.168-69; Dubow, *Racial Segregation*, pp.23-26.
117   Quoted in Dubow, *Racial Segregation*, p.26.
118   *Ibid.*, pp.27-29.
119   *Ibid.*, pp.7-8.
120   Rich, "Race, Science", p.673.
121   *Ibid.*, pp.683-86.

The work of Dubow and Rich in analysing segregationist thought reflects a recent growing interest in the history of ideas, and marks something of a departure from previous historiographical tendencies. It would be wrong, though, to characterise Dubow and Rich as conventional idealist historians. Both are concerned to situate intellectual history in a broader political, economic and social context. They clearly differ from an earlier generation of historians who had tended to view segregationism as a largely political, ideological phenomenon. Equally Dubow and Rich try to avoid the reductionism of the revisionist Marxist writers. So where does that leave us in the quest to better explain the segregation era of the first half of the twentieth century?

Recently Anthony Marx has put forward the argument that white racist ideology and the accompanying practice of discrimination and exclusion were necessary to build white unity from the early 1900s. In the aftermath of the bitter South African War, he argues, the two main white groups settled their ethnic differences by asserting a common white identity and pursuing a white supremacist agenda: 'Exclusion of the Africans helped to unify the nation of whites, defined them as such in an effort to use race to heal the previous rift'. This theme was, in Marx's view, to recur throughout the first half of the twentieth century: 'With every reemergence of the English-Afrikaner rift, the salve of racial domination was applied to keep the peace'.[122] This is an unsatisfactory argument. Certainly it was the case that a broad white supremacist consensus was achieved in South Africa for much of the twentieth century. But it is misleading to claim that policies of black racial subordination were imposed as a means to secure white unity. One can just as easily turn the argument around and say that white unity was necessary for effective black subordination. Indeed, the latter view is the more plausible one – that whites settled their differences so as to better maintain white domination, power and privilege.

Marx's interpretation is also too narrowly political, failing to show why white unity and white supremacy were so necessary at all. It therefore shares some of the shortcomings of previous attempts to explain segregationism in largely political terms. Tatz's argument, for instance, centred on the idea that Hertzog was determined to safeguard white political dominance against the seeming black electoral threat made possible by the Cape non-racial franchise. Accordingly, the argument continues, Hertzog's programme rested on a trade-off – Africans in the Cape would be deprived of the vote, but in

---

122 Anthony W. Marx, *Making Race and Nation* (Cambridge, 1998), p.117.

return more land would be added to the reserves. The 'substance' of the land would be compensation for the 'shadow' of the vote.[123] Tatz has been rightly taken to task, by Lacey in particular, for taking Hertzog's own utterances at face value, and thereby overstressing the political dynamic of segregation policy. The point has been made that by the 1930s the Cape African franchise posed no threat whatsoever to white political control. This was especially so after the enfranchisement of white women in 1930 doubled the number of white voters and significantly reduced the proportionate strength of black voters in the overall electorate.[124]

The implication of Lacey's critique of Tatz is that some other interest, not directly revealed, lay beneath Hertzog's political rhetoric. As an historical materialist Lacey would have seen that interest as economic. For Lacey the policy of segregation was designed to safeguard 'white economic supremacy, not white political majority'. The Cape African franchise was 'anathema to the ruling classes' because it 'threatened to undermine not only the traditional master-servant relationship but the State coercive system as well'.[125] Lacey's argument amounts to a forthright rendition of the 'cheap labour thesis', which gained considerable adherence among left-wing academics and activists during the 1970s and early 1980s. In her view the real concern of Hertzog's segregation policy was to secure an adequate supply of cheap black labour, especially for the white farming sector experiencing labour shortages. Lacey was following a line of analysis already propounded by other writers. Legassick, for instance, contended that segregation was not 'a policy produced by the imposition of earlier social attitudes on the new conditions of South African industrialization: nor were its proponents the more conservative of the white rural population'. In his view the policy had a clear purpose and significance: 'Along with other mechanisms of labour coercion, segregation created and perpetuated the system of migrant labour'.[126] In a similar vein, Wolpe centred his analysis of segregation on the African rural reserves. These made possible a system of migrant labour, which was cheaper than permanent, stabilised labour because the subsistence needs of migrant labourers and their families could be partly met from rural production in the reserves, thereby enabling the payment of lower wages to the

---

123 Tatz, *Shadow and Substance*, pp.38, 45, 79.
124 Lacey, *Working for Boroko*, pp.53, 70-73.
125 *Ibid.*, pp.73, 83.
126 Martin Legassick, "Gold, Agriculture, and Secondary Industry in South Africa, 1885-1970: From Periphery to Sub-Metropole as a Forced Labour System", in Robin Palmer & Neil Parsons (eds), *The Roots of Rural Poverty in Central and Southern Africa* (London, 1977), p.182.

labourers. Thus migrancy was essential to capitalist profitability, especially in the mining industry; and the migrant system in town rested on the reserves. For Wolpe therefore, 'The crucial function ... performed by the policy of segregation was to maintain the productive capacity of the pre-capitalist economies and the social system of the African societies in order to ensure that these societies provided portion of the means of reproduction of the migrant working-class'.[127]

While due recognition has been given in recent years to the pioneering insights of the revisionist writers of the 1970s, their work has also come in for criticism. Dubow, for instance, is critical of the economic reductionism implicit in the revisionist analysis of the segregation era. For him 'Segregationist policies were not simply a knee-jerk response to capitalist interests as a whole, much less to the particular needs of particular "fractions" of capital'. Dubow finds little empirical evidence to verify any close connection between the mining industry and segregation policies.[128] However, Dubow does not reject out of hand the essential thrust of the revisionist interpretation. He is fully aware that segregationism cannot be understood outside the social and economic context of the time – that a narrow idealist explanation, preoccupied with surface political factors, is inadequate. His main argument is that 'segregation should be seen as a *generalised* response on the part of the state to the problems wrought by industrialisation'.[129] Perhaps the chief of these problems was the perceived threat, arising from the processes of industrialisation and urbanisation, posed by a growing African proletariat. A rise in African militancy and protest in the decade after World War One seemed to give substance to this threat. Thus, even in Dubow's analysis, it is conceded that 'segregation worked in the long-term interests of capitalism by helping to secure the social conditions for the reproduction of capitalism as a system'.[130]

As South Africa industrialised, so did the racial order harden. Ideas of racial difference and white superiority, once loosely articulated, became more formalised in the realm of racial theory. The practice of racial differentiation and discrimination, once informal, resting on convention rather than law, became more institutionalised, codified and entrenched. In the first half of the

---

127 Harold Wolpe, "Capitalism and cheap labour-power in South Africa: from segregation to apartheid", *Economy and Society*, 1, 4, 1972, p.439.
128 Dubow, *Racial Segregation*, pp.52, 54.
129 *Ibid.*, p.52.
130 *Ibid.*, p.3.

twentieth century segregation was a multi-faceted phenomenon. It had an ideological dimension, and it comprised a set of policies and administrative practices. The ideological dimension itself contained various elements: pseudo-scientific theory with its special emphasis on race purity and its horror of miscegenation; benevolent paternalist thought with its idea of trusteeship and its concern to preserve African 'traditionalism' and 'tribalism' in the interest of social stability; and white supremacism with its unquestioning commitment to continuing white political control. At the policy level segregation provided for rural territorial segregation – the 1913 Natives Land Act was the most significant piece of legislation enacted during the segregation era. The foundations for urban apartheid were laid with the passing of the 1923 Urban Areas Act. But urban segregation was always going to be a contradictory process, as the state would struggle to balance the need for an adequate supply of African labour in urban areas against the concern to prevent the unlimited growth of a vast uncontrollable urban African population. The 1937 Native Laws Amendment Act clearly revealed this concern – with its provision that municipalities provide census figures with a view to limiting the urban African population according to labour needs.

The policy-makers of the segregationist state retained an unwavering conviction that political power should remain in white hands. At the same time they groped uncertainly towards establishing a system that would provide some kind of political space for the black majority. From the 1920s a policy of retribalisation and the indirect rule approach gained favour in official circles. But only a few tentative steps, such as the 1927 Native Administration Act, were taken to realise this approach. As a result the policy lacked any substance before 1950. The Natives Representative Council, established under the 1936 Representation of Natives Act, was merely a dummy institution – the notorious 'toy telephone' – that could never even begin to satisfy black political aspirations. And there was continuing uncertainty among white politicians as to where to draw the political colour line. In the 1920s Hertzog had toyed with the idea of incorporating coloureds into the enfranchised class. But nothing had come of this and the 1910 status quo remained, with coloureds retaining the vote at the Cape, but remaining disfranchised elsewhere. In the 1940s the United Party government made a fumbling attempt to deal with the question of Indian political rights. The 1946 Asiatic Land Tenure and Indian Representation Act was a clumsy measure which tried to restrict Indian land ownership and occupation in Natal in exchange for Indians being granted the right to vote for five white parliamentary representatives.

That the racial order hardened during the era of industrialisation is hard to dispute. Not only was there segregationist ideology and policy, but there was also the growing practice of segregation in most spheres of life, as we have seen. But did the racial order harden because of, or in spite of, industrialisation? The debate around this question has given rise to polarised positions. Materialists say 'because of', liberals 'in spite of'. During the past fifteen years there have been commendable attempts to break free from this polarisation. Some liberal writers have made concessions to the materialist position, which in turn has been modified so as to be less reductionist. Current thinking looks rather like a happy compromise – and perhaps lacking in any real edge. In my view, a renewed emphasis should be placed on material forces in the hardening of the racial order. That this process occurred contemporaneously with industrialisation was no coincidence. The two were closely connected. Industrial capitalism in South Africa was driven by imperatives and needs, many of which were more or less met by an institutionalised, legislated system of racial differentiation and discrimination. At the same time industrialisation wrought far-reaching social change – dislocation and dispossession for many. A more formal racial order was constructed in an attempt, albeit thoroughly misguided, to achieve social stability during this time of change. In any analysis of the segregation era these considerations must be prioritised. They carry greater weight than racial theories and racist attitudes. Segregation did not grow out of the theories of racial scientists, nor out of the ideas of liberal intellectuals, nor out of the prejudices of the white population at large. Segregationist policies and practices were forged in a particular socio-economic context, and cannot be properly understood outside that context.

6 Apartheid

Apartheid will for long stand out as one of the most monstrously inhuman systems of government that operated in the twentieth century. Some apartheid policies and practices were so ludicrous and bizarre as to be laughable.[1] But the horrendous impact of apartheid on the lives of millions of people, together with apartheid's continuing awful legacy, leaves one to question whether such a system could have had a 'lighter side'. The human devastation that it wrought also makes difficult a dispassionate analysis of the nature and dynamics of apartheid. However it is just such an analysis that will be attempted here. It is not the purpose of this book to try to assess or gauge the enormously destructive impact of white racism and apartheid, but rather to explore the history and historiography of these phenomena in an effort to uncover those forces, interests and processes that brought about the South African racial order.

A study of apartheid gives rise to certain questions that have preoccupied scholars in recent years. Did apartheid represent any significant departure from previous racial policies and practices, or was it essentially a continuation of segregationism? When the National Party came to power in 1948 did it have an apartheid master-plan ready at hand, and did it at once proceed with vigour and energy to implement that plan? Or was the new government's approach more cautious and pragmatic? How significant was the role of Verwoerd, first as Minister of Native Affairs and then as Prime Minister, in effecting apartheid? Was apartheid a product of white racism, white supremacism, or Afrikaner nationalism? Or did it arise out of a set of economic conditions during a particular phase of capitalism? These are large questions which will be given consideration. But first a brief description of apartheid's main features is required.

Apartheid is not easily encapsulated in a straightforward description. It was not a single, coherent system, and it changed its character, adapting to new circumstances, over three or four decades. There were, though, key interlocking elements that constituted the apartheid order. The most crucial element of this order – a prerequisite for the continuation of apartheid – was the ongoing system of racialised political exclusion and disfranchisement.

---

1 See Ben Maclennan, *Apartheid: The Lighter Side* (Cape Town, 1990).

This had been well established in 1910 with the vote being denied to people of colour in Natal, the OFS and Transvaal. The Cape African franchise was abolished in 1936. The process of racialised disfranchisement was taken further after 1948. Under the Asiatic Land Tenure and Indian Representation Act of 1946 Indians were to be offered token political representation (the right to elect five white representatives to parliament) as *quid pro quo* for restrictions on their land rights. The new NP government promptly abolished this token Indian franchise in 1948. It also set about disenfranchising coloured voters at the Cape. This turned out to be a long, fraught constitutional process requiring considerable machination and manipulation on the part of the government in order to obtain the necessary two-thirds parliamentary majority required for such a constitutional amendment. The Appeal Court was enlarged and packed with NP-aligned judges. So too was the membership of the senate increased, enabling the government to carry through coloured disenfranchisement in 1956.

These developments were essentially a continuation of segregationism. However in the 1950s the racialised political order began to take on a new form. This was the 'homeland' or bantustan policy, promoted by the government from the late 1950s. The first step in this new policy direction was taken at the beginning of the decade. The 1951 Bantu Authorities Act was a step towards retribalisation, setting up a three-tiered authority structure in the reserves at tribal, regional and territorial levels, with government-appointed chiefs in effect becoming the state's administrative agents in the reserves. The key measure was the 1959 Promotion of Bantu Self-Government Act. This proclaimed the existence of eight African 'national units', each of which was presumed to be ethnically and culturally distinct. These units would have their territorial base in the reserves and would gradually gain greater powers of self-government, perhaps even independence. The policy was implemented from the early 1960s, with Transkei being the first territory to pass through the various states of self-government, eventually obtaining its so-called 'independence' in 1976.[2]

The bantustans were supposed to perform a variety of functions for the apartheid government. They would be dumping-grounds for African people removed from the white rural and urban areas because they were deemed to be surplus to labour requirements in those areas. The bantustan policy was also a divide-and-rule strategy – a way of dividing the African majority into a set of

---

2   Paul Maylam, *A History of the African People of South Africa* (Cape Town, 1986), pp.167-68.

ethnic minorities in a (vain) attempt to undermine the broader African nationalist movement. The bantustans were supposed to provide a political home for Africans, to accommodate African political aspirations, and so to serve as a counter to the charge that apartheid represented a system of minority rule that denied political participation to the black majority. The bantustan policy was also a device to deny Africans full South African citizenship. Under the 1970 Bantu Homelands Citizenship Act all Africans would be compelled to become citizens of one of the bantustans even if a person's whole life had been spent in a white area of the country.

These were the objectives. The realities were to be rather different. During the 1970s it became increasingly evident that the bantustan policy was in tatters. The bantustans were in no way viable political or economic entities. Far from being drawn to the 'homelands' as arenas of political or economic activity, most Africans strove to escape the dire poverty and corrupt political elitism that characterised these territories. The government clung on to the policy through the 1980s even though it had long since been evident that the bantustan system was collapsing.

Spatial apartheid, the second main element of apartheid, was integral to the bantustan system. The aim, albeit an impossible one, was to achieve a correspondence between racialised political differentiation and racialised spatial separation. The 1913 Land Act had laid the foundation for rural spatial separation. In the 1960s territorial segregation came to be implemented with a new zeal and ruthlessness by the apartheid government. The forced removals programme brought about the coerced relocation of about 3.5 million people, virtually all of whom were black, between 1960 and 1983.[3] About half of those removed were Africans forcibly resettled from white rural areas to one or other of the bantustans. Over a million African tenants – cash tenants, sharecroppers or labour tenants – were removed from white-owned farms. Nearly half a million Africans were removed from 'black spots' – freehold land owned by Africans that fell inside territory demarcated for exclusive white ownership.[4] The overall objective of these rural forced removals was to relocate to the bantustans all Africans except those whose labour was required, and to destroy any independent access to land, in the form of ownership or tenancy, enjoyed by Africans in the rural areas of white South Africa.

---

3   Laurine Platzky & Cherryl Walker, *The Surplus People* (Johannesburg, 1985), p.9.
4   *Ibid.*, p.10.

As Evans has observed, '... apartheid administrators appreciated the central importance of space'.[5] And this was as true of urban space as it was of rural space. Urban spatial apartheid was a more complex phenomenon, riddled with internal contradictions, complicated by the vast labour needs of the industrial economy. Even so the NP government zealously set about implementing the basic principles of the 1923 Urban Areas Act. The 1950 Group Areas Act made compulsory what the 1923 Urban Areas Act had recommended – urban residential segregation. The 1950 act provided for demarcated urban areas to be set aside for particular racially defined groups. The measure led to further forced removals – the uprooting and relocation of whole urban communities, mostly coloured and Indian. The implementation of urban segregation involved the construction of vast townships for Africans, Indians and coloureds. According to apartheid principles these townships were to be sited as far as possible from white residential areas, but reasonably close to centres of employment. The spatial separation of residential areas was to be reinforced by buffer zones and by natural or other barriers.[6]

Spatial segregation depended on the state's capacity to control the mobility of people. Stricter influx control would be the chief mechanism – again the NP government resorted to the more vigorous enforcement of a policy applied during the segregation era. A key measure was the 1952 Native Laws Amendment Act. This restricted the right of permanent urban residence to Africans who fulfilled certain strict conditions relating to place of birth, duration of residence and employment in a particular urban area. The act also made stronger provision for the expulsion from urban areas of Africans who were deemed surplus to labour requirements. Even tougher restrictions upon entry into urban areas and more severe expulsion powers were introduced in 1964. These measures required uncompromising enforcement. Prosecutions under the pass laws increased significantly – from a total of about 280,200 in 1951 to about 631,300 in 1970.[7] Accompanying this process was a growing concentration of power as the central state and its agencies from the early 1970s took over from municipalities the administration of urban Africans. At the same time the continuing disfranchisement of black people at the local government level meant that defiance, protest and resistance became the only means to challenge the urban apartheid system.

---

5   Ivan Evans, *Bureaucracy and Race* (California, 1997), p.299.
6   Maylam, "The rise and decline of urban apartheid", pp.69-70.
7   *Ibid.*, p.69.

The racialisation of the labour field was a third main element of the apartheid order. Again, this was not new. The racial division of the labour force has a long history in South Africa. With the development of the mining industry the job colour bar came to be entrenched in legislation. Hertzog's government extended this colour bar in the mid-1920s, effectively reserving certain skilled trades for whites and coloureds. Job reservation was undermined during the Second World War which brought both economic growth and a shortage of white labour as many white men left the country to fight in the war. However, from the 1950s the NP government restored and strengthened the racial division of labour. Industrial conciliation legislation in 1956 and 1959 gave the Minister of Labour effective powers, through an industrial tribunal, to reserve specific jobs for particular race groups. The tribunal was to make a number of determinations reserving certain types of work for whites. There were also measures prohibiting mixed-race trade unions, outlawing strikes by African workers, and withholding official recognition for African trade unions.[8]

Political exclusion and differentiation, territorial segregation, the racialised control over African mobility, urban segregation, and the racial division of labour were the more significant elements of apartheid. But apartheid permeated all spheres of South African society. Segregated education became rigidified in the 1950s. The Bantu Education Act of 1953 provided for strictly racialised differentiation in education. Schools for Africans were brought firmly under central state control, and were subjected to a distinctive syllabus, geared more to practical learning to prepare Africans for subservient, menial roles. There continued to be a huge disparity between expenditure on the education of white children and that spent on children of colour. The 1959 Extension of University Education Act brought apartheid to the tertiary sector, which had long since been largely segregated anyway. The legislation extended and tightened the segregation of universities, and ethnicised the sector by providing for the establishment of separate universities for specific groups – initially institutions would be built for Indian, coloured, Zulu and Tswana students.[9]

Few areas of human activity and social life were left untouched by apartheid. The 1949 Prohibition of Mixed Marriages Act extended the provisions of the 1927 Act by outlawing marriages between whites and any persons of colour. The 1950 Immorality Act prohibited sexual relations

---

8   Doxey, *Industrial Colour Bar*, pp.140-51.
9   Davenport, *South Africa*, pp.533-36.

between whites and persons of colour. Sport and entertainment came to be more strictly segregated from the 1950s. Mixed sports clubs were banned, as were contests between white competitors and those deemed to belong to other race groups. Spectators were segregated into separate sections at sporting events. Most places of entertainment were almost entirely segregated, persons of colour being excluded from whites-only cinemas, theatres and restaurants. The Reservation of Separate Amenities Act of 1953 provided for racial segregation in a whole range of public facilities – toilets, lifts, public transport, post office counters, beaches, parks, park benches, and entrances to public buildings – interestingly, there was no generalised segregation of shops.

The application of this 'petty apartheid' was at times tragic, at times absurd. There were those cases where an ambulance would arrive at the scene of an accident and refuse to convey an accident victim to hospital if the victim's colour was wrong for that particular ambulance. People died as a result of this rigid adherence to apartheid rules. The absurdity of petty apartheid is well exemplified in the case of coloured usherettes employed to direct patrons to their seats in whites-only cinemas – on condition that they kept their heads down and did not look at the screen, in case they might catch a glimpse of the film.[10]

Apartheid was never a smoothly functioning system. That it functioned at all was due much to other key pillars that supported the whole edifice. Four such underpinnings were of crucial importance: the system of racial classification, the state's repressive apparatus, the apartheid bureaucracy, and racial ideology. First, the 1950 Population Registration Act was a cornerstone of apartheid. If people were to be separated along strict racial lines it became crucial that a person's racial identity be clearly defined. Thus under the 1950 measure all persons in South Africa were designated as members of one of four racial groups – white, African ('Bantu' in the terminology of the day), coloured, or Asiatic. Again, the application of the act could be both tragic and comic. Families were broken up as members of the same nuclear family, even siblings, were assigned to different racial groups. Ishmail Essop told the (coloured) House of Representatives in 1988 how he had been classified as Cape Malay, two of his brothers and two of his sisters as coloured, another brother as white, and another sister as Indian.[11] The business of determining a person's racial category showed up the absurdity. What were to be the criteria

---

10   Maclennan, *Apartheid*, pp.37, 106, 158.
11   *Ibid.*, pp.14-15.

and methods for determining race in borderline cases? There were eyelid tests and hair tests. Even sporting preference came into the picture; in the view of one Race Classification Board: 'A soccer player is a Native, a rugby player is a Coloured'.[12] Notwithstanding this absurdity, the 1950 act was crucial to other apartheid measures, determining a person's access to certain kinds of jobs, to particular residential areas, to educational institutions, among other things.

The second pillar of apartheid was state repression. This was exercised with ever greater might to curb protest and crush resistance. The state's repressive apparatus was steadily strengthened after 1948, especially from the 1960s. A series of harsh security laws were passed increasing the capacity of the government and the police to suppress political opposition, in the process undermining established judicial procedures. The first such measure was the 1950 Suppression of Communism Act. This outlawed the Communist Party (which had already disbanded in anticipation of the measure) and enabled the Minister of Justice, using a very broad definition of communism, to declare other organisations unlawful. The level of repression increased significantly after the political turmoil that followed the Sharpeville massacre in 1960. General Laws Amendment Acts passed in 1962, 1963 and 1964 strengthened the state's repressive capacity considerably. The Minister of Justice was given the power to place people under house arrest. The police could detain suspects for periods of 90 days, without bail, in solitary confinement. Much of this power was exercised in the early 1960s by the strong-arm Minister of Justice, B.J. Vorster, who made free use of his new-found authority.[13] At the same time the strength of both the police and defence force were increased in terms of personnel and coercive capacity. This was to be the trend throughout the 1960s, 1970s and 1980s – as the state faced mounting internal resistance, so did it depend more and more on extra-judicial procedures, the brute power of the police and defence force, and other repressive apparatus, to crush its opponents.

This other apparatus was essentially the apartheid bureaucracy – the third pillar underpinning the post-1948 racial order. Evans has made the important point 'that apartheid was installed not through military means, but largely through the everyday work of civil administration in the 1950s' – an administration that played a key role in 'routinizing oppression'.[14] From the

---

12 *Ibid.*, p.12.
13 Henry Kenney, *Power, Pride and Prejudice* (Johannesburg, 1991), pp.174-75.
14 Evans, *Bureaucracy and Race*, pp.277, 282.

1950s there was a change of style in the way that the racial order was administered. In the segregation era this administration had been characterised by a more *laissez-faire*, paternalist approach. Authority and responsibility had been devolved to regional native commissioners and to local magistrates. And these local white potentates had been expected to display a kind of paternalist sympathy towards the Africans they administered. But by the 1940s the Department of Native Affairs was increasingly being criticised, by white and African alike, for its inconsistent, ineffective performance which, in Evans' view, was 'centrally implicated in the administrative dissipation of the segregation state'.[15]

In the 1950s the situation changed. The once insignificant Department of Native Affairs took on a new importance. Here Verwoerd played a key role after becoming Minister of Native Affairs in 1950. Under his leadership the style and character of African administration changed. The Department expanded enormously – its white staff rose from 1750 in 1948 to over 3000 in 1960. The management style became less paternalist and more authoritarian. There was greater centralisation of power, with a shift of authority away from native commissioners and magistrates into the hands of the Department's own 'professional' administrators, many of whom had degrees in Bantu administration from Afrikaans universities. These people would be styled the 'experts' who would draw upon 'scientific' research to inform and legitimate their approach to administration. This was a 'modernising' administration, energised by Verwoerd's forceful leadership – so much so that the Department of Native Affairs became something of 'a state within a state' during the 1950s.[16]

Fourth, apartheid had ideological underpinnings. It would be a mistake to slip into the idealist assumption that apartheid was driven by ideas, that it derived primarily from a set of beliefs. Rather did apartheid ideology serve more of a legitimating function. And the legitimating power of the ideology was undoubtedly strengthened, at least in the eyes of its supporters, by the efforts of Afrikaner nationalists to ground apartheid policy in both theology and science. It became one of the core ideas of Afrikaner nationalism that apartheid was divinely ordained. God was the 'Great Divider'. The diversity of nations and ethnic groups was part of God's plan for the world, and therefore it was in keeping with God's will that nations and ethnic groups

---

15 *Ibid.*, pp.14-16.
16 *Ibid.*, pp.1-2, 6, 16, 293; Philip Bonner, Peter Delius, Deborah Posel, "The Shaping of Apartheid: Contradiction, Continuity and Popular Struggle", in Bonner, Delius & Posel (eds), *Apartheid's Genesis*, pp.30-31.

belong to their own separate territories and maintain their own distinct cultures, languages and political systems.[17] Apartheid theory also drew on scientific ideas, albeit ones that had become widely discredited in intellectual circles by the 1940s. In particular apartheid was fed by two ideas associated with racial science. One was the crude notion of white racial superiority and black inferiority – a notion that underpinned white supremacy and uncompromising white political domination, the *baaskap* approach of the 1950s. The second idea corresponded with the theological belief. Not only scripture but also science ordained that racial differences were real and fixed, and that biological and cultural diversity coincided.[18] Therefore South Africa's political system should accommodate this diversity. Such thinking supported the 'separate development' phase of apartheid from the 1960s. However, as Dubow has noted, racial science did not represent a main prong of apartheid ideology after 1948.[19] Rather did apartheid come to rest mostly on the fundamental tenets of nationalist thought. Nations and ethnic groups were deemed to be distinct entities with their own unique characters. Afrikaners cherished their own nationhood and so they would give to other ethnic groups what they had wanted for themselves – self-determination.[20] It was, of course, a thoroughly implausible attempt to justify apartheid – Afrikaner self-determination amounted in reality to an abhorrent system of white domination; and apartheid-style 'self-determination' was imposed forcibly on other groups with total disregard for their own wishes and aspirations. Apartheid ideology was riddled with contradictions and falsehoods. It gained adherence only from its own supporters while arousing world-wide condemnation.

This account of apartheid has been essentially descriptive, as much writing on the subject tends to be. It accordingly conceals the major analytical and historiographical issues, some of which must be addressed. Three broad questions will be considered here. First, were post-1948 race policies a continuation of a long pre-existing process of racial differentiation and discrimination, or did the election of the NP government in 1948 mark a significant turning-point? Second, was apartheid the product of an NP grand plan, a blueprint, or was it a set of pragmatic policies? Third, how is apartheid best explained? What was its main underlying dynamic (if it had one at all)?

---

17 Dubow, *Illicit Union*, p.250.
18 *Ibid.*, pp.271-74.
19 *Ibid.*, p.282.
20 Dan O'Meara, *Forty Lost Years* (Johannesburg, 1996), p.66.

The continuity/change debate has given rise to few clear-cut positions. The continuity argument had considerable appeal for Afrikaner nationalist politicians and writers. Early in his premiership D.F. Malan wrote that '... Apartheid, separation, segregation or differentiation ... is part and parcel of the South African tradition as practised since the first Dutch settlement at the Cape in 1652 ...'.[21] Similarly the historian, C.F.J. Muller, in the late 1960s described apartheid as 'South Africa's traditional colour policy which, in certain respects, was being carried to its logical conclusion'.[22] Such a view not only offered an historical interpretation of apartheid, but also formed part of apartheid's legitimating ideology. The view represented apartheid not as a piece of NP social engineering, but rather as a product of history. Apartheid had evolved over time, had grown out of the past, was grounded in tradition – and could therefore be regarded as enjoying some legitimacy.

Some defenders of apartheid did, though, qualify the continuity argument. Rhoodie and Venter, for instance, stressed the difference between segregation and apartheid. In their view segregation had been merely '... *a stage in the evolution* of apartheid' (original italics). Apartheid was an adaptation and crystallisation of segregationism – indeed, 'the apartheid idea rose out of the ruins of segregation ...'. The segregation policy had not made 'adequate provision for the national and political aspirations of the developing Bantu groups', whereas apartheid did do this. Moreover apartheid was preventing the interracial social mixing that had been on the increase during the segregation era.[23] Thus Rhoodie and Venter were concerned to hang on to the idea of apartheid as being rooted in tradition, but were also keen to represent apartheid policy-makers as innovative, logical, methodical, far-sighted and consistent.

There has been no clear-cut position on this continuity/change issue among social scientists and historians who can be loosely labelled anti-apartheid. One tendency among writers with liberal inclinations has been to stress the significance of the 1948 election as a watershed in the making of the South African racial order. According to this view 1948 marked the triumph of hard-line white supremacism associated with the tradition of the nineteenth century boer republics – suggesting continuity from boer republicanism to the apartheid era. But there is also an implied discontinuity with the immediate past – that the new NP government set about reversing the

---

21   Neame, *History of Apartheid*, p.80.
22   C.F.J. Muller, "Conclusion: Factors which shaped the History of South Africa" in C.F.J. Muller (ed.), *Five Hundred Years* (Pretoria, 1969), p.426.
23   Rhoodie and Venter, *Apartheid*, pp.146-50.

growing trend towards integration apparent during the 1940s. Neame, for instance, saw the two main white political parties of the 1950s as presenting 'two well-defined schools of thought'. First, 'The National Party, which was almost exclusively Afrikaans, demanded the rigid enforcement of segregation ...'. Second, 'The United Party, which contained the majority of the English-speaking section, favoured a more liberal attitude and suggested that attempts should be made to reach a better understanding with the Natives and the Coloureds'.[24] More recently Omer-Cooper has written in a similar vein:

> ... the election victory of 1948 enabled the new government under Dr Malan to launch a major re-organisation of South African society in accordance with Afrikaner nationalist ideals. This involved halting and reversing the trend towards the erosion of segregation which had been evident under the previous government. Instead, segregation was to be systematised as never before and applied rigidly and dogmatically in accordance with the theory of apartheid.[25]

In some respects these views have some validity. There is no doubt that after 1948 there was an attempt to systematise segregation and apply it more rigidly. But Omer-Cooper and others overstate the significance of 1948 and overemphasise the discontinuity between the segregation and apartheid eras. Even more misleading is the sharp contrast drawn by Neame between the policies of the NP and the UP, between Afrikaner and English. This kind of differentiation belongs to a historiographical tradition which pins the blame for racial segregation and discrimination on to the shoulders of Afrikaners, downplaying or ignoring the major contribution of white English-speakers to the making of South Africa's racial order.

It is difficult to deny either that there was continuity in the development of South Africa's racial order throughout the twentieth century, and before, or that the character of that racial order changed after 1948. As Dubow has put it, 'Apartheid is not merely an extension of segregation, as some have argued; nor does it represent a fundamental rupture from the past, as others have supposed'. Proponents of apartheid did not renounce segregation, but rather 'sought to reformulate it in a more consistent and radical form'.[26] Apartheid brought a more rigid and more vigorous enforcement of racial segregation. This in turn required a significant growth in the size and capacity of the state's

---

24 Neame, *History of Apartheid*, p.111.
25 J.D. Omer-Cooper, *History of Southern Africa* (London, 1987), p.193.
26 Dubow, *Racial Segregation*, p.177.

bureaucracy and security apparatus. The new departures that came with apartheid have been captured well by Evans:

> At the same time, apartheid introduced changes never even contemplated by segregationists: the conversion of racial segregation into a biblically derived moral project; the splintering of Africans into 'independent tribal states'; the disenfranchisement of 'coloureds'; the categorical denial that Africans would every qualify for citizenship; zealous attempts to enforce submission to a highly regimented state; and attempts to 'perfect' racial segregation in every sphere.[27]

While apartheid clearly did bring change, there is a popular impression that the extent of that change was far greater than it really was. To understand this one has to look at the changing international context in which apartheid occurred. South Africa's segregation policies of the first half of the twentieth century did not stand out as particularly abhorrent because they were much in keeping with the colonial policies of the European powers and with segregationist practice in the American South. However the NP government chose to rigidify and refine segregation after 1948 at the time when racial discrimination was rapidly being discredited around the world. Apartheid thus flew in the face of international trends, especially during the 1950s and 1960s when African countries were gaining independence from European rule and when the civil rights movement was gaining momentum in the United States.[28] In this context apartheid stood out as particularly obnoxious. Its break with developing international norms seemed therefore also to imply (wrongly) in the popular mind a significant break with the past.

Closely associated with the idea that apartheid brought a significant break with the past is the related notion that apartheid was the product of an Afrikaner nationalist 'grand plan'. According to this view the NP came to power in 1948 with the plan already devised, a blueprint for imposing a new racial order to replace the collapsing policy of segregation. As Posel has noted, this view has gained adherence across the ideological spectrum. For Afrikaner nationalists it implied that the NP leadership had a clear vision and strong sense of purpose on acceding to power.[29] Others writing in an anti-apartheid tradition have also shared the assumption that apartheid was based on a blueprint. Hepple, for instance, refers to the 'Grand Design of

---

27 Evans, *Bureaucracy and Race*, p.5.
28 Dubow, *Racial Segregation*, p.178; Sparks, *The Mind of South Africa*, pp.183-87.
29 Deborah Posel, *The Making of Apartheid 1948-1961* (Oxford, 1991), pp.1-2.

separate development'.[30] He goes further, developing another assumption that became embedded in conventional historical wisdom – that Verwoerd was the chief architect of this 'grand plan':

> The advent of Verwoerd as Minister in 1950 was the beginning of a new era in Native Affairs .... He was not interested in continuing along the old lines of trial and error. He had a plan which took account of both the present and the future. Henceforth the work of the Department of Native Affairs would be geared to that plan.[31]

Does this interpretation of apartheid stand up to careful scrutiny? There are some grounds for substantiating it. Certainly there is evidence that from the mid-1930s, and especially during the 1940s, Afrikaner nationalist intellectuals and policy-makers had been giving much consideration to the matter of race policy. The *Afrikaanse Bond vir Rassestudies* had been founded in 1935 – a body which Rhoodie and Venter described as 'the father of the concept of apartheid'.[32] By early 1947, according to Rhoodie and Venter, the Afrikaner nationalists' 'most important racial principles had crystallised into a defined synthesis so that the Nationalists were able to enter the political arena with a clearly formulated native policy'.[33] The spate of important legislation passed within a few years of the NP gaining power in 1948 would also suggest that the party had a clear sense of direction from the outset. The Prohibition of Mixed Marriages Act (1949), Population Registration Act (1950), Immorality Act (1950), Group Areas Act (1950), Bantu Authorities Act (1951), and Native Laws Amendment Act (1952) were all significant measures that served to tighten the racial order. Verwoerd's appointment as Minister of Native Affairs in 1950 ushered in a tougher managerial style and new approach to African administration. Verwoerd handled his portfolio with energy, zeal and conviction.

A critique of this orthodox interpretation of apartheid as a form of Verwoerdian social engineering has been developed in recent years, particularly by Lazar and Posel, effectively demolishing the conventional wisdom. Lazar and Posel argue that by the late 1940s apartheid, far from being a carefully devised programme, was little more than an electoral slogan. There were broad underlying apartheid principles – that racial segregation

---

30 Alexander Hepple, *Verwoerd* (Harmondsworth, 1967), pp.116-17.
31 *Ibid.*, p.110.
32 Rhoodie and Venter, *Apartheid*, p.170.
33 *Ibid.*, pp.168-69.

should be extended and applied more vigorously, and that urban Africans be regarded as temporary sojourners selling their labour, with no claim to citizenship rights. But there was no blueprint. Within NP circles there was still uncertainty around the practical implementation of these principles – about how soon and how far they could be applied. Verwoerd himself was not a great visionary, but rather a pragmatist, more concerned about immediate political issues and economic growth than about long-term master-plans.[34]

Apartheid, at least during the 1950s, should be viewed more as a reaction to immediate pressures and circumstances. What circumstances? One of the most pressing issues for Afrikaner nationalists was the growing rate of black urbanisation. During the 1940s, a decade of significant economic growth, there had been a massive migration of Africans to the cities. Between 1936 and 1946 the urban African population grew by over 57%. Accompanying this process was a rising tide of black militancy and protest, and worker organisation and action. The ANC Youth League was propounding a more assertive Africanist politics. Independent black trade unions were emerging. There was a wave of strikes across the country during the early 1940s, culminating in the massive African mineworkers' strike of 1946.

These trends posed a threat to key Afrikaner nationalist constituencies. White Afrikaner workers, preponderant in the less skilled industrial jobs, faced competition from black workers in the urban labour market. The African migration from rural areas aggravated the labour shortage that had been experienced by white farmers especially in the maize-producing areas of the Free State and Transvaal, since the 1930s. At the same time rising black organisation and protest seemed to endanger the whole fabric of white supremacy. Afrikaner nationalist policy-makers were alert to these trends, and devoted much attention in the early years of NP rule to tackling these immediate problems – not to implementing some 'grand plan'. Influx control was tightened. Uncontrolled black urban settlements were cleared, and new townships, more easily controllable and conforming to group areas principles, were constructed. Stabilising the urban social order was a pressing concern, as NP leaders were aware that one of the main keys to the 'native question' was the city.[35]

---

34   John Lazar, "Conformity and Conflict: Afrikaner Nationalist Politics in South Africa, 1948-1961" (unpublished Ph.D thesis, Oxford University, 1987), pp.29-30, 70.
35   Posel, *Making of Apartheid*, pp.24, 30-31, 38; O'Meara, *Forty Lost Years*, pp.24-25, 28-29; Bonner, Delius and Posel, "Shaping of Apartheid", pp.20-29.

Even if the NP government had wanted to implement an apartheid master-plan on its accession to power it lacked the political power base to do so. The 1948 election produced a thin parliamentary majority of only eight seats in the lower house; and the NP, with its allies, had obtained only 42% of the votes cast. So in the years after 1948 the party concentrated a great deal of energy on securing its position prior to the next election. This entailed strengthening party organisation, establishing new branches, fund-raising, and ensuring that supporters were on the voters' roll. This political activity brought a substantially increased majority in the 1953 election, but it also distracted attention away from any programme of apartheid social engineering.[36]

The NP was also far from united over the future direction of policy – a point which further undermined the 'grand plan' thesis. While the NP leadership had been particularly concerned about parliamentary survival, there were sections of the Afrikaner nationalist movement who were keen to pursue a more grandiose apartheid vision. These were the advocates of total apartheid – who have come to be called the 'visionaries'. Among such advocates was the *Suid-Afrikaanse Buro vir Rasse Aangeleenthede* (South African Bureau of Racial Affairs – SABRA), which was launched in 1948. SABRA's leading thinkers advocated vertical racial separation, or 'total apartheid'. This would require the consolidation and development of the reserves into viable states which would serve as the political, cultural and economic home for all Africans. This clearly implied full economic segregation – no longer could the South African economy depend on cheap black labour. Whites would be expected to make economic sacrifices in the cause of 'total apartheid', which was viewed by its proponents as more morally justifiable than a system of political and social segregation that operated in a context of economic integration. Support for 'total apartheid' came from sections of the Dutch Reformed Church (DRC). The main principles of the visionaries were set out in the report of the Tomlinson Commission, established in 1950 with the brief to make recommendations on the future of the African reserves. The Tomlinson Report, published in 1956, concluded that the government had to choose between total integration or separation, and firmly advocated the latter, recommending that the government plough capital into the reserves so that they might become economically viable.[37]

---

36 Lazar, "Conformity and Conflict", pp.44-53.
37 *Ibid.*, pp.169-89; Posel, *Making of Apartheid*, pp.50-53; Kenney, *Power, Pride and Prejudice*, pp.70-75.

According to the conventional wisdom Verwoerd was one of the 'visionaries'. More recent research, however, suggests that he was more of a pragmatist. Verwoerd believed that 'total apartheid' was an ideal, a goal to be worked towards, perhaps over a period of 300 years, but he also saw that it was impracticable in the short term. He recognised that there would have to be a continuing dependence on a permanent African labour force in urban areas, and he was wary of sacrificing white economic interests. Accordingly Verwoerd rejected some of the main recommendations of the Tomlinson Report. He refused to commit capital for the development of the reserves, or to allocate more land to them so as to make them more economically viable. Verwoerd's pragmatism was in tune with the attitudes of most NP supporters. Afrikaner nationalist farmers and business people would not give up their dependence on African labour. They did not wish to halt African urbanisation, but rather to regulate it more tightly according to the labour needs of different sectors.[38] The 'visionaries', the advocates of 'total apartheid', were clearly a minority among NP supporters, albeit a vociferous minority prepared to air their criticism of Verwoerd and the pragmatists. They kept the debate alive within the NP through the 1950s. Ultimately, though, pragmatic apartheid won through. Economic realities ensured this, and the 'ideal' of 'total apartheid' receded further and further beyond the horizon.

The picture emerging from recent research is one that portrays Verwoerd as a pragmatist and the NP government as pursuing, in the 1950s, policies that tightened the racial order but without endangering economic interests. It is also evident that apartheid changed over time. A key shift occurred in the years 1959-1961 when there was a change of direction away from a 'baaskap' approach, based on crude notions of white supremacy and racial differentiation, towards a policy known among its apologists as 'separate development'. This newer approach rested less on an ideology of racial differentiation – although continuing white supremacy and domination remained unquestioned – and more on ethnic differentiation within the black majority (while simultaneously playing down ethnic differences among the white minority, at a time when the NP was trying to attract more support from white English-speakers).

This change of approach came to be called 'Grand Apartheid', but it still stopped far short of the visionaries' ideal of 'total apartheid'. It was merely a

---

38 Lazar, "Conformity and Conflict", pp.176-98; Posel, *Making of Apartheid*, pp.53-57, 62; O'Meara, *Forty Lost Years*, pp.71-72.

step in that direction. 'Grand Apartheid' was marked by policy shifts, and by an intensification of existing measures. The bantustan system, initiated by the 1959 Promotion of Bantu Self-Government Act, was the cornerstone of 'Grand Apartheid'. The purpose of the system was to divide the African majority into ethnic groups and to channel African political and economic aspirations towards the bantustans which would be the 'homelands' for those ethnic groups. A further purpose was to deprive all Africans of South African citizenship thereby turning African workers in white areas into 'foreign' visitors. This in turn required a tightening of influx control and the pass laws, leading to the forced removal of hundreds of thousands of Africans from rural and urban areas deemed to be white and their relocation in one or other of the bantustans. As it turned out the bantustans did not, of course, provide any kind of political arena in which African aspirations could be met – only a small bantustan elite, lacking any real popular legitimacy, benefited from a system which accorded them the trappings and perks which went with a limited degree of power. African aspirations were geared to full political participation in a unitary South African state. Extraparliamentary opposition movements directed their energies towards that end, only to come up against the full force of state power which became increasingly repressive and authoritarian during the 1960s – another feature of 'Grand Apartheid'.[39]

'Grand Apartheid' was certainly not 'total apartheid'. After the policy shift of 1959-1961 there was no suggestion that the capitalist economy's dependence on black labour might be broken. One aim of 'Grand Apartheid' was to limit the black presence in 'white' areas as closely as possible to the labour needs of those areas. It was not envisaged that black labour would be replaced by whites or superseded by mechanisation, as the 'total apartheid' visionaries had planned. Indeed the record of the NP government suggests that it was not prepared to sacrifice capitalist economic interests in the cause of a more total application of apartheid. This is not to say that apartheid was essentially driven by economic interests (an issue soon to be addressed below). Nor is it to deny that apartheid policies had some consequences that were damaging to the capitalist economy. The point is that economic constraints placed limits on the extent to which a consistent, rigidly segregated racial order could be implemented. This is well illustrated by a debate that developed in the late 1960s between different Afrikaner

---

39 O'Meara, *Forty Lost Years*, pp.72-74, 118-20; Martin Legassick, "Legislation, Ideology and Economy in Post-1948 South Africa", *Journal of Southern African Studies*, 1, 1, 1974, pp.21-29.

nationalist factions around the issue of shop apartheid. The recently formed extreme right-wing breakaway party, the *Herstigte Nasionale Party* (HNP), called for segregation to be applied in shops. The NP Prime Minister, B.J. Vorster, rejected the call on the grounds that total shop apartheid would be inconvenient for whites, as shopowners depended in part on income derived from black customers; furthermore whites often relied on their black maids to do their shopping for them. Vorster's response revealed his priorities.

The shop apartheid issue is a microcosm of a much larger question – how does one best explain the dynamics of apartheid? This question has given rise to extensive debate among academics, activists and others. Again, as with the historiography of segregation, the great divide, but not the sole divide, has been between idealists and materialists. Nowadays many analysts would tend to frown upon any interpretation of apartheid that was too narrowly idealist or too rigidly materialist. And yet in the past many interpretations have been locked into one or other of these paradigms.

Idealist explanations have taken various forms, but have shared the common assumption that apartheid was primarily a product of white attitudes and ideas. Until about thirty years ago it seemed plainly obvious to most observers that apartheid was all about racial separation, differentiation and discrimination, and that therefore apartheid must have been a product of white racism and racial ideology. More particularly apartheid was viewed as a product of an especially virulent racism associated with Afrikaner nationalists. As Van den Berghe put it, 'From the ideological point of view, the advent of apartheid meant the triumph of the stern frontier paternalism of the Boer Republics over the more benevolent and sophisticated paternalism of the Cape'.[40] This was the old distinction between the northern tradition of boer racism and the Cape liberal tradition. Even Afrikaner nationalists themselves were supposedly divided along these regional lines, with Cape Afrikaners deemed to be more moderate than their northern counterparts. Thus it has been argued that when D.F. Malan, a Cape nationalist, retired as prime minister in 1954, to be replaced by J.G. Strijdom, a Transvaaler, 'northern' attitudes triumphed over the moderation of the Cape.[41] Verwoerd, who succeeded Strijdom as premier in 1958, was another Transvaaler seemingly obsessed with race. This is how Kenney characterises him: 'Of all the Nationalist leaders since 1948 Verwoerd was the most persistent

---

40   Van den Berghe, *South Africa*, p.115.
41   See, for instance, Kenney, *Power, Pride and Prejudice*, pp.86-87.

ideologue. He truly made a fetish of race. For him apartheid was genuine ideology, which stood or fell as a system'.[42]

The relationship between Afrikaner nationalism and apartheid is not as straightforward as some have made it appear. To say that apartheid was simply a product of a virulent Afrikaner racism is far too simplistic. Such a claim misses the class dimension and neglects the role of non-Afrikaner racism. However racial ideology was a fundamental element of Afrikaner nationalist thought. Racial theorists like Geoffrey Cronjé were obsessed about racial purity. The Dutch Reformed Church justified racial separation on scriptural grounds. Afrikaner nationalists generally presumed that there was a firm correlation between race and culture. As Rhoodie and Venter put it,

> The three foundation stones of apartheid are Western culture, Christian morality and a specific racial identity. In the case of the Afrikaner there is a powerful connecting link between these three elements. His own particular bio-genetic character is, for example, associated with a particular socio-cultural way-of-life and to give up either through amalgamation with a more primitive culture or race must necessarily result in the destruction of the other. To the Afrikaner cultural assimilation is synonymous with racial assimilation – there can be no *laissez-faire* middle path.[43]

In Afrikaner nationalist thought there was, though, an uneasy tension between its emphasis on a broad racial identity and its stress on a narrower ethnic nationalism. The former militated in favour of white solidarity, while the latter bred a more exclusive Afrikaner nationalism. Giliomee suggests that Afrikaners stressed different aspects of their identity at different times. From 1948 through most of the 1950s the main stress was on their racial identity – a period when they were an insecure white people needing legislation to ensure their survival. During Verwoerd's premiership from 1958 to 1966, with the colour line firmly established, Afrikaners came to emphasise their separate nationhood. By the 1970s Afrikaner nationalist ideology had become less overtly racist or nationalist, and generally more pragmatic, designed to secure the political and economic advances that Afrikaners had made in the previous two decades.[44]

---

42 *Ibid.*, p.186.
43 Rhoodie and Venter, *Apartheid*, p.30.
44 Hermann Giliomee, "The Growth of Afrikaner Identity", in Beinart and Dubow, *Segregation and Apartheid*, pp.200-203.

Does this mean that white Afrikaners were ultimately not so much concerned about their racial or national identity as about the basic matter of self-preservation? This suggests a rather instrumentalist view of apartheid – that the policy helped to forge Afrikaner unity, which in turn was the best means of ensuring Afrikaner survival and advancement. Thus apartheid was, according to this line of analysis, in large part a product of fear – the fear of racial 'others', the fear of being swamped in the cities, the fear of competition in the labour market, the fear of cultural norms being overturned. Even some defenders of apartheid have conceded that an instinct for self-preservation was at the root of apartheid[45] – a view which has some resonance across the historiographical spectrum, congruent with both idealist and materialist perspectives.

Much has been written on the ideology, policy and practice of apartheid. Some recent work, written in a postmodernist vein, has examined the discourse of apartheid. Aletta Norval focusses on the surface of apartheid, believing that attempts to probe beneath that surface are misguided. She takes as 'problematic attempts to account for apartheid by searching for an essence hidden from view, for such attempts tend to be bewitched by a metaphysical illusion of depth'. The object of her investigation is rather 'the discourse of apartheid: the multifarious practices and rituals, verbal and non-verbal, through which a certain sense of reality and understanding of the nature of society were constituted and maintained'.[46] It was a discourse that served to shape Afrikaners' identity in relation to others, and to represent apartheid as normal, just and moral. The discourse was particularly appealing to Afrikaners experiencing dislocation and insecurity at a time of social and economic upheaval during the 1940s. It enabled them to make sense of what was happening around them.[47]

Norval's application of Derrida's and Foucault's theoretical approaches to an analysis of apartheid has some value. She shows how the discourse of apartheid came to resonate among white Afrikaners. However, she too readily dismisses revisionist, materialist analysis for its reductionism. And her insistence on examining the surface features of apartheid means that we are given few new insights into the nature and dynamic of South Africa's racial order. Her interpretation is cast in a different style of language and is derived from theoretical work not previously applied to the study of apartheid, but one

---

45 Rhoodie and Venter, *Apartheid*, pp.34-36.
46 Aletta J. Norval, *Deconstructing Apartheid Discourse* (London, 1996), p.2.
47 *Ibid.*, pp.5, 51-52.

has the sense that she is stating in a different way what has been said before by writers like Dubow and Posel.

Norval's work follows a postmodernist trend which is highly critical of materialist approaches to history because of their essentialism and tendency to totalise the past. South Africanist social historians in the 1980s criticised the 1970s revisionists for their economic reductionism and rigid structuralism. In recent years postmodernists have taken that critique further. So why was it that the Marxist analysis of apartheid came to draw such strong criticism? We must now turn our attention to examining some of the main revisionist interpretations of apartheid.

Two crucial interventions were made by Wolpe and Legassick in the early 1970s. Wolpe dismissed out of hand the idealist assumption that apartheid was an expression of racial ideology. He also argued that apartheid should not be seen as 'a simple extension of segregation'.[48] His own argument centred on the function of the reserves in the changing capitalist economy of twentieth century South Africa. In the early decades of the century the reserves had performed the function of subsidising the capitalist sector, particularly the mining industry, because they provided, through rural subsistence production, supplementary income for the families of migrant labourers and therefore reduced the cost of that labour. The policy of segregation had by and large provided a political structure that enabled the reserves to fulfil that function. However, it was also becoming apparent, from as early as the 1920s, that the reserve economies were rapidly deteriorating so that they would be less and less able to perform the function of subsidising the cost of migrant labour. Thus, in Wolpe's view, apartheid was developed specifically in response to changing economic and social conditions – the collapse of the reserves, the accelerating rate of African urbanisation, and the growth of African militancy and protest from the 1940s. Apartheid was marked by a strengthening of the state's coercive apparatus and by a shift towards the policy of 'separate development' based on the bantustan system.[49] This was still 'centrally concerned, as in the past, with the control and supply of a cheap labour force, *but in a new form*'.[50] Whereas the reserves had once functioned to supplement the wages of the migrant labour force, under apartheid they became instruments of control used by the capitalist state to enforce low levels of subsistence on the African labour force. Rising

---

48   Harold Wolpe, "Capitalism and cheap labour-power in South Africa: from segregation to apartheid", *Economy and Society*, 1, 4, 1972, p.453.
49   *Ibid.*, pp.432-33, 439-41, 445-46.
50   *Ibid.*, p.448.

state coercion, the use of lackeys in the bantustan bureaucracy, the policy of industrial decentralisation, the Bantu education system, and the ideological shift from straight white supremacism ('*baaskap*') to ethnic differentiation ('separate development') were those features of apartheid that served to sustain the exploitation of cheap labour under changing social and economic conditions.[51]

Legassick's analysis of apartheid also proceeds within a materialist framework. Like Wolpe he examines changing economic conditions in South Africa in the middle decades of the twentieth century. But whereas Wolpe highlights the collapse of the reserves, Legassick stresses the rise of secondary industry. The growth of manufacturing created policy dilemmas as this sector required more skilled labour than mining or farming, and skilled industrial labour would normally be permanently urbanised. This was the dilemma for policy-makers: perpetuate the migrant labour system, which would have its disadvantages for manufacturing industry, or change the direction of policy and recognise a permanent urban African presence? In reality the choice was not as stark as this. It was more a matter of degree. The NP government, as we have seen, rejected the possibility of 'total apartheid' as an immediate policy option, recognising that there would be a continuing dependence on African labour. So the government tried to devise mechanisms whereby African labour could be secured without increasing the permanent presence of Africans in urban areas. One such device was the policy of industrial decentralisation – offering incentives to industrialists to locate their business in 'border areas' close to a bantustan so that African workers could live in the bantustan and still sell their labour to industry in 'white' South Africa. This, in Legassick's view, was one function of the bantustans in the apartheid era. At the same time the 'separate development' policy was a means of shifting to the bantustans both the problem of African unemployment and the burden of providing social welfare for those entitled to it.[52]

In the 1970s Wolpe and Legassick provided the two seminal revisionist interpretations of apartheid. They have been much debated ever since. Both have been criticised for being too narrowly economistic – for analysing apartheid too exclusively in terms of its economic function, and for neglecting its ideological, political and psychological dimensions. More specifically critics have suggested that Wolpe's emphasis on the changing

---

51 *Ibid.*, pp.450-53.
52 Legassick, "Legislation, Ideology and Economy", pp.14-17, 28-29.

state and role of the reserves does not hold. His thesis implies that policy-makers had an extraordinary awareness both of the economy's labour needs and the state of the reserves, and, what is more, were able to perform a delicate balancing act whereby the reserves would be sufficiently impoverished so as to continue to drive out workers into the labour market, but not so impoverished that they could no longer fulfil their function of providing subsistence for the families of migrant labourers. This kind of calculation could hardly have dictated the policy shift from segregation to apartheid, not the least because it overestimates the prescience of policy-makers.

The kind of analysis offered by Wolpe and Legassick has gone out of fashion in recent years. But it must be stressed that their work, and that of others, was pioneering and full of insight. At this time when historians are paying more attention to the history of ideas and culture than to material forces, it is worth reasserting the fundamental point that one cannot properly understand any historical process if it is removed from its economic context. So it is with apartheid. In order to explain the policy shifts of the 1950s and 1960s one has to look carefully at changing socio-economic conditions – the related processes of industrialisation and urbanisation, the decline of the reserves, and the growth of black protest and resistance. Analysts across the ideological spectrum, even those critical of historical materialism, whether conservative, liberal or postmodernist, have often acknowledged this fundamental point. Most writers who have attempted to explain apartheid have placed some emphasis on the growth of African urbanisation in the 1940s and the consequent rising insecurity felt by many whites. One must avoid the pitfall of economism – trying to explain everything in economic terms. But any historical explanation that ignores material forces will be inadequate.

Also unsatisfactory is any interpretation that represents South Africa's racial order as monolithic or unchanging. Apartheid was a complex phenomenon. It was riddled with internal contradictions. These posed enormous problems for policy-makers and the perpetrators of the abhorrent system. White supremacists may have agreed on the overall principle of racial domination, but the form of that domination was debated and contested among the supremacists themselves – not just between different political parties like the NP and UP, but also within the NP itself. In the 1950s and 1960s there was the debate between the 'total apartheid' visionaries and the pragmatists. By the 1980s the brand of pragmatism associated with Verwoerd was being questioned by a group within the NP, the so-called 'verligtes', who wanted pragmatism extended even further so that the racial order could be adapted to accommodate changing political and economic circumstances.

Apartheid was at one level a thoroughly rigid system of racial domination. It must have seemed as such to its victims; and many observers and commentators have represented it in this way. Yet close analysis reveals the contradictions within the apartheid order – contradictions that prevented apartheid from every being the smoothly functioning system that it appeared to be. One fundamental contradiction was between, on the one hand, segregation and racial exclusion at the political level, and, on the other, integration in the economic sphere. This contradiction lay at the heart of the debate between the apartheid 'visionaries' and the pragmatists. The 'visionaries' wished to eliminate the contradiction by bringing about economic segregation, to correspond with political segregation. The pragmatists believed that economic segregation would be impracticable, involving too many costs and sacrifices for the capitalist sector and white society. The pragmatists mostly had their way.

Once the 'total apartheid' vision had been abandoned this contradiction would become more and more evident, especially in the cities and towns. Although urban areas were racially divided according to group areas principles, the capitalist economy's dependence on black labour made clear the reality of economic integration in the urban industrial sphere. Successive NP governments tried to manage this contradiction and limit its consequences. Influx control was one key mechanism through which the state tried to limit the African urban presence according to the labour needs of any particular area. But this kind of balancing was impossible to achieve. Influx control required massive policing. Although millions of people were arrested under the pass laws, especially during the 1960s and 1970s, millions more evaded or resisted the system. As the bantustans became ever more impoverished so the incentive to defy influx control and migrate to the city became greater.

Industrial decentralisation was another mechanism developed in an effort to resolve this contradiction. The border industry policy would enable Africans to live in a bantustan and commute daily to their workplace in a border area of 'white' South Africa. This was a policy that might, it was thought, go some way towards realising the fuller apartheid vision. However, few industrialists were drawn to the border areas. And some major industrial centres – Johannesburg, Cape Town, Port Elizabeth, for instance – were too far removed from bantustans to make daily commuting practicable. Other devices were utilised in an attempt to resolve the contradiction. In some urban areas existing African townships were relocated at the stroke of a pen, by redrawing boundaries, from 'white' South Africa into a bantustan – as was the case with the Durban townships of Umlazi and KwaMashu, which were 're-situated' in KwaZulu in 1977.

Ultimately the contradiction was unresolvable. From the 1970s successive NP governments became more aware of this. This awareness, together with growing internal resistance, escalating international pressure, and steady economic decline, led these governments to resort to more and more pragmatic measures, tinkering with apartheid in an effort to stave off some of these pressures while still maintaining the system of racial domination. The tinkering took various forms. There was acknowledgement of the reality of economic integration in the late 1970s when job reservation was abolished and black trade unions were legalised. Social apartheid was relaxed, albeit at times in the most tortuous ways. Mixed sport was permitted on certain conditions in an effort to break out of international sporting isolation. In the 1980s the segregation of university education was gradually broken down. The ban on mixed marriages ended in 1985. At the political level there was an attempt to incorporate coloureds and Indians into the national political system through the tricameral constitution, which came into operation in 1984.

It is common to refer to 'the apartheid era', but it was not a single phase in the history of the South African racial order. In terms of my four-dimensional conceptualisation of racism, that racial order reached its zenith in the 1960s. Racial ideology, complemented by an ethnic discourse, was formally and unashamedly articulated by white power-holders in their effort to legitimate and reinforce white supremacy. Racial consciousness, authorised by the state and promoted by the media, became normalised, naturalised in the mindset of most whites. Similarly by the 1960s the South African racial order had become more institutionalised, more entrenched, than ever before. Racial discrimination and segregation was everywhere, pervasive throughout South African society. There was scarcely scope for the third dimension of racism, informal racial practice, because so many aspects of human interaction were shaped and constrained by formalised racial legislation.

Yet in the later phase of what is called the apartheid era – from the 1970s – the racial order changed character. State policy and official propaganda came to rest less and less on the articulation of racial ideology, and more and more on a discourse of survival. Ethnic difference superseded racial superiority in apartheid's legitimating discourse. And as South Africa became an increasingly embattled, besieged pariah state during the 1970s and 1980s, trying to withstand international pressure and internal resistance, the ideology of race largely disappeared from official propaganda, giving way to the idea of the 'total onslaught' – the concerted, communist-inspired, international assault on South Africa's political and economic order. Similarly during the later years of apartheid the institutionalised racial order weakened. Although all-pervasive the formalisation of racial segregation never went far enough in the direction of 'total apartheid' to overcome the internal contradictions of the system. Because successive apartheid governments always stopped short of 'total apartheid' they were never able to resolve the fundamental contradiction between racialised political separation and the reality of economic integration. This contradiction, together with internal resistance and international pressure, eroded the apartheid system. In response to this erosion the apartheid state slowly began to dismantle the institutionalised racial order from the late 1970s, at the same time trying to ensure that power remained in white hands – some called this 'modernising racial domination'. Policy-making became ever more pragmatic, designed to deal with short-term problems and pressures. As this trend continued so did the internal logic of apartheid evaporate. There was no longer an apartheid policy for the NP's supporters to believe in – only a set of arrangements that could secure white middle-class interests as best as possible. Those whites who still believed in a system of racial differentiation, and those who stood to lose most from the end of apartheid, joined far-right parties and organisations. For the new NP pragmatists like F.W. de Klerk the pressure of circumstances by the late 1980s was forcing their participation in a negotiated settlement. In 1994 the apartheid era formally ended, although the awful legacy of the system would continue to be felt for generations to come. No longer would the political and social order be formally structured along racial lines. But how long would it take to reduce, let along eradicate, the massive inequalities that had characterised that order for so many decades?

PART III:

CONCLUSION

7 South Africa's Racial Order: Historiographical and Historical Reflections

The task of historical reflection is inevitably coloured by the standpoint in time from which it is attempted and by the context in which it is undertaken. Six years after the demise of the NP apartheid government what historical perspectives on the South African racial order now provide the best analytical leverage? Some might say that we are not sufficiently removed in time to hit upon any particularly deep insights. After all, white racism is still very much a live issue in the public domain – as I write, newspaper editors are being summoned before the national Human Rights Commission to answer charges of racism. Only when the legacy of the past has been thrown off and South African society has become more fully deracialised, it might be argued, can the country's racial past be subject to a more sober, refined analysis. Such a view is altogether too rarefied. The present moment – a time of grappling with the country's ugly past, of dealing with the legacy of apartheid, of tackling ongoing racism – calls for historical analysis. In the day-to-day jostling for power and advancement the phenomenon of racism can be too easily reduced to crude rhetoric or bland assumptions – tendencies to which racists themselves have been so prone. The charge of racism is constantly being levelled at individuals and institutions: a charge that invariably draws a defensive reaction – given the country's history nobody today wants to be labelled racist. The charge can be used as a weapon against the former oppressor. In such a climate, where accusations of racism can generate heated exchanges, the phenomenon needs to be subjected to greater conceptual refinement and to careful historical analysis.

This study has been part-historiographical and part-historical (what is the difference between the two, some may ask?). Reflection on both dimensions is called for. The historiography of South African racism is of mixed quality. Much of it is based on assertion, unsubstantiated premise, or on ideas borrowed unquestioningly from previous writers. It is surprising how little careful, thorough research has been undertaken into the history of South Africa's racial order, particularly for the pre-1900 era. The most fruitful explorations occurred in a brief phase from the late 1970s to the mid-1980s –

the work of Elphick, Giliomee, Fredrickson and Ross. Before that rich historiographical phase much of the writing on South African racism had either been based on questionable assumptions or had lacked any solid empirical foundation. It had also tended to be ideologically loaded or paradigm-bound. Many writers were stuck in a mould, tied to a fixed concept of race and to rigid notions of racial difference, racial division and racial conflict. Others reacted so vehemently against this particular approach that they themselves became captive to an opposing class-based paradigm. Moreover, much of the earlier empirical research failed to move beyond the surface features of the racial order – the legislation, the institutional segregation, the overt forms of discrimination.

Since the 1980s interesting work on aspects of the racial order has been produced, but at the same time the theme has lost its historiographical salience. As one writer, Aletta Norval, has argued, 'The race-class debate between liberals and neo-Marxists ... seems antiquated from the point of view of theoretical developments in the 1980s and 1990s associated with the rubrics of post-structuralism, deconstruction and post-coloniality'.[1] This is too ready a dismissal of earlier analyses. Notwithstanding the rigidity of positions adopted in the race-class debate there are insights to be gleaned from the two contesting perspectives. They cannot just be discarded as 'antiquated'; and it remains to be seen whether 'post-theory' has significantly advanced our understanding of South Africa's racial past. All this suggests a need for the various historiographical tendencies to be subjected to reflection and overview – which will now be attempted.

In an earlier chapter the history of racial theory in the nineteenth century was briefly traced. This theory influenced historical writing about South Africa's racial order, more particularly a tradition of writing often labelled eurocentric. G.M. Theal was the founding father of this tradition – a prolific writer who produced numerous historical texts on South Africa from the 1870s up till his death in 1919. Theal's work is riddled with racist stereotypes representing blacks as barbarians with a natural propensity for thieving and warfare. At the same time Theal portrayed white colonisers as the bearers of order, progress and civilisation. His ideas about race were fairly standard in the European world at the time he was writing. He believed that humankind was divided into distinct racial groups, each demarcated from the others, there being a clear correlation of physical type and culture. Theal also slipped into the common assumption that there existed a racial hierarchy, at the bottom of

---

[1] Norval, *Deconstructing Apartheid Discourse*, p.59.

which were Bushmen hunter-gatherers, with African farmers only a few rungs higher.[2] These assumptions permeated Theal's work, and they obviated any need for him to try to explain the racial order. In his view that order was given, natural. It went without saying that whites were superior and blacks inferior; so power relations reflected what he saw as that basic fact. Theal's historiographical legacy was powerful. Generations of historians were influenced by his writing, sharing his assumptions. He was to have a particularly strong influence on Afrikaner nationalist historians.[3]

Saul Dubow has noted that 'Afrikaner nationalism was markedly slow to address directly the relationship between black and white South Africans'.[4] It was only from the 1930s that leading Afrikaner thinkers began to examine that relationship. When they did so they operated within a rigid racial pluralist framework. The existence and salience of racial categories went unquestioned. Racial groups were perceived as biological entities, and the distinctive character of each group was taken for granted. This basic assumption was propounded in the 1930s and 1940s by such writers as Badenhorst, Preller, Eloff and Cronjé – with Eloff even going so far as to define Afrikaners themselves as a separate biological race group.[5] As late as 1959 Du Preez was still able to proclaim '... it is an undeniable fact that racial differences actually exist, whether we can explain them or not. The Bantu and White man in South Africa belong to two different racial groups with distinctive and immutable racial characteristics'.[6] The proponents of this view drew upon both science and theology to back their claim. Preller, for instance, writing in the late 1930s, referred to scientific analysis which was 'gradually discovering the remarkable physiological differences between the brain of the white man ... and that of the Bantu – differences which are innate and constitute the measure of their respective intellectual capacities'.[7] Cronjé and Du Preez, among others, saw racial differences as divinely ordained, as part of God's creation.[8]

---

2   Saunders, *Making of the South African Past*, pp.26-34; Ken Smith, *The Changing Past* (Johannesburg, 1988), pp.36-39.
3   Saunders, *Making of the South African Past*, pp.41-43.
4   Dubow, *Illicit Union*, pp.248-49.
5   *Ibid.*, p.273; F.G. Badenhorst, *Die Rassevraagstuk* (Amsterdam, 1939), pp.14, 20; Gustav Preller, *Day-Dawn in South Africa* (Pretoria, 1938), pp.149-51; G. Cronjé, *Voogdyskap en Apartheid* (Pretoria, 1948), p.31.
6   A.B. Du Preez, *Inside the South African Crucible* (Pretoria, 1959), p.41.
7   Preller, *Day-Dawn*, pp.149-50.
8   J.M. Coetzee, "The Mind of Apartheid: Geoffrey Cronjé (1907-)", *Social Dynamics*, 17, 1, 1991, p.9; Du Preez, *South African Crucible*, pp.56,85.

This assumption had various implications. One was that there was no real need to explain, sociologically or historically, South Africa's racial order. Racial groups were deemed to be natural components of human society – as natural a component as the family. Race consciousness and a sense of identity with one's own race group was therefore equally a natural part of the human make-up. The race instinct was normal, and a consciousness that was not race-consciousness was deemed to be false.[9] This meant that the historical foundations of South Africa's racial order were taken for granted – racial separation was a natural process, in keeping with God's will.[10] Later there was a departure from this assumption among Afrikaner nationalist writers. By the late 1950s Rhoodie and Venter, two apologists for apartheid, were bemoaning the fact that, apart from Cronjé's writings, there was not 'a single work which gives a reasonably detailed socio-historical or fundamental exposition of apartheid'.[11] So from this time these old assumptions about racial difference came to be taken less for granted among Afrikaner nationalists, and attempts were made to explain the country's racial order in historical terms.

While there may have been a shift away from the crude primordialist assumptions of an earlier generation of Afrikaner nationalist writers, those who attempted to explain the racial order in historical terms still remained firmly tied to an idealist line of analysis. Central to this historical explanation were some key ideas. Foremost was the notion that the history of the boers/Dutch/Afrikaners should be read as a long struggle to protect their racial/national identity. Rhoodie and Venter, for instance, wrote of the Afrikaners' particular 'moral characteristics', based on Afrikaners' 'determination to preserve their racial identity and an inherent realisation of the 'difference' between themselves and the non-Whites'.[12] But there was more to it than simply protecting their identity. Other Afrikaner nationalist historians came to represent the history of the 'volk' as a history of sheer survival, suggesting that historical experience and the force of circumstance did much to shape boer racial attitudes from the nineteenth century. The voortrekkers who migrated into the South African interior after 1836, so the argument went, did not develop a race policy but rather engaged in a

---

9   Coetzee, "Geoffrey Cronjé", p.12.
10 Johannes du Bruyn, "Swartes in die Afrikanergeskiedskrywing", in H.C. Bredekamp (ed), *Afrikaanse Geskiedskrywing en Letterkunde: Verlede, Hede, en Toekoms* (Bellville, 1992), pp.72-73.
11 Rhoodie and Venter, *Apartheid*, p.6.
12 *Ibid.*, p.49.

straightforward struggle for survival. This was a quest for security which could only be achieved through the military subjugation of blacks, as well as their political exclusion and territorial separation. Thus security and survival became linked to the 'race question'. As one historian, Moolman, put it, for the boers in the nineteenth century the daily fight for survival became a racial fight.[13] In later Afrikaner nationalist historical writing attention was also paid to the development of racial attitudes. It was argued that virtually from the beginning of white colonisation at the Cape in the mid-seventeenth century the early Dutch colonists saw indigenous people as uncivilised and inferior. Three days after landing at the Cape Van Riebeeck referred to the indigenous Khoi people as 'wild' and 'brutal'.[14] According to this interpretation such attitudes soon became widely held among the white community. Because people of colour were deemed to be uncivilised and inferior it was therefore appropriate for them to be enslaved. A circular argument then developed: people of colour were inferior and therefore naturally servile – their enslavement and servitude confirmed their inferiority. When the trekboers came into contact with African communities on the eastern frontier in the late eighteenth century white racial attitudes strengthened. Contact with Xhosa chiefdoms, so the argument continued, seemed to reinforce the developing image of Africans as treacherous and savage. Thus in the minds of the early Dutch/boer colonists Christianity and civilisation came to be associated with whiteness, while heathenism and barbarism were equated with blackness.[15]

Racial segregation could therefore be represented by Afrikaner nationalist historians as the logical consequence of these different levels of civilisation. According to Van Jaarsveld, because whites regarded themselves as civilised and Christian and saw blacks as uncivilised and heathen, the idea and practice of race differentiation came into being.[16] Moolman argued that the difference in the levels of civilisation made political equality and social contact between white and black impossible.[17] And so it was easy for Afrikaner nationalist historians to claim that racial segregation developed

---

13   J.P.F. Moolman, "Die Boer se Siening van en Houding Teenoor die Bantoe in Transvaal tot 1860" (unpublished MA thesis, University of Pretoria, 1975), p.14. Se also G.D. Scholtz, *Die Ontwikkeling van die Politieke Denke van die Afrikaner: Deel II 1806-1854* (Johannesburg, 1970), pp.398, 401 and *Deel III 1854-1881*, pp.223, 228.
14   Moolman, "Die Boer se Siening", p.7.
15   *Ibid.*, pp.2, 7, 13, 16-17, 33, 35, 101; Scholtz, *Deel I 1652-1806* (Johannesburg, 1967), pp.206, 216-19, and *Deel II 1806-1854*, pp.213-14; F.A. Van Jaarsveld, *Die Evolusie van Apartheid* (Cape Town, 1979), p.3.
16   Van Jaarsveld, *Die Evolusie van Apartheid*, p.5.
17   Moolman, "Die Boer se Siening", pp.80-81.

naturally out of the historical relations between Dutch/boers/Afrikaners and indigenous communities.[18] Moreover, racial segregation was represented not only as logical and natural, but also as divinely ordained. In the nationalist version of South African history the boers were driven by devout Calvinist beliefs – by the idea that they were a chosen people, with a special calling. Any idea of black-white equality would have contravened the word of God – blacks were pre-ordained to serve whites.[19]

Afrikaner nationalist historical interpretations of South Africa's racial order display a few fundamental features. First, they fall within a crude pluralist framework. Racial difference was deemed to be a basic element of South African society and history. In its most raw form, as expressed in the 1930s and 1940s, this pluralist approach rested on the premise that races were distinct biological categories, and on the primordialist assumption that a strong sense of racial identity was an ingrained human instinct. Thus South Africa's racial order could be taken for granted, assumed to be part of the natural order of things. Such thinking was not at the time some bizarre South African aberration. It was a paradigm that enjoyed broad acceptance and legitimacy. As Saxton has remarked,

> Until about the third decade of the present century, most people in the so-called western world, including most social scientists and historians, took for granted the hereditary inferiority of non-white peoples. Differential treatment required no special explanation so long as it could be understood as a rational response to objective reality ... .[20]

Some of the early Afrikaner proponents of racial theory studied during the 1930s in Germany where Nazi ideas about race were gaining adherence.[21]

A later generation of Afrikaner nationalist writers moved away somewhat from these cruder racial theories, but still remained solidly within a basic pluralist, idealist paradigm. Attempts were now made to explain racial differentiation and segregation through recourse, not to racial science, but to

---

18 Du Bruyn, "Afrikanergeskiedskrywing", p.72.
19 Moolman, "Die Boer se Siening", pp.15, 23, 79, 83; F.A. Van Jaarsveld, *The Afrikaner's Interpretation of South African History* (Cape Town, 1964), pp.5-6. For a refutation of this view see A. du Toit, "No Chosen People: The Myth of the Calvinist Origin of Afrikaner Nationalism and Racial Ideology", *American Historical Review*, 88, 1983.
20 Alexander Saxton, *The Rise and Fall of the White Republic* (London, 1990), p.2.
21 Dubow, *Illicit Union*, pp.255, 270; Albert Grundlingh, "Politics, Principles and Problems of a Profession: Afrikaner Historians and their Discipline, c.1920-c.1965", *Perspectives in Education*, 12, 1, 1990, p.9.

history. Even so, the existence of distinct racial categories still went unquestioned; and it continued to be assumed that a sense of identification with one's race and nation was a key force motivating human behaviour – and, therefore, also a crucial factor explaining the course of South African history.

There was, of course, a strong ideological dimension to Afrikaner nationalist historical writing. Many of these historians claimed that they were producing 'objective-scientific' work in the Rankean tradition,[22] but in reality they were writing history to promote Afrikaner nationalism and to justify apartheid. Whereas the earlier generation of writers in the 1930s had had it somewhat easier in terms of the international acceptability of their ideas, however crude those ideas now seem, the later generation was engaged in an uphill battle. Amidst the post-war reaction against Nazism racial theory came to be widely discredited. From the 1950s African decolonisation proceeded apace. South Africa's apartheid policies flew in the face of the changing international order. Apartheid's apologists thus drew upon South African history to make their case. It was important that apartheid be represented, not as a crazy piece of National Party social engineering, but rather as a product of the country's past, as the culmination of a long evolutionary process of racial differentiation going back to the first days of white settlement, and therefore as a phenomenon that was 'traditional' to South Africa, a special feature of the country's unique character.[23]

Some have questioned whether one can talk of a 'liberal' school of South Africanist historians. However, during a period of four or more decades from the late 1920s there appeared a body of writing, produced by historians and social scientists, that investigated and analysed South Africa's racial order on the basis of key underlying ideas and premises. There were variations in these ideas from writer to writer, but there was also a common overall framework that enables one to view these works as a body of writing. This framework was essentially pluralist, and it was one that enjoyed a considerable degree of hegemony in South African historical discourse during these decades.

---

22   Grundlingh, "Afrikaner Historians", p.1.
23   It is worth noting that some Afrikaner nationalist writers found it necessary, particularly from the late 1950s when South Africa faced mounting international criticism, to produce work in English – in an attempt partly to appease international opinion and partly to win support from white English-speaking voters in South Africa. See, for instance, Du Preez, *South African Crucible*, and Rhoodie and Venter, *Apartheid*.

When liberal pluralist writers set about trying to explain the origins and evolution of the South African racial order they did so, of course, with a different political agenda from the Afrikaner nationalists. While the latter were trying to justify a system of racial differentiation, the former were striving for interracial cooperation and harmony. However, what is striking is the degree to which the two shared similar assumptions about South African society and history. Although each drew different conclusions and lessons from their study of the country's past, both proceeded from similar premises.

The single most important shared assumption was that racial categories could be viewed as fundamental realities of South African society, that relations between different racial and ethnic groups have been the central theme in South African history, and that those relations have been characterised by a high level of antagonism and conflict. By the 1950s and 1960s this assumption had come to pervade the literature on South African society and history. Marquard, for instance, in his brief survey of South African history, wrote that by 1700 'the three main elements of South Africa's population were present, European, African, and Coloured'.[24] These were the crucial categories in attempting to explain South Africa's past. For Van der Horst the census classification of South Africa's population into four major groups was 'not simply a statistical abstraction or a legal classification but a social reality'.[25] Perhaps the chief exponent of pluralist analysis in the South African case was Van den Berghe, who described South Africa as 'one of the world's most pluralistic societies'.[26] For him the deepest cleavage was the racial one, accompanied by significant cultural divisions and a general absence of value consensus among different groups.[27] His view of South Africa was asserted unequivocally: 'The only principle which pervades the whole society is that of "race" ...'.[28]

From this premise, that South Africa has long been a racially polarised society, there followed logically a further assumption – that racial division had, throughout South African history, given rise to racial conflict. Marquard stated this assumption explicitly: 'The history of South Africa is the story of strife between the various groups composing the political union ... Until 1910, when Union was established, the story is one of war between tribe and tribe,

---

24 Marquard, *Peoples and Policies of South Africa*, p.2.
25 Sheila Van der Horst, "The effects of industrialisation on race relations in South Africa", in Guy Hunter (ed.), *Industrialisation and Race Relations* (London, 1965), pp.99-100.
26 Pierre Van den Berghe, *Race and Ethnicity* (New York, 1970), p.81.
27 *Ibid.*, p.83; Van den Berghe, *South Africa*, p.38.
28 Van den Berghe, *South Africa*, p.72.

between black and white, and between English and Afrikaner'.[29] For Van den Berghe relations between South Africa's four main 'racial castes' were 'based mostly on conflict'.[30] Conflict was deemed to be the natural outcome of racial division. It was further assumed that one of the sources of conflict was white race prejudice. From the early days of white settlement, so the story goes, whites developed a strong racial identity and sense of superiority over racial 'others'. From white racism flowed many evils – labour exploitation, land-grabbing, and a host of discriminatory measures against people of colour. In Van den Berghe's view white race prejudice was, and had long been, South Africa's fundamental problem: 'At the very root of the "South African Dilemma",' he claimed, 'lies White racialism'.[31] Take away this and the course of South African history would have been very different: 'Had it not been for the development of a strong form of racial ... prejudice, South Africa could have developed into the same type of harmonious society, racially mixed and culturally Western, as is found in Latin America'.[32]

Not all writers belonging to this 'liberal' school saw race prejudice as being endemic from the very beginning of white settlement. As we have seen, there was debate among historians as to whether racism originated in Europe or developed in the particular conditions of South Africa. Some argued that racism was brought to the Cape from Europe by the Dutch.[33] Others stressed the colonial rather than metropolitan sources of white racism. Among the latter historians there were further differences. Some traced the origins of racism to Van Riebeeck, arguing that attitudes of white superiority developed from the 1650s. Others argued that the main cleavage in the early years of white settlement at the Cape was not racial, but religious – between Christian and non-Christian. Rather was the era of white frontier expansion, argued Walker and MacCrone, the crucial phase in the emergence of South Africa's racial order, because the racist attitudes that developed in the frontier environment were later carried over into the twentieth century – and so formed the basis of segregation and apartheid.[34]

---

29 Marquard, *Peoples and Policies*, p.32.
30 Van den Berghe, *South Africa*, p.267. See also K.L. Roskam, *Apartheid and Discrimination* (Leyden, 1960), p.9. It should, though, be recognised that not all liberal scholars stressed the conflictual nature of South African history – some focused on instances of interracial cooperation during the country's past.
31 Van den Berghe, *South Africa*, p.245.
32 *Ibid.*, p.41.
33 See above, chapter 1.
34 Walker, *Frontier Tradition in South Africa*, pp.7, 12, 22-24; MacCrone, *Race Attitudes*, pp.98-101, 109, 135-36. A number of other historians and social scientists adopted this

Liberal pluralist writing on South Africa stressed not only the racial cleavage and conflict between white and black, but also ethnic divisions. One such division deemed to be important historically was that between the English and the Afrikaners. In the view of many liberal writers this division reflected, at least in part, different degrees of racism, with the boers/Afrikaners deemed to be generally more racist than English-speaking colonists – and therefore more blameworthy for segregation and apartheid. It has been common to refer to two traditions of race relations in South Africa: the northern tradition of the nineteenth century boer republics, characterised by harsh race prejudice and rigid discrimination – a tradition which is contrasted with the Cape liberal tradition, supposedly less discriminatory and more open to assimilationism and interracial cooperation.[35]

This dichotomisation is seriously flawed. It is now well-known that the contribution of white English-speaking colonists and British imperial officialdom to the making of South Africa's racial order has been no less significant than that of the Dutch/boers/Afrikaners. It is also ironical that this idea of a distinction between two traditions should have been propounded by historians and social scientists who shared many of the premises and assumptions of Afrikaner nationalists when it came to explaining South African history and society. Both Afrikaner nationalist and liberal writers operated within the broad paradigm of racial pluralism, assuming race groups to be real categories and discrete entities, and deeming racial cleavages to be the primary divisions in South African society. Both, too, developed their analyses in the idealist tradition, stressing the significance of racial and ethnic consciousness as a major factor in South African history, and presuming political objectives to have been primary, while generally neglecting economic interests. According to both schools South Africa's racial order had deep roots in the country's past and evolved over a long period of time from the early colonial era.

Although both schools proceeded within a similar framework they were driven by different political agendas. Whereas Afrikaner nationalists were trying to present a view of South Africa's history that would legitimate both apartheid and Afrikaner nationalism, liberals were striving to promote

---

"frontier thesis" which was still being propounded in the 1950s and 1960s. See, for instance, Van den Berghe, *South Africa*, pp.23-24, and Patterson, *The Last Trek*, pp.9-11, 17-19.

35 Walker, *Frontier Tradition*, p.8; Marquard, *Peoples and Policies*, pp.14-16; Van der Horst, "Effects of industrialisation", pp.105-106; Ralph Horwitz, *The Political Economy of South Africa* (New York, 1967), pp.10-11.

interracial cooperation and individualist values. The liberal view of South African history gained ground from the 1930s. Before the 1930s a number of liberal thinkers in South Africa had supported segregationist polices as the best means to ensure social and political stability in South Africa.[36] However from the early 1930s liberals steadily moved away from segregationism. This was largely because they saw that greater economic and social integration was becoming a reality of South African life, and that a policy of racial segregation flew in the face of that reality. So they came to argue that the country's socio-political system should be amended along more liberal lines so as to adapt to this reality. Its failure to adapt, they believed, was largely the result of the ingrained, archaic, racist attitudes of most whites. As Van der Horst put it,

> Yet while economic forces have been drawing black and white together, social and political adaptation on the part of the dominant white group has not kept pace. There has been a constant attempt by the whites to retain the benefits of economic integration and yet to insist upon a large measure of social and geographic segregation; to retain a monopoly of political power ... .[37]

As part of their effort to promote interracial cooperation and harmony some liberal writers argued that South Africa's past had been marked not only by racial division and conflict. These writers drew attention to past interracial cooperation, trying to downplay the emphasis on conflict.[38]

How was it that liberal writers came to pin the responsibility for segregation and apartheid on to the boers/Afrikaners? This tendency became more pronounced in the 1950s and 1960s – for the fairly obvious reason that during these decades the Afrikaner-dominated National Party government was tightening its system of racial discrimination and oppression at the very time when racism was being reviled in international circles. In this context it became much easier to represent boers/Afrikaners as the chief proponents of racist thought and practice throughout South African history. In the eighteenth and nineteenth centuries the Enlightenment, it was argued, had passed by isolated, inward-looking boer communities. Similarly, in the second half of the twentieth century narrow-minded Afrikaners shut themselves off from the international trend towards liberalisation and deracialisation. It was not just a political agenda that shaped the liberal

---

36 See Dubow, *Racial Segregation*, pp.21-45.
37 Van der Horst, "Effects of industrialisation", p.101.
38 Saunders, *Making of the South African Past*, pp.95-96.

idealist approach to South African history. Idealists were working within a paradigm that enjoyed a degree of hegemony in western social science circles at that time, especially in the USA. A social psychologist recently recalled how his 'work of the 1950s was still largely conducted within the theoretical frame that dominated race relations research during the decade. That frame involved an emphasis on attitudes and stereotypes while paying scant attention to the macroinstitutional level of analysis ...'.[39]

Pluralist analysis, 1950s-style, now seems antiquated and simplistic. The preoccupation with 'race' and 'race relations' may have been understandable in the aftermath of World War Two. The ugly, brutish racial theories that had come to the fore during the 1930s and 1940s needed to be countered and demolished. However, liberals fought back on the same terrain, shackled by the concept and discourse of race. Their approach was informed by too easy a categorisation of races; they too readily correlated race and culture; they failed to pay sufficient attention to cross-cutting class divisions. And they clung on to the dream that the South African racial order could be reformed away if the country's white leaders would see the light, 'move with the times', and step into the second half of the twentieth century. During the 1960s it became more and more obvious that this was not going to happen. A different political strategy, accompanied by a fresh line of analysis, was required. This came in the 1970s.

It was fifty years ago that Oliver Cox suggested that 'The interest behind racial antagonism is an exploitative interest – the peculiar type of economic exploitation characteristic of capitalist society'.[40] It was not to be for another twenty years or more before this idea gained significant or widespread application to the South African case. But when the analysis of racial oppression in South Africa did come to be based on this premise, the idea took root. The growth of Marxist analysis in the 1970s marked a significant paradigm shift in South African studies. The emergence of a 'school' of radical, revisionist South Africanist scholars at that time is well known – a story that has been told many times. All that is required here is a brief recapitulation of some of the salient points – or, more particularly, those aspects of the revisionist analysis which related to the history of South Africa's racial order.

---

39   Thomas F. Pettigrew, "How events shape theoretical frames: A personal statement" in John H. Stanfield II (ed.), *A History of Race Relations Research* (California, 1993), p.164.
40   Cox, *Caste, Class and Race*, p.xxxi.

The first thrust of this radical challenge was a forthright rejection of those pluralist and idealist assumptions which had for long held sway. Pluralist analysis was deemed fundamentally flawed because it treated racial and ethnic categories as given realities, and because it saw relations between racial and ethnic groups as the crucial dynamic in divided societies. As Wolpe put it, such an approach wrongly conceived of race '... as the irreducible constituent and determinant of social relations'.[41] Johnstone rejected out of hand the very concept of 'race relations' in his study of the South African gold mining industry.[42] Hand-in-hand with this critique of pluralism went an assault on idealist explanations of South Africa's racial order. These were deemed to focus too heavily on race attitudes and prejudice, and rested on the false presupposition that the racial order was essentially a political/ideological phenomenon.[43] For Legassick, such an emphasis on white race attitudes failed to explain 'the unfolding dynamics of South African society'.[44] Segregation and apartheid were not primarily about separating races. Two further common liberal assumptions about the history of South Africa's racial order were also challenged by the revisionists. First, they rejected the notion that the racial order evolved over a long period of time, from the early years of white colonisation, preferring to view racial oppression as an essentially modern phenomenon, integrally bound up with the development of industrial capitalism in South Africa. Second, they questioned the assumption that the boers/Afrikaners had been the most virulent racists in South African history and the main culprits responsible for segregation and apartheid. The racial order was not an outgrowth of Afrikaner ethnicity, but rather a product of material forces.

So how did revisionist writers explain the making of the racial order in South Africa? There was no single explanation – different writers had different emphases – but there clearly was a dominant theme, within which there were variations. An unequivocal, perhaps extreme, statement of the revisionist interpretation was put forward by Davies, O'Meara and Dlamini: 'The national oppression of black people in South Africa is a product of, and was indeed the necessary historical condition for, the development of

---

41   Harold Wolpe, *Race, Class and the Apartheid State* (London, 1988), p.12. For another trenchant critique of pluralism see Johnstone, *Class, Race and Gold*, pp.5-6, 208-10.
42   Johnstone, *Class, Race and Gold* , p.5.
43   *Ibid.*, pp.8, 206; Wolpe, *Race, Class*, p.25.
44   Martin Legassick, "South Africa: Forced Labour, Industrialization and Racial Differentiation", in Richard Harris (ed.), *The Political Economy of Africa* (Cambridge, Massachusetts, 1975), p.232.

capitalism in that country'.[45] They are quite explicit in stating that racial discrimination was 'a product of' capitalism. Similarly, Johnstone set out to explain '... the racial system not as some dysfunctional intrusion on the economic system from such outside, non-material factors as prejudice, racism and "social and cultural pluralism", but as a system generated and determined by the economic system of which it formed a part'.[46] The racial order was essentially a system of class domination, designed to further the interests of capital.

The close connection between racial oppression and capitalism was central to this line of analysis. To establish this connection it became necessary to argue that the racial order was born of capitalism – hence the rejection of the older view that apartheid had deep roots in the past. If racial oppression grew out of capitalism such oppression could not have occurred on any significant scale in the precapitalist era. The growth of the racial order could only be explained if it was viewed in the context of South Africa's mining revolution in the last third of the nineteenth century. The revisionist argument started from a structural analysis of the gold-mining industry in its early phase when it came up against serious constraints on its profitability. These constraints placed an absolute imperative on the minimisation of production costs. From this imperative there developed a system of racial oppression which made possible the ultra-exploitation of cheap black labour. A number of revisionist writers propounded the 'cheap labour thesis' in the 1970s and 1980s. It is stated succinctly, for instance, by Lacey, for whom the policy of racial segregation 'was designed as a coercive labour system geared to ensure capitalist profitability'.[47]

An examination of one specific issue – the racial division of labour – serves to illustrate the difference between the pluralist, idealist interpretation and the materialist approach. According to the former there was a racial division of labour in the mining industry because white workers had since the seventeenth century developed an aversion to performing unskilled manual labour which they deemed to be degrading and the preserve of black people.

---

45 Rob Davies, Dan O'Meara and Sipho Dlamini, *The Struggle for South Africa* (London, 1984), i, p.2.
46 Johnstone, *Class, Race and Gold*, p.215.
47 Lacey, *Working for Boroko*, p.xi. See also, Johnstone, *Class, Race and Gold*, pp.22-25; Harold Wolpe, "Industrialism and Race in South Africa", in Sami Zubaida (ed.), *Race and Racialism* (London, 1970), pp.168-70; Magubane, *Political Economy,* p.14; Legassick, "Gold, Agriculture, and Secondary Industry in South Africa, 1885-1970", p.193.

The racial division of labour was thus explained as a manifestation of this long-held, irrational prejudice.[48] In contrast some revisionists argued that the racial division of labour was a deliberate strategy of the mining industry and the state to divide the working class along racial lines so as to eliminate any threat that a united, organised working class might have posed to capitalist profitability. This position has been clearly stated by Ticktin: '... the rigidities in the system, the common superiority of the whites, do not derive from previous history or from a shared "whiteness" or common culture but rather from the need of the capitalist class, in order to survive, to find a means of dividing the working class'.[49]

This shift away from pluralist, idealist approaches to the history of South Africa's racial order was not simply a change of intellectual direction in South African studies. It was part of a wider tendency. As one American sociologist recently recalled, 'During the sixties and seventies there was this strong tendency to privilege structural explanations of all types and to downplay – almost with scorn – the relevance of cultural values or the importance of racial prejudice'.[50] This was the case among revisionist South Africanist social scientists and historians who dismissed cultural, ideological and psychological factors, as having little significance in explaining the history of racial oppression in South Africa. At best it was conceded that racial ideologies could take on a life of their own once formulated.[51] But the general view was that the main function of racial ideology was to justify the extreme exploitation of black labour, and that the apparatus of racial discrimination was designed to facilitate such exploitation.

Although influenced by international theoretical tendencies, the work of revisionist South Africanist writers was also fashioned in a particular political context. The new wave of Marxist writing appeared in the early 1970s, after the heavy political repression of the 1960s, when the apartheid system was being tightened and when extra-parliamentary opposition movements had been quelled. The prospects for a white change of heart and reform of the racial order – the hope of liberals – had all but vanished. Equally bleak was the likelihood of any popular uprising to overthrow the apartheid regime, at least

---

48 See Doxey, *Industrial Colour Bar in South Africa*.
49 Hillel Ticktin, *The Politics of Race Discrimination in South Africa* (London, 1991), p.12. See also Davies, *Capital, State and White Labour in South Africa*, p.100; Magubane, *Political Economy*, p.16.
50 Bob Blauner, "'But things are much worse for the negro people': Race and Radicalism in my Life and Work", in Stanfield (ed.), *Race Relations Research*, p.30.
51 Magubane, *Political Economy*, p.225.

in the near future. The situation demanded new lines of analysis and innovative ways of conceptualising South African society and history. Marxist theory and class analysis seemed to point to a new way forward.

The revisionist analysis of South African history and society was highly influential and had a considerable impact in the 1970s. However, the shortcomings of the approach soon became apparent. A number of historians and social scientists broadly sympathetic to the overall materialist approach were, by the 1980s, critically reevaluating some of the earlier revisionist assumptions about the history and nature of South Africa's racial order. The thrust of the critique was that the earlier writing had been too determinist, reductionist, functionalist, and mechanistic. The connection between capitalism and racism had been represented in a too stark and oversimplified way. Racism could not, argued the critics, be viewed simply as the invention of capitalism.[52] The racial order could not just be viewed as a modern phenomenon with minimal roots in the distant past.

Those revisionist writers of the 1970s who were drawing conclusions about the history of the South African racial order were for the most part concentrating their focus on the era of industrial capitalism.[53] Apart from Legassick and Freund, few revisionist historians at that time were concerned to explore the history of racial division and discrimination in the preindustrial era.[54] So the view that racism was not rooted in the distant South African past tended to be asserted rather than substantiated with reference to historical evidence.

It may well have been this revisionist assumption, with its rather thin foundations, that prompted a rush of research into the history of South Africa's racial order in the pre-industrial era. Within a period of four years, between 1979 and 1983, there were published a number of important historical works which aimed to throw light on the subject of white racism

---

52 Shula Marks and Richard Rathbone, "Introduction", in Shula Marks and Richard Rathbone, *Industrialisation and Social Change in South Africa* (London, 1982), p.5. See also, Belinda Bozzoli, "Class, Community and Ideology in the Evolution of South African Society", in Belinda Bozzoli (ed.), *Class, Community and Conflict* (Johannesburg, 1987), pp.1-2; and D.B. Posel, "Rethinking the 'Race-Class Debate' in South African Historiography", *Social Dynamics*, 9, 1, 1983.

53 I am here excluding those historians (like Guy, Bonner, Wright, Peires, and Delius) who worked in the field of precolonial African history – they were generally not trying to explain the history of South Africa's racial order.

54 See Legassick, "Frontier tradition" and Freund, "Race in the social structure of South Africa".

during the first two hundred years or so of white settlement.[55] One significant feature of these works is that none of them can be fitted into the paradigms that have been considered thus far. They avoided the assumptions of pluralist analysis; and, although open to the materialist perspective, they were wary of its reductionist conclusions. Ross, for instance, was struck by 'the general lack of a cogent Marxist theory on the origins of racist stratification in South Africa ...'.[56] And Fredrickson set out 'to comprehend the interaction and inter-relationship of 'race' and 'class' – of ethnic consciousness and economic advantage – without assigning a necessary priority to either'.[57] Their conclusions accordingly represented a departure from orthodox pluralist and materialist views. They rejected, for instance, the idea that rigid white racist attitudes had been ever-present since the early days of white settlement. Fredrickson saw a pattern of free fraternisation between racial groups in Cape Town well into the twentieth century – what he refers to as the city's 'special tradition of multi-racialism'.[58] Ross, Elphick and Giliomee agree that in the pre-industrial Cape there was no systematic expression of race attitudes, no racist ideology or racial theory, no system of racial classification.[59] As Ross observes, 'The eighteenth-century Cape was in no way a plural society in the sense that Furnivall, M.G. Smith, or Leo Kuper would define it, with specific ethnic blocks maintaining identities of their own and meeting only under specific, defined conditions'.[60]

Miscegenation has been a central issue in the historiography of the preindustrial racial order at the Cape. For primordialist pluralists and the apologists of apartheid the incidence of miscegenation in the early Cape was an awkward topic. Their stance was usually one of denial – claiming that the only white men to consort with women of colour were transient sailors and soldiers. By contrast revisionist writers highlighted the occurrence of miscegenation to prove that racism was not a significant feature of the

---

55 Elphick and Giliomee (eds), *Shaping of South African Society*; Fredrickson, *White Supremacy*; Ross, "Pre-industrial and Industrial Racial Stratification in South Africa"; Ross (with D. van Arkel and G.C. Quispel), "Going Beyond the Pale" - this essay was originally published (in Dutch) in 1983.
56 Ross, "Pre-industrial and Industrial Racial Stratification in South Africa", p.83.
57 Fredrickson, *White Supremacy*, p.xx.
58 *Ibid.*, pp.258-60. This assumption has recently been challenged – see Vivian Bickford-Smith, "South African Urban History, Racial Segregation and the 'Unique' Case of Cape Town", *Journal of Southern African Studies*, 21, 1, 1995.
59 Ross, "Going Beyond the Pale", pp.85-86, 90; Elphick and Giliomee, "Origins and entrenchment", p.532.
60 Ross, "Going Beyond the Pale", p.72.

preindustrial order. Both views were too simplified. The work of Elphick, Shell and Fredrickson, based on more careful historical research, provides a necessary corrective. They show that in the seventeenth and eighteenth centuries, especially in Cape Town, it was common for white men to take women of colour as concubines, and there was a regular occurrence of intermarriage. White masters might cohabit with slave women, and by the late eighteenth century white trekboers in the eastern frontier districts were consorting with Khoi women. There was at the time no commonly held view that white racial purity should be preserved, that miscegenation was a form of contamination. However, these writers do qualify their view. Elphick and Shell suggest that miscegenation was more common in Cape Town than in the rural districts of the western Cape; and they insist that miscegenation and intermarriage did not threaten white dominance at the Cape.[61]

It is on this last point that this group of writers part company with the revisionist view that the racial order was barely developed before the nineteenth century. Elphick and Giliomee see 'the racial order as largely in place by the end of the eighteenth century'.[62] They argue that there was a high coincidence of race and class in early Cape society: whites exercised power and made up the landholding class, while Khoisan and slaves formed the labouring class.[63] Fredrickson reinforces this point, arguing that the long experience of black servitude and enslavement 'established a presumption that whites were naturally masters and members of a privileged group while nonwhites were meant to be their servants and social inferiors'.[64] Ultimately Fredrickson adopts a compromise position in the race-class debate: 'One way to comprehend the social structure of the late eighteenth- and early nineteenth-century Cape is to see it as a class society in which race mattered in the determination of status but was not all-important'.[65]

These historians adopting an intermediate position also addressed the teleological question – was the eighteenth century racial order an antecedent of twentieth century segregation and apartheid? Ross is somewhat ambivalent on this issue. He states that apartheid institutions 'must have had their roots in pre-industrial South Africa', but also argues that 'the racial order of modern South Africa was in no way inherent in colonial society from its

---

61 Elphick and Shell, "Intergroup Relations", pp.194-204; Fredrickson, *White Supremacy*, pp.110-17, 122-23.
62 Elphick and Giliomee, "European Dominance", p.522.
63 *Ibid.*, pp.559-60.
64 Fredrickson, *White Supremacy*, pp.92-93.
65 *Ibid.*, p.88.

foundation'.[66] These two statements can be reconciled with each other, but they do reflect the author's attempt to steer a course between the older liberal position with its emphasis on continuity and the revisionist stress on discontinuity. Elphick and Giliomee are less equivocal in their conclusion. They have no doubt that whites in the eighteenth century Cape had a conviction of their own distinctiveness and enjoyed 'virtually exclusive access to power and wealth'. The long-term implications of this are made clear in the final sentence of the book: 'These convictions and social realities formed the fateful legacy of the pre-industrial Cape to the modern people of South Africa'.[67]

Four main approaches to explaining the history of South Africa's racial order have been identified – loosely labelled as primordialist pluralist, liberal pluralist, materialist, and 'intermediate'. Not all writing can necessarily be placed squarely in one or other of these categories. But most historians who have ventured interpretations of the history of racial division in South Africa can probably be identified more or less with one of those four schools – although there are exceptions. What is striking about the first three of these approaches in particular is that each fitted into a paradigm that enjoyed a level of international credibility at the time. For instance, the idea of racial groups being real, discrete entities displaying distinctive cultural traits was standard fare in the early decades of the twentieth century.[68] From the 1930s this idea gained extreme expression in some Afrikaner nationalist writing, reinforced by Nazi ideology. The idea also informed liberal pluralist analysis which was a widely supported tendency in western social science in the 1950s and 1960s. What separated the primordialist pluralists from the liberal pluralists was their different political agendas. The primordialists saw racial difference as an essential feature of human society and therefore argued that political systems should accommodate this deep-seated difference – an argument presented as an obvious apologia for apartheid. Liberal pluralists on the other hand, while recognising that racial division and conflict had been a major factor shaping the course of South African history, still believed in an individualist ethos and a sense of common humanity, both of which could transcend or erode racial and ethnic divisions. Hence the agenda of the primordialists was

---

66   Ross, "Going Beyond the Pale", pp.71, 90.
67   Elphick and Giliomee, "European Dominance", p.561.
68   Dubow, *Illicit Union*, pp.20, 74.

conservative, and that of the liberals was reformist, even though both shared pluralist and idealist assumptions.

The revisionist approach tended, at least in its most determinist form, to reduce racial ideology and racial discrimination to material forces. Again, this was a fashionable approach in the 1960s and 1970s, and it was adopted by a number of South Africanist social scientists and historians. In disavowing liberal reformism it seemed to offer a fresh, more radical approach to challenging the apartheid regime of the time. Only the fourth of the four lines of analysis, the so-called 'intermediate' approach, cannot be linked to any dominant paradigm or to any particular political agenda at the time. This approach is labelled 'intermediate' because its practitioners tried to steer a middle course in the race-class debate, avoiding the pitfalls of pluralism and economic determinism. Each of the scholars pursuing this line was an historian working in an empirical tradition according to which interpretations of the past had to be based on a careful examination of available evidence. (This, of course, does represent a paradigm in itself – a long-standing one within the discipline of history.) Moreover, each of the scholars would have been, in their private lives, firmly opposed to apartheid, even if there is little in their historical writing to suggest a particular strategy for opposing or ending apartheid. It appears that their project was more purely historical – to explain the origins and evolution of South Africa's racial order.

The second edition of Elphick and Giliomee's *Shaping of South African Society* appeared in 1989. So, one might ask, what developments have occurred since then in the historiography of South Africa's racial order? Some might say that the historiography has taken an idealist turn. Certainly there has been a growing interest in the history of the ideas that informed (perhaps even shaped?) the practice of racial oppression in South African history. Racial theory, as expressed in scientific, medical, anthropological, sociological and political thought, has become a growing field of study for South Africanist historians.[69]

Another tendency has been to subject segregation and apartheid to discourse analysis. Ashforth has analysed the reports of a series of twentieth century official commissions of enquiry set up to investigate the 'native question' in South Africa. He has studied these reports as texts which used certain metaphorical techniques in order to convey an authoritative sense of South African realities, based on 'expert', 'scientific' knowledge.[70]

---

69 See, for instance, Dubow, *Illicit Union*; Rich, "Race, Science, and the Legitimization of White Supremacy in South Africa, 1902-1940"; Bank, "Liberals and their Enemies".
70 Adam Ashforth, *The Politics of Official Discourse in Twentieth-Century South Africa* (Oxford, 1990).

Ashforth's work is a valuable inquiry into the nature of domination in South Africa. It does not attempt to explain the origins or dynamic of South Africa's racial order. Indeed, postmodernists generally disavow such attempts anyway. The quest for origins is deemed to give rise to a flawed teleological analysis. And the effort to probe for an underlying dynamic or pattern leads only to essentialism or a totalising discourse.

Norval attempts to apply 'post-theory' to an analysis of segregation and apartheid in the twentieth century. The focus of her project is 'the discourse of apartheid: the multifarious practices and rituals, verbal and non-verbal, through which a certain sense of reality and understanding of the nature of society were constituted and maintained'. She chooses to concentrate on the surface of apartheid, rejecting as problematic any attempt to search for some hidden, underlying essence, 'for such attempts tend to be bewitched by a metaphysical illusion of depth'.[71] She disavows class reductionism, preferring to examine those elements of apartheid discourse which enabled whites, particularly Afrikaners, to make sense of their everyday life.

Norval, like Ashforth, provides some useful insights, but she is too readily dismissive of materialist analysis and other approaches. It is one thing to reject crude class reductionism and economic determinism, but quite another to throw out materialist analysis altogether. One cannot begin to understand racism, segregation and apartheid by removing them from an economic context. And to focus just on the surface of these phenomena can only produce a limited understanding. The idealist turn and postmodernist interventions of recent years have served in some respects to enhance our historical understanding of South Africa's racial order. But the postmodernist rejection of essentialism and totalisation places unnecessary limits on the kinds of question that might be asked and the kinds of project that might be pursued. Instead of closing off lines of inquiry, we should be opening them up. Instead of dismissing previous analyses, we should be building on their insights.

The postmodernist turn away from macro-history, rejected as an impossible project, towards the micro-study of the particular, the unique, and the exceptional, is in some respects regrettable. Indeed, even before the advent of postmodernism the historiography of the South African racial order was lacking in any kind of thorough synthesis or overview. There have been

---

71 Norval, *Deconstructing Apartheid Discourse*, p.2.

excellent studies of particular phases – the early Cape, the mid-nineteenth century, the segregation era, apartheid – but no single work that surveys the whole, drawing out the continuities and discontinuities, the interconnections and linkages over time and space. An overview, which this book attempts, makes possible a more refined periodisation of the South African racial order. Crucial questions can be addressed. How is the history of South Africa's racial order best periodised? What have been the key points of origin and the main watersheds in the evolution of that order? Has that evolution been marked by a steady continuity, or have there been striking discontinuities?

Most historians and analysts have stressed the continuity of South Africa's racial order, seeing it as evolving gradually over 300 years or more. Afrikaner nationalists, as we have seen, generally took this teleological view. It suited their purpose for apartheid to be represented as having deep roots in the South African past, so much so that it became simply an expression of 'the traditional South African way of life'. This was just one way in which history was used by Afrikaner nationalists in an effort to legitimate apartheid. Liberal idealists have also tended to emphasise the continuity. For them white racism evolved in the particular conditions of colonial society, especially in frontier zones where there was no effective authority to restrain white colonists from riding roughshod over indigenous people. And so a sense of antagonism towards racial 'others' became more and more embedded in the mindset of whites, particularly boers, from generation to generation. Apartheid was thus explained as the ultimate expression of this mindset. Revisionist writers, on the other hand, rejected the teleological argument, rather stressing the discontinuity that marked the history of the racial order. In their view the colour line was blurred in the preindustrial era, and it was the process of industrialisation that more than anything shaped South Africa's racial order.

All of these interpretations are unsatisfactory. The continuity argument in its starkest form, conceals the significant shifts that occurred in the racial order over time. The argument carries the flawed teleological assumption that the racial order unfolded according to some preordained logic. The standard Afrikaner nationalist version served an obvious ideological function and therefore has to be viewed with scepticism. The revisionist attempt to play down the extent of white racism in the preindustrial era also fails. Their stress on discontinuity was vital to their fundamental claim that the racial order was essentially the product of capitalism. To establish this link it was necessary to show that in the precapitalist era there was only a limited degree of racial discrimination. But in fact there was little research by revisionists into the preindustrial racial order, with the exceptions of Legassick and Freund. So the claim that white racism was of little significance before the mid-nineteenth century was not firmly established at all. The work of Elphick, Giliomee, Fredrickson, Ross and Shell, among others, shows that the revisionist position was too far-reaching and too stark in its conclusion.

Just as one cannot view the history of South Africa's racial order as unfolding gradually and continuously over 300 years, nor can one drastically shorten its history to cover the century or so after the mining revolution. There have been continuities in the history of this racial order – a white racial consciousness, based on a sense of physical and cultural difference from racial 'others', has been more or less loosely articulated from the beginning of white settlement. At the same time, the revisionist stress on discontinuity does carry some weight. After all the very structuring of this book, with its two main parts divided by a major economic break, implies that the process of industrialisation changed the character of the racial order. What is required is a periodisation that captures some of the complexities of the South African racial order, as well as its short-term twists and turns and its more imperceptible shifts.

The trail of South African history is littered with turning-points. Historians have come up with their own favourites – those key moments when South African history changed course, when events occurred or decisions were made that set the country even more inexorably on its racial path. Let us examine some of these possibilities. The beginning of white settlement in the 1650s is an obvious watershed phase, and one that raises the question addressed at the start of the book – did the Dutch bring racism to the Cape, or did it arise only in the colonial situation? The Winthrop Jordan line of analysis has suggested that racism was deeply ingrained in European consciousness by the early modern era. Guelke has applied this analysis to the Dutch, arguing that they arrived at the Cape with pronounced racial attitudes. Others like Fredrickson have argued that the Dutch were primarily concerned about their commercial interests and that race mattered little to them. There can be no clear-cut answer to this question. Dutch commercial interests certainly did take priority, but these would not have precluded the growth of race consciousness and the practice of racial exclusion. It is probable that the Dutch did arrive with perceptions of white superiority and with a strong sense of cultural and religious difference. Contact with indigenous people undoubtedly reinforced these perceptions – the early utterances of Van Riebeeck himself bear this out.

Historians have also emphasised key decisions on labour policy taken within the first 70 years of white settlement at the Cape. One was the Dutch East India Company's decision to allow the importation of slaves, with the first two shipments arriving as early as 1658-59. Thereafter all slaves would be people of colour; no whites were enslaved. In the seventeenth century there was no definite commitment to the continuing use of either slave labour or other forms of black servile labour. However, a momentous decision was made during 1716-17 by the Company to the effect that a white labour policy would be impractical and unwise. So one central element of the racial order, the racial division of labour, was determined, if not fixed for all time, in the early decades of white colonisation. At later junctures the possibility of a white labour policy was reconsidered – in the eastern Cape in the 1820s, in the mining industry in the early twentieth century, and during the 'total apartheid' debate of the 1950s. But in practice there would be little deviation from a pattern whereby only people of colour performed menial, servile labour.

The work of Elphick and Giliomee and others suggests that by the end of the eighteenth century Cape society was implicitly ordered along racial lines. This does not mean to say that there was formalised or institutionalised discrimination, but rather that a social, political and economic hierarchy had emerged – a hierarchy that had a visibly racial character. Elphick and Giliomee place particular emphasis on the Company's creation of four main legal status groups: Company employees, freeburghers, slaves and Khoisan. Although the first three of these groups were not racially defined in practice, the first two were almost entirely white, and no whites belonged to the other two.

Another period identified as a key formative phase has been the frontier era, the time when colonial expansion brought white colonists in close proximity to settled indigenous African communities. Writers like Walker and MacCrone argued that the competition for resources and consequent tensions that characterised these frontier zones bred a strong, hostile racial consciousness among the white colonists. This, in their view, was a crucial point of origin in the making of South Africa's racial order in that it set a pattern of white racism that continued into the twentieth century, culminating in the apartheid system. Revisionist critics of this frontier thesis have argued that its characterisation of white frontier attitudes is flawed, and that race relations in frontier zones were in reality much more flexible and fluid. Again one sees in this debate two positions that are too starkly opposed to each other. The Walker/MacCrone thesis was undoubtedly faulty. They missed some of the complexities of frontier interaction. They were guilty of trying to read the present – in MacCrone's case, the growth of segregation in the 1930s – back into the past. And there is no clear thread connecting the twentieth century racial order to the frontier era. At the same time the revisionists overstated the extent to which frontier zones were marked by interracial cooperation and exchange. This interpretation was necessary to support their overall thesis that the precapitalist era was marked by much less white racism than the capitalist era. Guelke's distinction between two different types of white frontierspeople – between those who were racially exclusive and whose who interacted across the racial lines – is useful. However, in spite of the shortcomings of their position, the revisionists were undoubtedly right to play down the supposed connection between the frontier era and the later institutionalised racial order of the twentieth century. There is little to support the view that the frontier era was especially significant in the making of segregation and apartheid.

The mid-nineteenth century has more recently been emphasised as a crucial formative phase in the history of the racial order, especially by Crais. This is an appropriate emphasis. It correctly draws closer attention to the connection between British imperialism and racism. It links the emergent racial order to growing contact and conflict between white colonisers and indigenous African communities, chiefdoms and states, and situates it in the context of the competitive struggle for key resources, especially land, cattle and labour. It is no coincidence that colonial authorities became preoccupied with labour matters in the middle decades of the nineteenth century, and that the labour issue became increasingly racialised. During this phase the ideological dimension of the racial order also took on a more pronounced form. Racial difference was brought into the realm of theory, articulated more explicitly and virulently, no longer a matter of imprecise perception.

For revisionists the mining revolution of the last third of the nineteenth century has been the great turning-point in South African history, the key moment in the making of the racial order. Again this argument was overstated, especially during the 1970s phase of revisionist historiography. It was almost as if industrial and agrarian capitalism created the racial order in the service of capitalist interests. And the continuities between the preindustrial and industrial orders were played down to the extent that race seemed to have been barely a factor before the development of mining. However, there is also little doubt that the mining revolution was a key moment. The racial order took on a much clearer shape and became more firmly structured as the country industrialised. The ownership and control of the means of production in the industry came to rest entirely in white hands. The division of labour in mining became racialised. The colour line dividing black unskilled workers from white skilled workers came to be formalised in law. And this racial division of labour came to be reinforced by a pattern of residential segregation.

Within thirty years of the discovery of gold on the Witwatersrand South Africa's racial order was becoming more defined. A key phase was the period 1902-13. Between 1902 and 1910 the question of extending the Cape qualified non-racial franchise was up for consideration. The British imperial authorities and white political leaders in South Africa combined to maintain a racially exclusive franchise outside the Cape. The 1903-05 South African Native Affairs Commission produced a report which set out a broad framework for a policy of racial segregation. Labour legislation, passed before and after South African union, formalised the racial division of labour on the mines. The 1913 Natives Land Act entrenched the principle of territorial segregation and laid the basis for the future bantustan system.

While revisionists overstated the lack of continuity between the preindustrial and industrial eras, they were correct to highlight the early decades of the mining revolution as a key phase in the development of South Africa's racial order. Political discrimination, territorial segregation, the racial division of labour, and residential separation were all, in varying degrees, being implemented or tightened within thirty years of the Rand gold discoveries. That these developments were contemporaneous with the growth of mining capitalism was far from being merely coincidental. These first dozen years or so of the twentieth century were more significant than other later turning-points often identified by historians – such as the years 1924 and 1948. In 1924 the first Nationalist government came to power, headed by Hertzog, sometimes viewed as the father of segregation. Hertzog did indeed espouse strong segregationist principles, and he devoted considerable energy in trying to push a package of segregation laws through parliament. But Hertzog did not introduce any major new policy departures. Rather did he try to extend and entrench existing patterns, most notably in the racial division of labour, territorial segregation, and racial disenfranchisement. It is true that the 1927 Native Administration Act was an important measure in the development of a retribalisation policy, but in practice it was only a pointer to the later bantustan policy. 1924 should not be viewed as a key turning-point in the development of the South African racial order.

1948 would seem to carry more obvious significance. As we have seen, the apparatus of discrimination tightened under the new NP government. Policies of racial separation were pursued and implemented with greater zeal than before. A strict system of racial classification was introduced. Social, residential, and educational segregation was applied more thoroughly. And the bantustan policy was a new departure. However, the continuities across the 1948 divide are more striking than the policy shifts. So much of what the NP government did after 1948 was an extension and more rigorous implementation of what had gone before. This was certainly the case with urban policy. Influx control was tightened according to principles laid down in the 1937 Native Laws Amendment Act. In destroying black settlements like Sophiatown in Johannesburg, and District Six in Cape Town, the NP government was carrying through what had been recommended by UP administrations before 1948. Moreover segregation had long been normal practice in many spheres of South African life – in education, sport and recreation, and in the spatial ordering of residential and commercial life. After 1948 the racial demarcations in these spheres were not new, but more rigid.

This periodisation becomes more refined, more instructive, if linked to a sharper conceptualisation of the racial order. It is useful to bear in mind the four elements of that order identified at the start of this book: a loosely articulated racial consciousness, explicit racial ideology and theory, informal racial practice, and formalised, institutionalised racism. During the seventeenth and eighteenth centuries the first two of these elements were present at the Cape, but not the latter two. The early white settlers had a strong sense of cultural and religious difference between themselves and both indigenous people and imported slaves. There was also a sense that cultural difference corresponded to difference of colour. And this sense of difference gave rise to a degree of separation in the social and economic spheres. However, white racial consciousness was not expressed in any kind of racial theory. Nor did it bring about a rigid, institutionalised racial order before the end of the eighteenth century. The third element, racial theory, as articulated by scientists and other thinkers and writers, came to the fore during the nineteenth century. But this did not lead to the immediate emergence of an entrenched, formalised racial order. Certainly in the nineteenth century many laws were passed and policies pursued – by imperial, colonial and republican authorities alike – that had racial implications. Numerous racially based labour measures were enacted throughout the century. Similarly constitutional arrangements, especially franchise laws, generally contained racially exclusive provisions. But in many spheres of life racial separation and discrimination were not formalised in law.

That formalisation came in the twentieth century with the growth of an institutionalised racial order. During the past hundred years or so all of the four elements have been present. They reached their most developed form in the early apartheid era, during the 1950s and 1960s. From the 1970s the racial order remained in place, albeit under great strain, but explicit racial theory lost its salience and ceased to underpin apartheid in the way that it once had. In the 1990s the racial order has been largely dismantled. The formal structures of discrimination have been broken down; and overt, explicit racial ideology and theory has largely disappeared from the public domain. At the same time, however, white race consciousness and informal racial practice – the two elements present from the early days of white settlement – have survived into the post-apartheid era. This race consciousness is still very much alive, often denied by its owners, perhaps held privately, or expressed only in safe company around the dinner-table. It also gains expression, implicitly rather than explicitly, in a more public arena, most noticeably in the media. News coverage regularly displays a racial bias in that, for instance, crimes against whites are given far more extensive reporting than crimes against people of colour. Moreover much newspaper writing is now based on a code, unstated but evident, that colour equals criminality, corruption and inefficiency. The end of apartheid has certainly not brought the end of white racial consciousness.

Related to the problem of periodisation is the question of culpability – who should bear the most blame for South Africa's racial order? Many possible culprits come to mind. There are individuals, ranging from Van Riebeeck to Verwoerd. There are particular groups who might be said to carry collective responsibility – the Dutch/boers/Afrikaners have often been singled out for blame. White farmers have been represented as a particularly racist section of South African society. Links have been drawn between the 'northern tradition' of the boer republics and the later growth of apartheid; the roots of segregation have also been traced to the mid-nineteenth century eastern Cape and to colonial Natal. Blame has been pinned on capitalists, seen by some as the prime movers in the making of the modern racial order. Successive governing regimes during the course of the twentieth century can each be accorded some responsibility – the British imperial government in the first decade of the century; the South African Party government from 1910 to 1924; the NP government from 1924 to 1933; the UP government till 1948; and the NP government after 1948.

It is not a useful historical exercise to apportion blame to particular individuals or groups. Behind such an exercise there is always a suggestion of scapegoating. There has long been a tendency on the part of white English-speakers to blame Afrikaners and their ancestors for racial discrimination. This tendency has often been no more than an attempt to deflect attention away from the major contribution of English-speakers to the making of the country's racial order. Today many whites, Afrikaner as well as English, target Verwoerd as the arch-villain. This is evident from the widespread obliteration of Verwoerd from public historical memory. His statue is removed from outside display; and in the name-changing process Verwoerd's is the one name to be consistently eradicated from places, streets and other sites. Verwoerd serves as a convenient scapegoat for English-speakers, even though it was during his premiership that English-speakers flocked to support the National Party in ever-increasing numbers. More recent generations of Afrikaner nationalists have also distanced themselves from Verwoerd, trying to absolve themselves with the excuse that they were trapped by Verwoerd's legacy.

It is wrong to single out Verwoerd as the arch-culprit. Indeed it is surprising that the name-changing process in post-apartheid South Africa has not included other major figures in the making of South Africa's racial order – men like D'Urban, Harry Smith, Rhodes, Milner and Smuts, to name a few. It is also wrong to ethnicise racism – to view one particular ethnic or cultural group as being more racist than another. In the nineteenth century the boers were certainly no more racist in their thinking and practice than English settlers in the eastern Cape and Natal. Certainly the policies of the trekker republics were highly discriminatory. Their constitutions were racially exclusive; and their labour regimes were particularly harsh. However boer communities do not seem to have produced anything like the venomous racist discourse that came out of setter society in the eastern Cape and Natal in the nineteenth century. And the exploitation of black labour in the latter two regions was no less harsh than it was in boer territories. Racism pervaded white colonial society – it was no less virulent among one section of that society than another.

It is also misleading to draw a contrast, as some have done, between the racism of white colonists and the supposedly more liberal outlook of the British imperial authorities. Many writers have suggested, wrongly, that British imperialism in the nineteenth century was a liberalising force that placed a restraining hand on white colonists, curbing their excesses and limiting their capacity for racial oppression. Exponents of this view point to the emancipation of slaves in 1833, and to the non-racial qualified franchise introduced in the Cape in 1854. However, slave emancipation only brought to an end an extreme form of labour oppression. After 1833 imperial policy continued to allow for the harsh exploitation of black labour by white colonists. Moreover the Cape non-racial franchise did nothing to prevent white domination of the Cape political system; and the imperial government did not stop the introduction of what amounted to a racially exclusive franchise in colonial Natal during the second half of the nineteenth century. Furthermore, successive British governors and high commissioners slipped easily into the dominant racist discourse. The record of the imperial authorities in the first decade of the twentieth century firmly belies any idea of British imperialism as a liberalising force. From 1902 the imperial government was in a strong position to take steps towards the deracialisation of the country. Instead it did the opposite. Nothing was done to extend the non-racial franchise beyond the Cape. And during those years between 1902 and 1910 when all four territories in South Africa fell under British imperial suzerainty there was a clear policy drift in the direction of segregationism.

If it is not useful to single out boers or Britons as bearing the prime responsibility for the racial order, can one then identify specific classes as being particularly culpable? Perhaps white farmers, or mining capitalists, or white workers? Certainly white farmers consistently, over two centuries, called for a racial order that would meet their need for land and labour. It has been argued that in the nineteenth century eastern Cape the most virulent racist discourse emanated from the settler elite, among whom farmers were prominent. In colonial Natal white farmers represented a powerful constituency and were among the chief exponents of racist thought and practice in the colony. During the twentieth century capitalist farmers carried considerable electoral weight. Their support for successive NP governments meant that their interests were given careful attention. The racial order guaranteed them sufficient land and labour as well as favourable access to credit, subsidies, and protected markets. Farmers have consistently been party to racial oppression – they have supported the racial order and benefited from it. However it is less easy to label them as prime culprits. Although a significant constituency they never enjoyed sufficient collective power to have played the key determining role in shaping the racial order. That order was shaped to their liking, but it was not shaped by them.

Much the same can be said of industrial capitalists. Revisionist writers in the 1970s stressed the significant role of mining capital in the making of the twentieth century racial order. Critics of the revisionists argued that the notion of 'mining capital' was too amorphous and that attention had to be paid rather to the role of mining capitalists. In the critics' eyes the revisionists took too instrumentalist a view of the state, assuming that it simply implemented policies at the behest of capitalists, or of dominant branches of the capitalist sector. There is point to this criticism. There is insufficient evidence of mining capitalists dictating policy. However, at least until the 1920s mining was at the forefront of the industrialisation process in South Africa, and successive governments were bound to look after the interests of mining capital. Some mining capitalists were politically prominent. One thinks of Rhodes who enjoyed considerable political power in the 1890s at a time when he was the foremost mining capitalist in southern Africa. Even after his fall from grace in the mid-1890s various governments – from the post-1902 imperial administration through to union governments from 1910 to 1924 –

pursued policies that were generally favourable to mineowners. Measures were implemented to secure the labour needs of the industry. The force of the state was brought to bear to crush white worker strikes in 1907, 1913 and 1922. Moreover, as we have seen, the late nineteenth and early twentieth century was both a significant period in the emergence of the racial order and the crucial initial phase of the mining industry when it was striving towards profitability. There has to be a link between the two. But one must still hold back from labelling mining capitalists as prime culprits.

To what extent can blame be pinned on the shoulders of white workers? After all, they too have benefited from the racial order. For much of the twentieth century white workers have enjoyed the formal protection of the job colour bar which has secured for them a relatively privileged position in the job hierarchy. Under the racial division of labour they were also accorded trade union rights denied to black workers. And state policies and programmes meant that the spectre of unemployment, which had once afflicted a significant proportion of the white population, had virtually disappeared by the 1960s. Again though, it would be misleading to argue that white workers somehow manipulated the racial order to bring themselves greater economic and social security. Although white workers came to form a significant electoral constituency they never had it in their power to shape policy. As with farmers and industrialists, successive twentieth century governments pursued racial policies that privileged white workers, and in return received the latters' electoral support. But white workers were not the driving-force behind the making of the South African racial order.

By not singling out culprits, in not apportioning primary responsibility to particular groups or individuals, is everybody therefore being absolved? No, this study is not designed to offer exoneration, but rather to emphasise the collective responsibility of the white community at large. All sections of that community – Afrikaner and English, middle class and working class – have been party to racial oppression in South Africa. However, this question of culpability is highly problematic. In assigning collective responsibility, in broadening the base of culpability, is one therefore not letting some off the hook? All may be guilty, but surely some more so than others? Conversely, in apportioning blame to specific groups and individuals is one not tacitly pronouncing the innocence of others who do not deserve exoneration? Does not the scapegoating of the Malans, Verwoerds and Vorsters lead to a false presumption of innocence on the part of the greater white community who had no immediate, direct responsibility for the apparatus of racial discrimination? Alternatively, there is the problem encountered by the Truth and Reconciliation Commission in its deliberations during the late 1990s.

Many have argued that the amnesty process has allowed the political leaders who gave the orders – the PW Bothas and FW De Klerks – to get off scot free for apartheid's crimes, while the foot-soldiers, apartheid's 'willing executioners', have had to take the brunt of the blame and in some cases face court proceedings and jail sentences.

These are all complex ethical, judicial and political issues. How might an historian attempting to unravel the history of the racial order contribute to the conversation around these questions? It is the task of the historian to historicise – in this case to examine the South African racial order in its changing contexts over time. This endeavour can, though, degenerate into an extreme relativism – so much so that the perpetrators of racial discrimination and oppression become mere pawns, victims of their context and circumstances, and thus absolved. In this study I have attempted to historicise the racial order, but certainly with no intention of exonerating its makers and its practitioners.

The endeavour to historicise carries a further danger. It can give rise to a project that is largely academic, confined to the ivory tower and the realm of professional historians. In many respects this study does fall into that realm – the weight of the analysis has centred on the work of historians and social scientists. But my purpose has not just been to offer historical explanation, or simply to pursue academic debate. Exploring and understanding the history of the South African racial order can help guide an approach to dealing with the numerous surviving monuments to the country's racial past. Such monuments are still spread throughout South Africa – not just statues and memorials, but also names of places, streets, buildings and institutions. On the walls of the Anglican Cathedral in the town where I live, Grahamstown, there are plaques commemorating British soldiers killed in nineteenth century frontier wars. Some of these plaques contain offensive racist language. Members of the largely white, English-speaking congregation have been unwilling to remove these plaques. Similarly the university were I work continues to carry the name of Rhodes – Cecil Rhodes, the arch-imperialist and white supremacist.

The matter of name-changing does have practical implications – it can be costly. But it also requires white people to offer a collective acknowledgement of their complicity in the South African racial order. This acknowledgement has generally not been forthcoming. Instead there has been widespread denial – denial of responsibility, complicity or culpability. This study has tried to show that the responsibility cannot be pinned on specific individuals and groups, that all classes of white society have been complicit in making the racial order. The recent widespread tendency of whites to deny rather than to acknowledge is shameful.

Such an acknowledgment does not have to become self-flagellation. One can still avoid the pitfalls of relativism in recognising that white racism is a conditioned attitude, born of circumstances. This study has proceeded on the assumption that people are not naturally or normally racist – rejecting the view of Winthrop Jordan that racism has been deep-seated and long ingrained in the white psyche. Rather do racist attitudes, racial ideologies, and institutionalised racism emerge and take shape in particular historical contexts. A process of racialisation occurs whereby racial meanings are attached to identities, practices and institutions.[72] This requires the historian to look closely at those contexts, to examine the forces shaping the South African racial order, in an effort to capture something of the dynamics of that order. Such an endeavour inevitably brings us back to the tension between idealist and materialist perspectives.

Idealist explanations vary, with different writers emphasising different dimensions. Many have stressed the importance of white racist attitudes, so that legalised and institutionalised racial discrimination simply becomes an outgrowth of those attitudes. This approach can be taken even further. According to some, racial orders can be seen as the almost inevitable outcome of a diseased white psyche. This kind of interpretation is unsatisfactory. It is not enough to say that racism has been ingrained in the white mindset for centuries. Rather must one examine the particular circumstances in which racial thought takes on, asking why racist discourse has more appeal at some times than it does at others. Then a further conceptual exploration is required – to consider the link between racial consciousness and the practice of racial discrimination and exclusion.

Where there is a racial order, formalised to a greater or lesser degree, one would expect to find a pervasive racial consciousness among the dominant caste. But that consciousness may not have been a significant causal factor behind the making of that order. Racial consciousness might have been actively promoted by the ruling class as a way of reinforcing the racial order, so racial thought becomes a legitimating ideology. This is the most likely connection between racial thought and the practice of racial discrimination. It is much less likely that the apparatus of racial discrimination and exclusion is established because those responsible for creating the apparatus hold strong racist attitudes. Thus any argument which

---

72 Ran Greenstein, "Racial Formation: Towards a Comparative Study of Collective Identities in South Africa and the United States", *Social Dynamics*, 19, 2, 1993, p.4.

highlights white race prejudice as a significant moving force behind the growth of a racial order lacks any real explanatory weight.

The same can be said for interpretations which stress racial theory, racial science and religion. These are all interesting fields of inquiry, as the work of Dubow and others has shown. But it cannot be argued that more formal bodies of racial thought, whether articulated by scientists, religious figures or other intellectuals, provide the foundation for a racial order. We have seen that racial science has been propounded in South Africa for much of the nineteenth century and well into the twentieth. This work did not shape the country's racial order or inform leading policy-makers. However racial theory did serve a legitimating function. If the racial order could be endorsed by the claims of a particular brand of scientific theory, however spurious the theory, then that order could carry greater legitimacy. The same goes for religious thought. Many Afrikaner nationalist leaders proclaimed that South Africa's racial order was divinely ordained, that it was God's will that different races be kept apart. Many scriptural justifications were produced to support this claim. Again, though, it would be entirely wrong to suggest that the makers of the South African racial order were driven by some divine mission to carry through God's will that different races be separated. Rather was religious authority being drawn upon in an attempt to add moral justification to racially oppressive policies and practices which were totally immoral.

Materialist perspectives have naturally played down the importance of white racist attitudes, beliefs, and ideas in the making of the racial order. For materialists racist policies, practices, institutions and beliefs are developed essentially to serve material interests. As we have seen, such a perspective was fashionable in the 1970s but has come to be heavily criticised in the last fifteen years or so. There is certainly point to the criticisms, but the critics have tended to throw out the baby with the bath-water. In the reaction against materialist analysis many of its insights have been lost. The practice of racial oppression in South African history cannot be separated from material forces. In the pre-industrial era, for instance, whites' quest for land, labour and other resources led to conflicts and struggles on the ground, and to the growth of racial discourse. Racial 'others' occupied desirable land, or they offered a potential supply of labour. These material needs could best be met if those 'others' were treated differentially, subjugated and oppressed.

In the industrial era the connection between material forces and the racial order is even more pronounced. It cannot be a coincidence that that racial order took firmer shape at the very time when the country was going through its first phase of industrialisation. During the course of the twentieth century all sections of the white population – in particular industrialists, farmers, workers, the unemployed – have benefited materially, at one time or another, from the racial order. Not surprisingly the vast majority of whites have consistently supported policies and structures that have been racially discriminatory and oppressive. And, as we have seen, the policy of racial separation only gained support as long as it did not seriously jeopardise material interests. Hence the idea of 'total apartheid' was never seriously entertained as a viable option precisely because it would have required material sacrifices on the part of whites.

Some materialist analyses of the South African racial order have undoubtedly been too determinist, reductionist and mechanistic, as many critics have rightly observed. But there can be no denying the connection between material interests and the racial order. Racism has been much more an expression of class interest than a manifestation of some primordial identity. Race consciousness can be manipulated, mobilised and promoted so as, perhaps, to bring security or solidarity, or to confer privilege and prosperity on its exponents. This is not to reduce the history of white racism in South Africa to material interests. There are other important factors that require consideration if that history is to be better understood. Indeed, there is one factor that stands out – one that to some extent bridges the idealist/materialist divide. That is, fear. This can be found at the root of much white racism in South African history. There has been the fear of racial 'others' who can be enemies, actual or potential, in war. These 'others' might also be feared as criminals, as sources of contaminating disease, as a threat to racial purity through miscegenation, as competitors in the labour market or in the commercial arena, or as rebels who might seek revenge by turning the table on their oppressors and doing to them what had for long been done to themselves.

It is significant that outbursts of white racial hysteria in South Africa have often occurred during times of interracial war. A long series of frontier wars from the late eighteenth century bred insecurity and anxiety among white settler communities, and this fear easily manifested itself in racist discourse. For instance, the 1834-35 war on the eastern frontier did much to harden racial attitudes among the settlers. During the late 1870s and early 1880s there was an upsurge of warfare and rebellion across southern Africa. These events aroused racial hysteria in white communities, and reinforced the colonial image of Africans as being inherently savage and war-like. There was a similar hardening of colonial racist attitudes during and after the 1906-08 Bambatha Rebellion in Natal.

Across frontiers indigenous people seemed remote and alien to white colonists. They were unknown 'others' whose apparent propensity for war made them seem dark and threatening. Racist thought and practice later developed in situations of interracial proximity and contact, most particularly in urban areas. Urbanisation fuelled racism in a variety of ways. Again fear was often at the root of this racism. There was the fear of contamination, based on the belief that people of colour were carriers of disease. The 1882 smallpox epidemic in Cape Town was followed by growing calls among whites for racial segregation, in the belief that people of colour were a source of infection. It was no coincidence that the bubonic plague outbreak which swept around South Africa between 1901 and 1904 was followed by concerted efforts to establish segregated townships for Africans. During the 1920s and 1930s it was believed that the best way to control the spread of tuberculosis was to clear slums and segregate Africans. In the last two decades of the twentieth century when social facilities were gradually being desegregated many whites objected to the desegregation of public swimming pools on the grounds of hygiene.[73]

Just as racist discourse has grown around stereotypes of black people as carriers of disease, so too has this discourse been fuelled by assumptions about black criminality. In the colonial mindset people of colour were naturally 'thievish', not to be trusted. They also represented a dangerous, uncontrolled sexuality. There have been in South African history instances of white hysteria arising from black rape scares – those in Durban and Pietermaritzburg in the late 1860s and early 1870s, and in Johannesburg between 1897 and 1912 have been documented by historians. Again, white fears of this kind lived on well into the twentieth century. In the 1980s one of the white arguments against bus desegregation was that white women travelling on buses would become vulnerable to harassment from black male commuters.[74]

Black urbanisation aroused other fears and antagonisms among whites. The white commercial class resented the competition of Indian traders. This gave rise to racially restrictive measures against Indians in Natal from the late nineteenth century. White workers feared being undercut and displaced by cheaper black labour. When the mining industry did precisely that during and after World War One, employing more black workers in semi-skilled jobs, the white miners resorted to militant strike action. The 1922 Rand Revolt was a

---

73 Gerhard Schutte, *What Racists Believe* (London, 1995), pp.186-87.
74 *Ibid.*, p.186.

racial strike by white miners in defence of their privileged position in the racialised job hierarchy. Later in the century, after the NP government had largely abolished the job colour bar in 1979 many white workers came to support far-right parties and movements that defended the older, more rigid, racial order.

Fear has to be an important factor in any explanation of white racism in South African history. This is not to say that all racism is based on fear. Racism may grow out of contempt for racial 'others', or out of a desire to exploit some resource or capacity, perhaps land or labour, held by those 'others'. But white fear has been ever-present, particularly during the nineteenth and twentieth centuries. Blackness came to be seen as threatening – as a threat to physical safety, to property, to health, to job security, and ultimately to white political domination. In the post-apartheid era much of the old overt, explicit racist discourse has disappeared from the public domain. But white fears are still very much alive, and these are now expressed in a less overt, more implicit racial discourse centred on crime, corruption and incompetence. Racism has had a long history in South Africa. It has changed its form and been expressed in different ways through different phases. Racial consciousness, race categorisation and racial differentiation have not disappeared. A racial order with such a long history will inevitably leave an awful and enduring legacy.

Bibliography

Agar-Hamilton, J.A.I., *The Native Policy of the Voortrekkers* (Cape Town, Maskew Miller, 1928).
Agar-Hamilton, J.A.I., 'The voortrekkers and the natives', *Race Relations*, V, 4, November, 1938.
Allen, Theodore W., *The Invention of the White Race* (New York, Verso, 1994).
Archer, R. and Bouillon, A., *The South African Game: Sport and Racism* (London, Zed Books, 1982).
Ashforth, Adam, *The Politics of Official Discourse in Twentieth Century South Africa* (Oxford, Clarendon Press, 1990).
Baines, G., 'The origins of urban segregation: Local government and the residence of Africans in Port Elizabeth, c.1835-1865', *South African Historical Journal*, 22, 1990.
Bank, Andrew, 'Of "native skulls" and "noble caucasians": Phrenology in colonial South Africa', *Journal of Southern African Studies*, 22, 3, 1996.
Bank, Andrew, 'Liberals and their Enemies: Racial Ideology and the Cape of Good Hope, 1820 to 1850' (unpublished Ph.D thesis, Cambridge University, 1995).
Banton, Michael, *Racial Theories* (Cambridge, Cambridge University Press, 1987).
Banton, Michael, *Racial Consciousness* (London, Longman, 1988).
Barker, Anthony J., *The African Link: British Attitudes to the Negro in the Era of the Atlantic Slave Trade, 1550-1807* (London, Frank Cass, 1978).
Beinart, William and Bundy, Colin, *Hidden Struggles in Rural South Africa* (Johannesburg, Ravan Press, 1987).
Beinart, William and Dubow, Saul (eds), *Segregation and Apartheid in Twentieth Century South Africa* (London and New York, Routledge, 1995).
Benedict, Ruth, *Race: Science and Politics* (New York, Viking Press, 1945).
Bickford-Smith, Vivian, *Ethnic Pride and Racial Prejudice in Victorian Cape Town* (Cambridge, Cambridge University Press, 1995).
Bickford-Smith, Vivian, 'South African urban history, racial segregation and the "unique" case of Cape Town', *Journal of Southern African Studies*, 21, 1, 1995.
Bonner, Philip, 'Factions and fissions: Transvaal/Swazi politics in the mid-nineteenth century', *Journal of African History*, 19, 2, 1978.

Bonner, P., Delius, P., and Posel, D. (eds), *Apartheid's Genesis 1935-1962* (Johannesburg, Witwatersrand University Press, 1993).

Boxer, C.R., *Race Relations in the Portuguese Colonial Empire 1415-1825* (Oxford, Clarendon Press, 1963).

Bozzoli, Belinda (ed.), *Class, Community and Conflict* (Johannesburg, Ravan Press, 1987).

Bradford, Helen, *A Taste of Freedom: The ICU in Rural South Africa 1924-1930* (New Haven and London, Yale University Press, 1987).

Bradlow, Edna, 'Emancipation and Race Perceptions at the Cape', *South African Historical Journal*, 15, 1983.

Bredekamp, H.C., (ed.), *Afrikaanse Geskiedskrywing en Letterkunde: Verlede, Hede, en Toekoms* (Bellville, Institute for Historical Research, University of the Western Cape, 1992).

Brookes, Edgar H., *White Rule in South Africa 1830-1910* (Pietermaritzburg, University of Natal Press, 1974).

Brookes, E.H. and Webb, C. de B., *A History of Natal* (Pietermaritzburg, University of Natal Press, 1965).

Burton, D.R., 'Sir Godfrey Lagden: Colonial Administrator' (unpublished Ph.D thesis, Rhodes University, 1989).

Cell, John W., *The Highest Stage of White Supremacy* (Cambridge, Cambridge University Press, 1982).

Christopher, A.J., 'Apartheid Planning in South Africa: The case of Port Elizabeth', *The Geographical Journal*, 153, 2, 1987.

Coetzee, J.M., 'The mind of apartheid: Geoffrey Cronjé (1907-)', *Social Dynamics*, 17, 1, 1991.

Comaroff, Jean and John, *Of Revelation and Revolution: Christianity, Colonialism and Consciousness in South Africa*, Volume One (Chicago, University of Chicago Press, 1991).

Cope, Nicholas, *To Bind the Nation* (Pietermaritzburg, University of Natal Press, 1993).

Cox, Oliver C., *Caste, Class and Race* (New York, Modern Reader Paperbacks, 1970).

Crais, Clifton C., 'The vacant land: The mythology of British expansion in the Eastern Cape, South Africa', *Journal of Social History*, 25, 1991.

Crais, Clifton C., *The Making of the Colonial Order* (Johannesburg, Witwatersrand University Press, 1992).

Crais, Clifton C., 'Race, the State, and the Silence of History in the Making of Modern South Africa: Preliminary Departures' (unpublished paper, University of Cape Town, 1992).

Cronjé, G., *Voogdyskap en Apartheid* (Pretoria, Van Schaik, 1948).

Curtin, Philip D., *The Image of Africa: British Ideas and Action, 1780-1850* (Madison, University of Wisconsin Press, 1964).
Davenport, Rodney, 'African Townsmen? South African natives (Urban Areas) legislation through the years', *African Affairs*, 68, 1969.
Davenport, T.R.H., *South Africa: A Modern History* (London, Macmillan, 1991).
Davies, Robert H., *Capital, State and White Labour in South Africa 1900-1960* (Brighton, Harvester Press, 1979).
Davies, Rob, O'Meara, Dan, and Dlamini, Sipho, *The Struggle for South Africa*, 2 vols (London, Zed Books, 1984).
Deacon, Harriet, 'Racial segregation and medical discourse in nineteenth-century Cape Town', *Journal of Southern African Studies*, 22, 2, 1996.
Degler, Carl N., 'Slavery and the genesis of American race prejudice', *Comparative Studies in Society and History*, 2, 1959-60.
De Kiewiet, C.W., *British Colonial Policy and the South African Republics 1848-1872* (London, Longmans, Green, 1929).
De Kiewiet, C.W., *A History of South Africa* (London, Oxford University Press, 1957).
De Kiewiet, C.W., *The Imperial Factor in South Africa* (New York, Russell and Russell, 1966).
De Kock, Leon, *Civilising Barbarians* (Johannesburg, Witwatersrand University Press, 1996).
Delius, Peter, *The Land Belongs to Us* (Johannesburg, Ravan Press, 1983).
Denoon, Donald, *A Grand Illusion* (London, Longman, 1973).
Doxey, G.V., *The Industrial Colour Bar in South Africa* (London, Oxford University Press, 1961).
Dubow, Saul, *Racial Segregation and the Origins of Apartheid in South Africa 1919-36* (London, Macmillan, 1989).
Dubow, Saul, 'Afrikaner Nationalism, Apartheid and the Conceptualization of "Race"', *Journal of African History*, 33, 1992.
Dubow, Saul, *Illicit Union: Scientific Racism in Modern South Africa* (Johannesburg, Witwatersrand University Press, 1995).
Duminy, Andrew and Guest, Bill (eds), *Natal and Zululand from Earliest Times to 1910* (Pietermaritzburg, University of Natal Press, 1989).
Du Preez, A.B., *Inside the South African Crucible* (Cape Town, HAUM, 1959).
Du Toit, A., 'No chosen people: the myth of the Calvinist origin of Afrikaner nationalism and racial ideology', *American Historical Review*, 88, 1983.

Du Toit, A. and Giliomee, H., *Afrikaner Political Thought* (Cape Town, David Philip, 1983).

Edgecombe, Ruth, 'The Glen Grey Act: Local origins of an abortive "Bill for Africa"', in J.A. Benyon *et al* (eds), *Studies in Local History* (Cape Town, Oxford University Press, 1976).

Elphick, Richard and Giliomee, Hermann (eds), *The Shaping of South African Society, 1652-1840* (Cape Town, Maskew Miller Longman, 1989).

Etherington, Norman, *Preachers, Peasants and Politics in Southeast Africa, 1835-1880* (London, Royal Historical Society, 1978).

Etherington, Norman, 'Natal's black rape scare of the 1870s', *Journal of Southern African Studies*, 15, 1, 1988.

Evans, Ivan, *Bureaucracy and Race* (Berkeley, University of California Press, 1987).

Fouché, Leo, 'The historical setting of the Great Trek', *Race Relations*, V, 4, November 1938.

Fredrickson, George, *White Supremacy* (Oxford, Oxford University Press, 1981).

Fredrickson, George, *The Arrogance of Race* (Middletown, Wesleyan University Press, 1988).

Freund, W.M. 'Race in the social structure of South Africa, 1652-1836', *Race and Class*, 18, 1, 1976.

Furlong, Patrick, *The Mixed Marriages Act* (Cape Town, University of Cape Town Centre for African Studies, 1983).

Galbraith, J.S., *Reluctant Empire* (Berkeley, University of California Press, 1963).

Gie, S.F.N., 'The Cape Colony under Company Rule, 1708-1795', in *The Cambridge History of the British Empire* (Cambridge, Cambridge University Press, 1993) vol.viii.

Giliomee, Hermann, 'Eighteenth century Cape society and its historiography: culture, race and class', *Social Dynamics*, 9, 1, 1983.

Goldberg, David Theo, *Racist Culture* (Oxford, Blackwell, 1993).

Gossett, Thomas F., *Race: The History of an Idea in America* (Dallas, Southern Methodist University Press, 1963).

Greenberg, Stanley B., *Race and State in Capitalist Development* (Johannesburg, Ravan Press, 1980).

Greenstein, Ran, 'Racial Formation: Towards a Comparative Study of Collective Identities in South Africa and the United States', *Social Dynamics*, 19, 2, 1993.

Grundlingh, Albert, 'Politics, principles and problems of a profession: Afrikaner historians and their discipline, c.1920-c.1965', *Perspectives in Education*, 12, 1, 1990.

Grundlingh, Albert, Odendaal, André, and Spies, Burridge, *Beyond the Tryline: Rugby and South African Society* (Johannesburg, Ravan Press, 1995).

Guelke, Leonard, 'The making of two frontier communities: Cape Colony in the eighteenth century', *Historical Reflections*, 12, 3, 1985.

Guelke, Leonard, 'The origin of white supremacy in South Africa: An interpretation', *Social Dynamics*, 15, 2, 1989.

Hart, D., 'Master Plans: The South African Government's Razing of Sophiatown, Cato Manor and District Six' (unpublished Ph.D thesis, Syracuse University, 1990).

Heese, H.F., *Groep Sonder Grense* (Bellville, University of the Western Cape Institute for Historical Research, 1984).

Hellmann, Ellen (ed.), *Handbook on Race Relations in South Africa* (Cape Town, Oxford University Press, 1949).

Hemson, David, 'Class Consciousness and Migrant Workers: Dock Workers of Durban' (unpublished Ph.D thesis, University of Warwick, 1989).

Hepple, Alexander, *Verwoerd* (Harmondsworth, Penguin Books, 1967).

Hindson, Doug, *Pass Controls and the Urban African Proletariat* (Johannesburg, Ravan Press, 1987).

Horwitz, Ralph, *The Political Economy of South Africa* (London, Weidenfeld and Nicolson, 1967).

Hunter, Guy (ed.), *Industrialisation and Race Relations* (London, Oxford University Press, 1965).

Huyser, J.D., 'Die Naturelle-Politiek van die Suid-Afrikaanse-Republiek' (unpublished thesis, University of Pretoria, 1936).

Hyam, Ronald, *Empire and Sexuality* (Manchester, Manchester University Press, 1990).

Jeeves, Alan H., *Migrant Labour in South Africa's Mining Economy* (Johannesburg, Witwatersrand University Press, 1985).

Johnstone, Frederick A., *Class, Race and Gold* (London, Routledge and Kegan Paul, 1976).

Jordan, Winthrop D., *White Over Black: American Attitudes Towards the Negro 1550-1812* (New York, Norton, 1977).

Kallaway, Peter (ed.), *Apartheid and Education* (Johannesburg, Ravan Press, 1984).

Katz, Elaine, 'Revisiting the Origins of the Industrial Colour Bar in the Witwatersrand Mining Industry, 1891 to 1899', *Journal of Southern African Studies*, 25, 1, 1999.

Keegan, Timothy, 'Crisis and catharsis in the development of capitalism in South African agriculture', *African Affairs*, 84, 1985.

Keegan, Timothy, 'The dynamics of rural accumulation in South Africa: Comparative and historical perspectives', *Comparative Studies in Society and History*, 28, 4, 1986.

Keegan, Timothy, *Colonial South Africa and the Origins of the Racial Order* (Cape Town, David Philip, 1996).

Kenney, Henry, *Power, Pride and Prejudice* (Johannesburg, Jonathan Ball, 1991).

Keppel-Jones, A., *South Africa* (London, Hutchinson, 1963).

Klausen, Susanne, '"For the sake of the race": eugenic discourses of feeblemindedness and motherhood in the *South African Medical Record*, 1903-1926', *Journal of Southern African Studies*, 23, 1, 1997.

Lacey, Marian, *Working for Boroko* (Johannesburg, Ravan Press, 1981).

Lamar, Howard and Thompson, Leonard (eds), *The Frontier in History* (New Haven and London, Yale University Press, 1981).

Lambert, John, *Betrayed Trust: Africans and the State in Colonial Natal* (Pietermaritzburg, University of Natal Press, 1995).

Lazar, John, 'Conformity and Conflict: Afrikaner Nationalist Politics in South Africa, 1948-1961' (unpublished Ph.D thesis, Oxford University, 1987).

Le Cordeur, B.A., 'The relations between the Cape and Natal, 1846-1879', *Archives Year Book for South African History*, i, 1965.

Legassick, Martin, 'South Africa: capital accumulation and violence', *Economy and Society*, 3, 1974.

Legassick, Martin, 'Legislation, ideology and economy in post-1948 South Africa', *Journal of Southern African Studies*, 1, 1, 1974.

Legassick, Martin, 'South Africa: forced labour, industrialization and racial differentiation' in Richard Harris (ed.), *The Political Economy of Africa* (Cambridge, Massachusetts, Schenkman, 1975).

Legassick, Martin, 'Gold, agriculture, and secondary industry in South Africa, 1885-1970: from periphery to sub-metropole as a forced labour system' in Robin Palmer and Neil Parsons (eds), *The Roots of Rural Poverty in Central and Southern Africa* (London, Heinemann, 1977).

Legassick, Martin, 'The frontier tradition in South African historiography' in *Societies of Southern Africa*, vol.2 (Institute of Commonwealth Studies, London, 1971), later published in Shula Marks and Anthony Atmore (eds), *Economy and Society in Pre-Industrial South Africa* (London, Longman, 1980).

Legassick, Martin, 'British hegemony and the origins of segregation in South Africa, 1901-14' in William Beinart and Saul Dubow (eds), *Segregation and Apartheid in Twentieth Century South Africa* (London and New York, Routledge, 1995).

Legassick, Martin, 'The State, Racism and the Rise of Capitalism in the Nineteenth Century Cape Colony', *South African Historical Journal*, 28, 1993.

Lemon, A. (ed.), *Homes Apart: South Africa's Segregated Cities* (Cape Town, David Philip, 1991).

Lester, Alan, 'Cultural construction and spatial strategy on the Eastern Cape frontier, 1806-c.1838', *South African Geographical Journal*, 78, 2, 1996.

Lester, Alan, 'The margins of order: Strategies of segregation on the Eastern Cape frontier, 1806-c.1850', *Journal of Southern African Studies*, 23, 4, 1997.

Lewsen, Phyllis, 'The Cape liberal tradition – myth or reality?', *Race*, 13, 1, 1971.

Lipton, Merle, *Capitalism and Apartheid* (Cape Town, David Philip, 1985).

Lorimer, Douglas A., *Colour, Class and the Victorians* (Leicester, Leicester University Press, 1978).

Mabin, Alan, 'Labour, capital, class struggle and the origins of residential segregation in Kimberley, 1880-1920', *Journal of Historical Geography*, 12, 1, 1986.

Mabin, A., 'Origins of segregatory urban planning in South Africa, c.1900-1940', *Planning History*, 13, 3, 1991.

MacCrone, I.D., *Race Attitudes in South Africa* (Johannesburg, Witwatersrand University Press, 1937).

Maclennan, Ben, *A Proper Degree of Terror* (Johannesburg, Ravan Press, 1986).

Maclennan, Ben, *Apartheid: The Lighter Side* (Cape Town, Chameleon Press, 1990).

Macmillan, W.M., *The Cape Colour Question* (London, Faber and Gwyer, 1927).

Magubane, Bernard, *The Political Economy of Race and Class in South Africa* (New York, Monthly Review Press, 1979).

Magubane, Bernard M., *The Making of a Racist State: British Imperialism and the Union of South Africa, 1875-1910* (Trenton, Africa World Press, 1996).

Malik, Kenan, *The Meaning of Race* (New York, New York University Press, 1996)

Mamdani, Mahmood, *Citizen and Subject* (Princeton, Princeton University Press, 1996).

Mansergh, Nicholas, *South Africa 1906-c1961: The Price of Magnanimity* (London, George Allen and Unwin, 1962).

Marais, J.S., *The Cape Coloured People 1652-1937* (Johannesburg, Witwatersrand University Press, 1962).
Marks, Shula, *Reluctant Rebellion* (Oxford, Clarendon Press, 1970).
Marks, Shula, 'Natal, the Zulu Royal family and the Ideology of Segregation', *Journal of Southern African Studies*, 4, 1978.
Marks, Shula, *Divided Sisterhood* (Johannesburg, Witwatersrand University Press, 1994).
Marks, Shula and Atmore, Anthony (eds), *Economy and Society in Pre-Industrial South Africa* (London, Longman, 1980).
Marks, Shula and Rathbone, Richard (eds), *Industrialisation and Social Change in South Africa* (London, Longman, 1982).
Marks, Shula and Trapido, Stanley, 'Lord Milner and the South African State' in P. Bonner (ed.), *Working Papers in Southern African Studies* (Johannesburg, Ravan Press, 1981), vol.ii.
Marks, Shula and Trapido, Stanley (eds), *The Politics of Race, Class and Nationalism in Twentieth Century South Africa* (London, Longman, 1987).
Marquard, Leo, *The Peoples and Policies of South Africa* (London, Oxford University Press, 1962).
Marx, Anthony W., *Making Race and Nation* (Cambridge, Cambridge University Press, 1998).
Maylam, Paul, *A History of the African People of South Africa* (Cape Town, David Philip, 1986).
Maylam, Paul, 'The rise and decline of urban apartheid', *African Affairs*, 89, 1990.
Maylam, Paul, 'Explaining the apartheid city: 20 years of South African urban historiography', *Journal of Southern African Studies*, 21, 1, 1995.
McCracken, J.L., *The Cape Parliament 1854-1910* (Oxford, Clarendon Press, 1967).
'Mnguni' (Hosea Jaffe), *Three Hundred Years* (Cape Town, New Era Fellowship, 1952).
Moleah, Alfred T., *South Africa: Colonialism, Apartheid and African Dispossession* (Wilmington, Disa Press, 1993).
Moolman, J.P.F., 'Die Boer se Siening van en Houding Teenoor die Bantoe in Transvaal tot 1860' (unpublished M.A. thesis, University of Pretoria, 1975).
Morrell, Robert (ed.), *Political Economy and Identities in KwaZulu-Natal* (Durban, Indicator Press, 1996).
Mostert, Noël, *Frontiers* (London, Pimlico, 1992).
Muller, C.F.J. (ed.), *Five Hundred Years* (Pretoria, Academica, 1969).
Nash, Gary B. and Weiss, Richard (eds), *The Great Fear: Race in the Mind of America* (New York, Holt, Rinehart and Winston, 1970).

Neame, L.E., *The History of Apartheid* (London, Pall Mall Press, 1962).
Nel, E.L., 'Racial Segregation in East London, 1836-1948', *South African Geographical Journal*, 73, 1991.
Newton-King, Susan, 'The labour market of the Cape Colony, 1807-28' in Shula Marks and Anthony Atmore (eds), *Economy and Society in Pre-Industrial South Africa* (London, Longman, 1980).
Noel, Donald L., (ed.). *The Origins of American Slavery and Racism* (Columbus, Charles E. Merrill Publishing Co., 1972).
Norval, Aletta J., *Deconstructing Apartheid Discourse* (London, Verso, 1996).
Odendaal, André, *Vukani Bantu!* (Cape Town, David Philip, 1984).
O'Meara, Dan, *Forty Lost Years* (Johannesburg, Ravan Press, 1996).
Omer-Cooper, J.D., *History of Southern Africa* (London, James Currey, 1987).
Pachai, B. (ed.), *South Africa's Indians* (Boston, Univesity Press of America, 1979).
Packard, Randall M., *White Plague, Black Labor* (Pietermaritzburg, University of Natal Press, 1989).
Parker, Kenneth, 'Fertile land, romantic spaces, uncivilized peoples: English travel-writing about the Cape of Good Hope, 1800-1850' in Bill Schwarz (ed.), *The Expansion of England* (London, Routledge, 1996).
Parnell, S., 'Racial segregation in Johannesburg: The Slums Act, 1934-39', *South African Geographical Journal*, 70, 2, 1988.
Parnell, S., 'Creating racial privilege: The origins of South African public health and town planning legislation', *Journal of Southern African Studies*, 19, 1993.
Parnell, Susan and Mabin, Alan, 'Rethinking Urban South Africa', *Journal of Southern African Studies*, 21, 1, 1995.
Parry, Richard, '"In a sense citizens, but not altogether citizens ...": Rhodes, race and the ideology of segregation at the Cape in the late nineteenth century', *Canadian Journal of African Studies*, 17, 3, 1983.
Patterson, Sheila, *The Last Trek* (London, Routledge and Kegan Paul, 1957).
Peires, J.B., *The House of Phalo* (Johannesburg, Ravan Press, 1981).
Pieterse, Jan Nederveen, *White on Black* (New Haven, Yale University Press, 1992).
Platzky, Laurine and Walker, Cherryl, *The Surplus People* (Johannesburg, Ravan Press, 1985).
Posel, D.B., 'Rethinking the "Race-Class Debate" in South African historiography', *Social Dynamics*, 9, 1, 1983.
Posel, Deborah, *The Making of Apartheid 1948-1961* (Oxford, Clarendon Press, 1991).
Preller, Gustav, *Day-Dawn in South Africa* (Pretoria, Wallach's P&P, 1938).

Pyrah, G.B., *Imperial Policy and South Africa 1902-10* (Oxford, Clarendon Press, 1955).

Rhoodie, N.J. and Venter, H.J., *Apartheid: A Socio-historical Exposition of the Origin and Development of the Apartheid Idea* (Cape Town, HAUM, 1960).

Rich, Paul, 'Race, science, and the legitimization of white supremacy in South Africa, 1902-1940', *International Journal of African Historical Studies*, 23, 4, 1990.

Riekert, Julian, 'Race, sex and the law in colonial Natal', *Journal of Natal and Zulu History*, 6, 1983.

Robertson, H.M., '150 years of economic contact between black and white', parts one and two, *South African Journal of Economics*, 2, 4, 1934 and 3, 1, 1935.

Robinson, J., 'The Power of Apartheid: Territoriality and State Power in South African Cities – Port Elizabeth 1923-1972' (unpublished Ph.D thesis, Cambridge University, 1990).

Roskam, K.L., *Apartheid and Discrimination* (Leyden, Sijthoff, 1960).

Ross, R. (ed.), *Racism and Colonialism* (The Hague, M Nijhoff, 1982).

Ross, Robert, *Beyond the Pale* (Johannesburg, Witwatersrand University Press, 1994).

Rotberg, Robert I., *The Founder: Cecil Rhodes and the Pursuit of Power* (Johannesburg, Southern Book Publishers, 1988).

Roux, Edward, *Time Longer Than Rope* (Madison, University of Wisconsin Press, 1964).

Russell-Wood, A.J.R., 'Iberian expansion and the issue of black slavery: Changing Portuguese attitudes, 1440-1770', *American Historical Review*, 83, 1, 1978.

Saayman, Willem, *Christian Mission in South Africa* (Pretoria, University of South Africa, 1991).

Saunders, Christopher, *The Making of the South African Past* (Cape Town, David Philip, 1988).

Saunders, C., 'District Six and urban history in South Africa', *South African Historical Journal*, 26, 1992.

Savage, Michael, 'The imposition of pass laws on the African population in South Africa 1916-1984', *African Affairs*, 85, 1986.

Saxton, Alexander, *The Rise and Fall of the White Republic* (London, Verso, 1990).

Scholtz, G.D., *Die Ontwikkeling van die Politieke Denke van die Afrikaner*
    Deel I 1652-1806 (Johannesburg, Voortrekkerpers, 1967)
    Deel II 1806-1854 (Johannesburg, Voortrekkerpers, 1970)
    Deel III 1854-1881 (Johannesburg, Voortrekkerpers, 1974).

Schreuder, D.M., 'The cultural factor in Victorian imperialism: a case-study of the British "civilising mission"', *Journal of Imperial and Commonwealth History*, 4, 3, 1976.
Schutte, Gerhard, *What Racists Believe* (London, Sage, 1995).
Scully, Pamela, *Liberating the Family?* (Portsmouth, Heinemann, 1997).
Shell, Robert C-H., *Children of Bondage* (Johannesburg, Witwatersrand University Press, 1994).
Sherwin-White, A.N., *Racial Prejudice in Imperial Rome* (Cambridge, Cambridge University Press, 1967).
Simons, H.J. and R.E., *Class and Colour in South Africa 1850-1950* (Harmondsworth, Penguin Books, 1969).
Smith, Andrew B. (ed.), *Einiqualand: Studies of the Orange River Frontier* (Cape Town, University of Cape Town Press, 1995).
Smith, Ken, *The Changing Past* (Johannesburg, Southern Book Publishers, 1988).
Snowden, Frank M., *Before Color Prejudice* (Cambridge, Harvard University Press, 1983).
Sparks, Allister, *The Mind of South Africa* (London, Mandarin, 1991).
Stanfield, John H., (ed.), *A History of Race Relations Research* (London, Sage, 1993).
Stepan, Nancy, *The Idea of Race in Science: Great Britain 1800-1960* (Basingstoke, Macmillan, 1982).
Swanson, M.W., 'The sanitation syndrome: bubonic plague and urban native policy in the Cape Colony, 1900-1909', *Journal of African History*, 18, 1977.
Swanson, Maynard W., 'The urban factor in Natal native policy, 1843-1873', *Journal of Natal and Zulu History*, 3, 1980.
Swanson, M.W., '"The Asiatic Menace": Creating Segregation in Durban, 1870-1900', *International Journal of African Historical Studies*, 16, 3, 1983.
Switzer, Les, *Power and Resistance in an African Society* (Madison, University of Wisconsin Press, 1993).
Tankard, K., 'Urban segregation: William Mvalo's "celebrated stick case"', *South African Historical Journal*, 34, 1996.
Tatz, C.M., *Shadow and Substance in South Africa* (Pietermaritzburg, University of Natal Press, 1962).
Thompson, L.M., *The Unification of South Africa 1902-1910* (Oxford, Clarendon Press, 1960).
Thompson, Leonard, *The Political Mythology of Apartheid* (New Haven, Yale University Press, 1985).
Thompson, Lloyd A., *Romans and Blacks* (London, Routledge, 1989).

Ticktin, Hillel, *The Politics of Race Discrimination in South Africa* (London, Pluto Press, 1991).
Tomaselli, Keyan, *The Cinema of Apartheid* (Sandton, Radix, 1989).
Torrance, David E., *The Strange Death of the Liberal Empire: Lord Selborne in South Africa* (Montreal and Kingston, McGill-Queen's University Press, 1996).
Trapido, S., 'Natal's non-racial franchise, 1856', *African Studies*, 22, 1963.
Trapido, Stanley, 'The origins of the Cape franchise qualifications of 1853', *Journal of African History*, V, 1, 1964.
Trapido, Stanley, '"The friends of the natives": merchants, peasants and the political and ideological structure of liberalism in the Cape, 1854-1910' in Shula Marks and AnthonyAtmore (eds), *Economy and Society in Pre-Industrial South Africa* (London, Longman, 1980).
Turrell, R.V., *Capital and Labour on the Kimberley Diamond Fields 1871-1890* (Cambridge, Cambridge University Press, 1987).
Van Aswegen, H.J., *History of South Africa to 1854* (Pretoria, Academica, 1990).
Van den Berghe, Pierre L., *South Africa: A Study in Conflict* (Middletown, Wesleyan University Press, 1965).
Van den Berghe, Pierre, *Race and Ethnicity* (New York, Basic Books, 1970).
Van Jaarsveld, F.A., *The Afrikaner's Interpretation of South African History* (Cape Town, Simondium Publishers, 1964).
Van Jaarsveld, F.A., *Die Evolusie van Apartheid* (Cape Town, Tafelberg, 1979).
Van Onselen, Charles, *Studies in the Social and Economic History of the Witwatersrand 1886-1914* (Johannesburg, Ravan Press, 1982), vols. 1 and 2.
Van Onselen, Charles, 'Race and Class in the South African Countryside: Cultural Osmosis and Social Relations in The Sharecropping Economy of the South-Western Transvaal, 1900-1950', *American Historical Review*, 95, 1, 1990.
Van Schoor, W.P., 'The origin and development of segregation in South Africa' in Maurice Hommel (ed.), *Contributions of Non-European Peoples to World Civilization* (Johannesburg, s.n., 1989).
Vaughan, Alden T., *Roots of American Racism* (New York, Oxford University Press, 1995).
Walker, Eric A., *The Frontier Tradition in South Africa* (Oxford, Oxford University Press, 1930).
Walker, E.A., *The Great Trek* (London, Adam and Charles Black, 1965).
Walker, Eric A., *A History of Southern Africa* (London, Longmans, 1965).

Walvin, James B., *Black and White: The Negro and English Society 1555-1945* (London, Allen Lane, 1973).
Walvin, James, *Questioning Slavery* (London, Routledge, 1996).
Wells, Julia C., 'Eva's Men: Gender and Power in the Establishment of the Cape of Good Hope, 1652-74', *Journal of African History*, 39, 1998.
Welsh, David, *The Roots of Segregation: Native Policy in Colonial Natal, 1845-1910* (Cape Town, Oxford University Press, 1971).
Williams, Eric, *Capitalism and Slavery* (London, Deutsch, 1964).
Wilson, M. and Thompson, L. (eds), *The Oxford History of South Africa*, vol.i (Oxford, Oxford University Press, 1969) and vol.ii (Oxford, Oxford University Press, 1971).
Wolpe, Harold, 'Industrialism and Race in South Africa' in Sami Zubaida (ed.), *Race and Racialism* (London, Tavistock, 1970).
Wolpe, Harold, 'Capitalism and cheap labour-power in South Africa: from segregation to apartheid', *Economy and Society*, 1, 4, 1972.
Wolpe, Harold, *Race, Class and the Apartheid State* (London, James Currey, 1988).
Worden, Nigel, *Slavery in Dutch South Africa* (Cambridge, Cambridge University Press, 1985).
Worden, N. and Crais, C. (eds), *Breaking the Chains* (Johannesburg, Witwatersrand University Press, 1994).
Worger, William H., *South Africa's City of Diamonds: Mine Workers and Monopoly Capitalism in Kimberley, 1867-1895* (Johannesburg, Ad. Donker, 1987).
Wright, Harrison M., *The Burden of the Present* (Cape Town, David Philip, 1977).
Young, Robert J.C., *Colonial Desire: Hybridity in Theory, Culture and Race* (London, Routledge, 1995).
Yudelman, David, *The Emergence of Modern South Africa* (Cape Town, David Philip, 1984).

Index

Afrikaanse Bond vir Rassestudies 191
Afrikaner Bond 129
Afrikaner, Klaas 62
Afrikaner nationalism 30, 35, 64, 192, 228, 235, 240
   historians 30, 34, 35, 67, 68, 93, 109, 188
   and racial ideology 197-9, 209-13, 216
Agar-Hamilton, J.A.I. 94, 98
America, North
   frontier thesis 52
   race attitudes 16-18, 45-6
   slavery 45-7
Anglo-Zulu War 134, 138, 169
anthropology 64, 89, 167, 172, 226
Apartheid
   and Afrikaner nationalism 197-9
   bantustan policy 180-1
   bureaucracy 185-6
   contradictions within 201-4
   education 183
   'Grand Apartheid' 194-6
   ideology 186-7
   interpretations of 196-204
   main elements of 179-84
   NP 'grand plan' 190-5
   race classification 184-5
   relaxation of 203
   and segregation 188-90
   social 183-4
   spatial 181-2
   state repression 185
   total 193-6, 201-2, 241
Ashforth, Adam 226-7
Asiatic Land Tenure and Indian Representation Act (1946) 177, 180

Badenhorst, F.G. 209
Baines, Thomas 92
Bank, Andrew 78-9, 80-2, 85, 91-2, 109
Banton, Michael 6-7
Bantu Authorities Act (1951) 180, 191
Bantu Education Act (1953) 183

Bantu Homelands Citizenship Act (1970) 181
bantustans 180-1, 193, 195, 202, 232
Barrow, John 49
Basotho 97
Bender, Gerald 25-6
Benedict, Ruth 16
Bickford-Smith, Vivian 130, 134
Bloem, Jan 62
Bourke, General 71
Bowker, John 85, 91
Boxer, C.R. 19, 20
Bradford, Helen 157
Brazil 25
Brookes, Edgar 63, 64, 94, 173

Caledon Code (1809) 70-1
Caledon, Earl of 70
Cape Colony
   early racial discrimination 20-3, 29, 31-51, 233
   education 164-5
   franchise 107, 110, 128-9, 133, 146, 232, 235
   liberal tradition 5, 51, 64, 65, 98, 106-8, 110, 127-8, 196, 216
   policy towards Africans 107-9, 110
   racist discourse 131-3
   trekboers 52-3, 54, 61, 64, 211
Cape Mounted Yeomanry Act (1875) 130
Cape Native Laws and Customs Commission (1883) 132
Cape Town 42, 70, 107, 133, 134, 158, 163, 202, 223, 224, 242
   segregation 130-1, 159, 160
Carlyle, Thomas 85
Catholic Church 24, 25
Cell, John 106
Chamberlain, Joseph 147
chiefs
   as state functionaries 151
   curtailed power of 75, 108, 135, 139
   in colonial Natal 102-4

Christopher, A.J. 76
coloureds 171, 177, 180, 182, 183-5, 189, 190, 203
Cox, Oliver 15-16, 19, 27, 218
Cradock, Sir John 74, 75
Crais, Clifton 61, 78-83, 85, 110-11, 231

Darley-Hartley, W. 168
Dart, Raymond 167
Davenport, T.R.H. 23, 95
Davies, Robert 50, 124, 219-20
Davis, R. Hunt 164
Degler, Carl 17, 18, 20, 21, 45
De Kiewiet, C.W. 22, 30, 49, 54, 63, 68-9, 84, 97
De Kock, Leon 93
Derrida, Jacques 198
diamond mining
    compounds 119, 162
    racial division of labour 116-20
    white ownership 116
discourse analysis 226-7
District Six 160, 233
Dlamini, Sipho 219-20
Doxey, G.V. 123, 126
Dubow, Saul 149-51, 154, 166-9, 172, 174, 176, 187, 189, 199, 209, 240
Du Preez, A.B. 209
Durban 105, 159-63, 169, 203, 242
D'Urban, Sir Benjamin 74-5, 84, 235
Dutch East India Company 20, 22, 32-4, 37, 40, 47-8, 56, 229-30
Dutch Reformed Church 130, 140, 193, 197

East London 77, 158
Eastern Cape (see also 'frontier wars')
    frontier 59-61, 66
    imperial expansion 74-5
    racist discourse 78-85, 91-2, 128-9, 235-6
    segregation 75, 76-7, 110, 234
education 70, 108
    segregation 131, 164-5, 173, 183, 203, 232-3
Elizabethan England 16, 17-18
Eloff, G. 209
Elphick, Richard 21, 29, 31, 34, 35, 37-9, 41-3, 57, 208, 223-6, 229-30

Entertainment Act (1931) 165
essentialism 2, 9, 27, 227
Essop, Ishmail 184
Etherington, Norman 169
eugenics 167-8, 171
Eva 41
Evans, Ivan 182, 185-6, 190
Evans, Maurice 173
Extension of University Education Act (1959) 183

Fantham, H.B. 168
Fingoes/Mfengu 83
forced removals 181, 182
Foucault, Michel 106, 198
franchise
    Cape Town municipal 70, 107
    in boer republics 95-6
    in Cape Colony 59-61, 66, 107, 110, 128-9, 133, 146, 232, 235
    in colonial Natal 101-2, 136
    in twentieth century 145-7, 150-1, 161, 174-5, 179-80, 233, 236
Franchise and Ballot Act (1892) 128
Fredrickson, George 8, 18, 22, 31, 33, 41, 43, 48, 51, 81, 107, 208, 223-4, 229
Freund, Bill 31, 35, 65, 222, 228
frontier wars 81-2
frontiers 5, 6, 30, 44, 59-61, 62, 66, 97
    frontier thesis/debate 35, 38, 52-66, 79, 154, 158, 215, 230-1
    1811-12 74, 76
    1834-35 74-5, 81-2, 92, 94, 241
    1846 75
    1877-78 134

Galbraith, J.S. 69
German immigrants 41
Giliomee, Hermann 21, 29, 31, 34-5, 37, 39, 41-2, 57, 59-61, 197, 208, 223-6, 229-30
Glen Grey Act (1894) 129-30, 148
Glenelg, Lord 75
Godlonton, Robert 81-2
gold mining
    and cheap labour 121, 220
    job colour bar 121-7
Goldberg, David 6, 7, 16

Gossett, Thomas F. 15, 25
Graham, John 74
Grahamstown 82, 92, 128, 238
Graham's Town Journal 78, 81-2, 83
Great Trek 93-4, 99
Greeks, ancient 14-15
Greenberg, Stanley 125
Grey, Sir George 106, 108-9, 127, 131
Griqua 116
Griqualand West 116, 119
Group Areas Act (1950) 158, 182, 191
Guelke, Leonard 20-1, 44, 55, 58-9, 66, 229, 231

Handlin, Oscar and Mary 46
Hart, Deborah 163
Heese, H.F. 41
Hepple, Alexander 190-1
Herstigte Nasionale Party 196
Hertzog, J.B.M. 150-3, 156, 174-5, 177, 183, 232
Hume, David 86
Hyam, Ronald 169

idealist analysis 4, 9, 13, 18, 24, 26, 33, 45, 69-70, 163, 196-8, 212, 216-21, 225-6, 228, 239-40
Immigration Law Amendment Act (1895) 136
Immorality Act
  (1927) 151, 171;
  (1950) 183-4, 191
imperialism, British 67, 235-6
  expansion 74-5
  humanitarianism 69-70, 84
  labour measures 70-3
  and racism 16, 23, 67-77, 109-10, 144, 147, 216, 231, 235-6
Indians
  discrimination against 136, 138, 140-1, 146, 162, 172, 177, 182, 183, 203, 242
Industrial Conciliation Act (1924) 150
influx control (see also 'pass regulations') 149, 152, 160, 182, 192, 195, 202, 233
intermarriage, interracial sex (see 'miscegenation')

interracial military alliances 57, 60, 66, 98

Jaffe, Hosea 36-7, 48
Jeeves, Alan 125
job reservation (see 'labour/racial division of labour')
Johannesburg 159, 160, 163, 170, 202, 242
Johnstone, Frederick 120-2, 123-5, 219-20
Jordan, Winthrop 16-17, 18, 20, 21, 23, 24, 45, 229, 239

Katz, Elaine 126
Keegan, Timothy 61, 65, 79, 99-100, 148, 155
Kenney, Henry 196
Keppel-Jones, Arthur 33
Khoisan 32, 33, 41, 42, 44, 58, 60-2, 78, 80, 81, 224, 230
  labour measures 70-2
  stereotypes of 32, 38, 39, 80, 211
Kimberley 115, 119, 159, 162
Knox, Robert 91-2
Kora 62, 116
Kruger, Paul 122
KwaMashu 203

labour
  discriminatory measures 70-3, 107-8, 110, 116-19, 121, 131, 134-5, 139, 149-50, 183, 232, 233
  exploitation and racism 27, 80, 83, 96, 97, 99, 101, 105, 136-7, 139-40, 155-8, 199-200, 235
  racial division of 116-27, 131, 150-1, 183, 203, 220-1, 230-2, 237, 243
  white attitudes 47-50, 115-27
  white labour policy 47-8, 80, 117, 230
Lacey, Marian 155, 156, 175, 220
Lagden, Sir Godfrey 144
land (see 'racism/and demand for land/and access to land')
Langalibalele Rebellion 138
Lazar, John 191-2
Legassick, Martin 30, 31, 35, 56-62, 64-6, 145, 175, 199-201, 219, 222, 228
Lester, Alan 76, 81, 82, 110
Leuchars, Col. G. 137

Index

liberal
  historiography and racism 4, 30, 35, 52-6, 57, 63-4, 67, 93-4, 178, 188, 213-18, 219, 225, 228
  segregationism 149, 172-4, 217
  view of British imperialism 67-70, 76, 84
Lipton, Merle 125-6, 156
Location Acts (1869, 1876, 1884, 1892, 1899) 130
Long, Edward 86-7
Loram, Charles 63, 173
Lorimer, Douglas 90

Mabin, Alan 162
Macartney, H.E. 92
MacCrone, I.D. 30, 32-5, 49, 52-9, 60-2, 65-6, 215
Macmillan, W.M. 30, 52, 62, 72
Magubane, Bernard 124-5
Maitland, Sir Peregrine 75
Malan, D.F. 188, 189, 196, 237
Malik, Kenan 6
Marks, Shula 105, 152, 170-1
Marquard, Leo 98, 99, 214
Martindale 160
Marx, Anthony 174
Master and Servants' Law Amendment Act (1926) 156
Masters and Servants Act (1856) 107-8
Masters and Servants Ordinance (1841) 73
materialist/Marxist analysis 4, 10, 13, 24, 26-7, 36, 37, 45-6, 109, 115, 127, 162-4, 174-6, 178, 198-202, 218-22, 225-6, 240-1
Medieval era 15
Milner, Lord 122, 144, 145-7
Mines and Works Act (1911) 122
Mines and Works Amendment Act (1926) 150-1
Mining Act (1883) 119
miscegenation 19, 20-2, 24-6, 36, 39-44, 58, 60, 62, 66, 85, 151, 168, 170-1, 223-4
missionaries 92-3, 94
Moleah, Alfred 23, 26
Molema, Silas 167
Moolman, J.P.F. 211
Mostert, Noël 76, 81, 82
Muller, C.F.J. 188

Nash, Gary 17
Natal 95, 100-1, 161, 164, 170, 172, 177, 180
  racial discrimination and discourse 100-4, 106, 134-8, 141, 146, 234-6, 242
Natal Native Affairs Commission (1906-07) 137
Natalia 95
National Party 5, 6, 30, 41, 64, 65, 99, 151, 160, 179, 183, 187-96, 201-3, 204, 213, 217, 232-4, 236, 243
Native Administration Act (1875) 135; (1927) 151, 177, 232
Native Affairs Act (1920) 148
Native Labour Regulation Act (1911) 121
Native Laws Amendment Act (1937) 152, 161, 177, 233; (1952) 182, 191
Native Service Contract Act (1932) 156
Native Strangers' Location 77
Native Trust and Land Act (1936) 152
Natives' Land Act (1913) 145, 147-8, 155-6, 177, 181, 232
Natives Land Commission (1916) 156
Natives' Representative Council 151-2, 177
Natives (Urban Areas) Act (1923) 149, 159-61, 177, 182
Nazism 212, 213, 225
Ndebele 97
Neame, L.E. 189
Newclare 160
Newton-King, Susan 72
Nicholls, Heaton 153
Niven, Rev. 78
Northern Cape frontier 62, 66
Norval, Aletta 198-9, 208, 227
Noyes, John 26

O'Meara, Dan 219-20
Omer-Cooper, J.D. 189
Orange Free State 5, 96, 138-41, 164, 180
Orange River Colony 145-6, 170
Ordinance 50 (1828) 71-3, 80, 94
Ordinance 54 (1903) 122

Packard, Randall 172
Parliamentary Voters Registration Act (1887) 128
Parnell, Susan 162

261

pass regulations (see also 'influx control') 70-1, 95, 97, 101, 118, 121, 135, 139, 145, 160-1, 182, 195, 202
Patterson, Sheila 34, 54
Pedi 97
Penn, Nigel 62
Philipps, Thomas 78
phrenology 89, 92
Pietermaritzburg 105, 159, 169, 242
Pieterse, Jan 15
Pim, Howard 63, 172-3
pluralist analysis 212-16, 218-21, 225-6
Population Registration Act (1950) 41, 184, 191
Port Elizabeth 76-7, 158, 159, 162, 163, 202
Portugal 16
  colonialism 19, 24-6
  culture and racism 19-20, 25-6
Posel, Deborah 190-2, 199
postmodernism 4, 27-8, 106, 198-9, 208, 227
Potchefstroom Republic 96
Preller, Gustav 167, 209
Pringle, Thomas 78
Prohibition of Mixed Marriages Act (1949) 183, 191
Promotion of Bantu Self-Government Act (1959) 180, 195
Public Health Act (1919) 159

race, concept of 6-7, 16
racial theory/science 4, 8, 10, 99, 109, 133, 176, 203-4, 209-10, 223, 226, 231, 233-4, 240
  absence of in early Cape 39, 44, 66
  apartheid theory 186-7, 209-13
  during segregation era 166-9
  idea of racial hierarchy 7, 89, 169, 208-9
  in Britain 88-90
  in the Cape 91-2
  racial categorisation 4, 167, 169, 171, 208, 209, 213-14, 218, 225
racism
  and abolition of slavery 72-3, 86-8
  and access to land 71, 97, 130, 139, 145-6, 147-8, 181
  and Afrikaner nationalism 188-9, 197-9, 209-13
  and British imperialism 16, 23, 67-77, 109-10, 144, 216, 231, 235-6
  and capitalism 23, 27, 30-1, 36, 115-27, 176-8, 219-20, 231, 236-7
  and Christianity 15, 23, 24-5, 53, 61, 92-3, 186-7, 240
  and crime 163, 242
  and demand for land 81, 83, 99, 105, 138, 155, 241
  and disease 134, 138, 163-4, 171-2, 241-2
  and labour discrimination 70-2, 107-8, 110, 116-19, 121, 131, 134-5, 139, 149-50, 183, 232-3
  and labour exploitation 27, 80, 83, 96, 97, 99, 101, 105, 136-7, 139-40, 155-8, 199-200, 235
  and mining 6, 30-1, 115-27, 133, 138, 219-21, 231-2, 236-7
  and sexuality 26, 39-44, 169-70, 171, 242
  and skin colour 22, 24, 33, 83, 233
  and slavery 6, 13, 16, 17, 20, 39, 45-51, 66, 86-7, 229-30
  and warfare 81-2, 92, 95, 128, 133-4, 138, 241-2
  and white farmers 83, 136-8, 154-8, 234, 236
  and white workers 115-27, 237, 243
  as a rural phenomenon 154-8
  as an urban phenomenon 158-64
  attitudes/consciousness/discourse 7-8, 10, 38-40, 43-5, 47, 49-51, 53, 66, 77-88, 90-1, 103-5, 117, 123, 125-6, 131-3, 134, 136-8, 144, 157, 210-11, 215, 223, 229, 233-4, 239, 243
  attitudes of settlers/English-speakers 5, 25, 64, 66, 77-85, 93, 103-5, 189, 216, 235
  concept of 7
  cultural dimension of 5, 15, 17-18, 22, 24, 26, 45, 115, 221, 233
  different dimensions of 7-8, 233
  discrimination in boer republics 95-7, 110, 138-41
  discrimination in colonial Natal 100-3, 106, 134-8
  European origins of 13-26
  historiography of 207-41

idealist interpretation of 4, 9, 13, 18, 24, 26, 33, 45, 163, 196-8, 220-1, 239-40
   in Britain 85-90
   in classical times 14-15
   in colonial Natal 100-6, 134-8
   in early Cape 20-3, 29, 31-51
   in North America 17-18, 25
   in South America 25-6
   in Spanish and Portuguese culture 19-20, 24, 25-6
   in the Netherlands 20-3
   materialist interpretation of 4, 10, 13, 24, 26-7, 45-6, 115, 162-4,166, 175-6, 178, 198-202, 218-22, 225-6, 240-1
   of Cape governors 73-6, 84, 235
   on the frontier 52-66, 79, 154, 158, 215, 230-1
   pluralist analysis of 212-18, 219-21, 225-6
   psychological dimension of 5, 17-18, 26, 45, 81, 105, 115, 134, 163, 169-71, 198, 221, 241-3
   racial classification 184-5, 232
   racial division of labour 116-27, 131, 150-1, 183, 203, 220-1, 230-2, 237, 243
   South African origins of 6, 20-3, 29-66, 228-34
Rand Revolt 123, 242-3
Refugee Law (1854) 101
Representation of Natives Act (1936) 151, 177
Reservation of Separate Amenities Act (1953) 184
reserves, African 145, 148, 150, 155, 175-6, 180, 193, 194, 199-201
Rhodes, Cecil 129, 132, 133, 235, 236, 238
Rhoodie, N.J. 30, 32, 188, 191, 197, 210
Rich, Paul 174
Robertson, H.M. 56, 63
Robinson, Jennifer 163
Romans, ancient 14-15
Ross, Robert 31, 34, 39, 41, 44, 72-3, 84, 208, 223-5, 229
Rotberg, Robert 132
Roux, Edward 30, 34
Russell-Wood, A.J.R. 19

Saunders, Christopher 57-8

School Boards Act (1905) 131
Schreiner, Olive 167
Schreuder, D.M. 131
segregation 10, 65, 76, 115, 143-78, 188-90, 216, 219, 226, 228, 232
   administrative 139, 145, 151
   in education 131, 164-5, 173, 183, 203, 232, 233
   in hospitals 37, 130, 170-1
   in local government 161-2
   in prisons 130
   in sport and recreation 131, 165-6, 184, 203, 233
   in the church 130, 140
   in the eastern Cape 75, 76-7, 110
   interpretations of 174-8, 199
   judicial 102
   political 129, 138-9, 145, 148-9
   prohibition of interracial sex 140, 151, 170-1, 183-4, 203
   territorial 32, 95, 100, 102, 139, 145, 147-8, 152, 177, 181-2, 211, 232
   transport 130-1
   urban 76-7, 119, 130-1, 136, 140, 149, 158-64, 172, 177, 182, 231-2
Selborne, Lord 144
Shell, Robert 40-3, 51, 224, 229
Shepstone, Theophilus 100, 102-3, 105-6, 108-9, 132-3, 137, 141
slavery (see also 'racism/and slavery') 6, 13, 16, 17, 45-51, 97, 229-30
   abolition of 69, 70, 72-3
   sexual exploitation of slaves 40-1
Slums Act (1934) 159
Smith, Andrew 91
Smith, Sir Harry 75, 82, 235
Smuts, Jan 63, 151, 153, 235
Snowden, Frank 14-15
Social Darwinism 167-8, 172
Somerset, Lord Charles 74
Sophiatown 160, 233
South African Bantu Rugby Board 166
South African Bureau of Racial Affairs 193
South African Native Affairs Commission (1903-05) 144-5, 147, 172, 232
South African Party 234
South African Republic/Transvaal 5, 96-7, 138-41, 145-6
Spain 16

colonialism 19, 24
culture and racism 19-20
Sparks, Allister 23, 55
Sprigg, Sir Gordon 128
Stepan, Nancy 88-90
Stockenström, Andries 75, 79
Strijdom, J.G. 196
Stuart, James 137
Swanson, Maynard 105, 163-4, 171-2

Tatz, Colin 174-5
taxation 135-6
Theal, G.M. 29, 208-9
Thompson, L.M. 23, 144, 147
Ticktin, Hillel 221
Tlhaping 116
Tomlinson Report (1956) 193-4
Transkei 180
Treaty of Vereeniging 146
Truth and Reconciliation Commission 1, 237
Tswana 39, 62, 97, 183
Tulbagh, Governor 37
Turner, Frederick J. 52
Turrell, Robert 118

Umlazi 203
Union constitution 146
United Party 151, 177, 189, 201, 233, 234
University of Cape Town 165
University of Fort Hare 165
University of Natal 165
University of the Witwatersrand 165

Van Aswegen, H.J. 70, 71
Van den Berghe, Pierre 54, 69, 98-100, 196, 214-15

Van den Boogart, Ernst 21-2, 24
Van der Horst, Sheila 214, 217
Van Imhoff, Baron 49
Van Jaarsveld, F.A. 211
Van Onselen, Charles 157, 170
Van Riebeeck, Jan 5, 21, 32, 41, 211, 215, 229, 234
Van Schoor, W.P. 36-7
Venter, H.J. 30, 32, 188, 191, 197, 210
Verwoerd, Hendrik 6, 179, 186, 191-2, 194, 196-7, 201, 234-5, 237
Voortrekkers 53, 64-5, 76, 93-5, 98-100, 210-11
Vorster, B.J. 196, 237

Walker, Eric 32, 52, 59, 62-3, 65-6, 79, 94, 98, 215, 230
Walvin, James 17-18, 26, 46, 85-7
Weiss, Richard 17
Welsh, David 100, 104, 106
West Indies 25, 43, 45, 86
White, Charles 89
Wilberforce, William 87
Williams, Eric 45-6
Wilson, Monica 10
Winter, H.D. 11
Wolpe, Harold 175-6, 199-201, 219
Worden, Nigel 48-9, 110
Worger, William 118

Xhosa 39, 57, 59, 60, 61, 78, 80, 83, 91, 92, 211
  stereotypes of 74, 75, 81-2

Zulu 97, 101, 169, 183